Pier Vittorio Aureli
Architecture and Abstraction

THE MIT PRESS   Cambridge, Massachusetts   London, England

Pier Vittorio Aureli
Architecture
and Abstraction

Writing Architecture Series

Introduction

> The abstraction, or idea, however, is nothing more than the theoretical expression of those material relations which are their lord and master.

Karl Marx, *Grundrisse: Foundations of the Critique of Political Economy*, 1857

In his essay "Abstraction and Culture" the American painter Peter Halley lamented the persistent belief that abstraction is a stylistic device or invention, born out of the artist's formal concerns.[1] For Halley, abstraction unfortunately continues to be seen as a free play of form that is completely self-referential and detached from social and political issues. "In thinking about this most rarefied of visual languages," Halley writes, "it seems we intellectually retreat into the cloister of high culture; we deny that abstraction is a reflection of larger historical and cultural forces. We deny that the phenomenon of abstraction only gains meaning to the extent to which it does reflect larger forces and is embedded with their history."[2] The understanding of abstraction as a retreat from the world is dominant within the discipline of architecture, where it is associated with modernist formal simplicity and the reduction of architecture to Platonic objects. This book aims to overcome this interpretation by situating the relationship between architecture and abstraction within a wider social and political context.

What Is Abstraction?

"To abstract" means to pull something out from the totality of which it is a part. It comes from the Latin verb *trahere*, which means to draw or drag out. To put it in very simple terms, abstraction is a process through which humans seek generic frameworks rather than specific solutions. For example, when two objects are compared in order to find common properties, those objects undergo a process of abstraction, because they are being addressed not in their singularity but only in those terms that support the comparison. Perhaps the most basic form of abstraction is language, in which existing things are translated into words that address classes of objects rather than describing them one by one. The word "apple" does not refer to a specific apple but to an idea which brings together in one class of things all existing apples regardless of their contingency. Precisely because of its high level of generality, language is abstract. It is not surprising that in Diderot and D'Alembert's *Encyclopédie* the entry "abstraction" is discussed in terms of language. For César Chesneau Dumarsais, who wrote the entry, abstraction consists in the process of forming a concept by separating it from the sensible reality that stimulated its formation.[3] In order to express this concept, the abstraction of words is necessary. He wrote: "We live in a real and physical place, but we speak, if I may, the language of the country of *abstractions*. We say: *I'm hungry, I want, I've mercy, I fear, it's my intention* etc. in the same way as we say *I have a clock*."[4] This definition of abstraction centered on language was clearly indebted to John Locke, who, at the end of the seventeenth century, was responsible for claiming abstraction as a central philosophical theme.[5] Notably, Locke's understanding of abstraction did not emerge from metaphysics or idealism but from an empirical approach to the world. Locke argued that due to the abundance of stimuli in the sensible experience of the world, it would be impossible to name them one by one.[6] For this reason, the human mind synthesizes each particular aspect of reality into general ideas that are independent of sensible reality. According to Locke, sensible reality is abstracted not only by language but also by signs—the study of which Locke defined as *semiotike* (semiotics), the science that concerns the way signs such as written words are used to understand things and transmit knowledge. This understanding of language and signs as abstractions grounded in our experience of sensible reality constituted a materialist interpretation of abstraction that counters the customary idealist interpretation. With Locke, abstractions are not understood as the outcome of some metaphysical conception of the world, but as something derived from material conditions. Besides being concerned with abstraction as a central faculty of human understanding, Locke was also busy with very concrete and political problems: the writing of a constitution for a newly founded (colonial) state in America, and the definition of the modern conception of private property as a "natural" right founded on the cultivation of land. In both efforts, the bridge between concrete material conditions and abstract law became a fundamental weapon which imposed colonial government not only through military coercion but also, and especially, with the power of civilian law.[7] Indeed, property and law—which Locke considered the essential aspects of government—can be considered abstractions that emerge from the concrete ground of power relationships.

Although abstractions are fabricated by the human mind, the stimulus motivating their formation comes from outside the mind. Therefore, abstractions are not timeless, but contingent on given social and political conditions. Within human history, the power of abstractions developed in proportion to social complexity, and indeed abstractions became a *conditio sine qua non* with the rise of early large-scale societies.

The administration of large quantities of people, animals, and goods required their reduction into abstract signs in order to be computed. Early forms of written language appeared not for writing poems or stories, but for counting the surplus of goods accumulated in the storage of rulers. Even before the invention of mathematics and geometry, many ancient societies functioned as machines of social organization in which abstractions such as numbers, algorithms, and systems of measure played a crucial role. These abstractions emerged from tangible human actions such as ritual, labor, disciplining, marking, and counting. In summary of this first definition of abstraction, it is evident that abstractions are rooted in real things and in turn inform how things work. To paraphrase Karl Marx, who analyzed the dominance of capitalism by abstractions: *abstractions are concrete*.[8]

Exemplary of a concrete abstraction is geometry, which evolved—as the name itself reveals—from the act measuring land in order to give it an economic value. Geometry played a fundamental role in architecture because it made buildings measurable, allowing those who initiated a construction project to control built form with exactitude and thus estimate the amounts of materials and labor needed for the project's completion.

Although geometric ordering is common to many cultures around the world, within the historical lineage that links the Near East, ancient Egypt, and ancient Greece it acquired an unprecedented level of abstraction in measuring and ordering the world. It is for this reason that I trace the prehistory of the project as we understand it today within this lineage. In this book I argue that the rise of abstraction within architecture consists not in the visible form of a structure—its appearance—but rather in the way it is produced, especially in the way the exactitude of measurement has been systematically applied to building in order to control construction and separate intellectual from manual labor.

Architecture has always been a labor-consuming undertaking that requires careful planning. Planning—the very idea of a *plan*—concerns both the ideation of the structure to be built and the logistics of its implementation: instructions for the builders, estimation of labor force required and amounts of resources, transportation of materials. Since ancient times, geometry and calculation were considered inevitable frameworks for the realization of large-scale buildings. In the Western tradition of architecture, the plan became a *project*, a strategy that guides the production or materialization of a thing. My thesis, which I present in the first chapter, is that the project's planning is geared toward the prefiguration of the building form, the organization of the labor force, and the management of resources. In many ancient cultures, building a large-scale artifact was a ritual that communities performed to reinforce social ties. There is archaeological evidence that the building of large-scale complexes such as temples predates the advent of cities or even of sedentary cultures. Yet in some early cities and states such as the civilization of Sumer, building large-scale structures by mobilizing massive quantities of people and resources coordinated by the ruling class was one of the most powerful representations of sovereign power. The making of architecture was thus deeply intertwined with the institutional functioning of societies and their power relationships. While this is already implicit in the way architecture—especially monumental architecture—was produced since antiquity, it would be explicitly theorized in the Renaissance, when the project became the prerogative of the professional architect. Geometrizing, measuring, calculating, and drawing architecture empowered the architect and the engineer (as ancillaries of the patron) to take control of the building process, widening the gap between intellectual and manual labor in architecture.

But the project became even more crucial with the rise of capitalism in the sixteenth century, since the extraction of profit from everything was possible only if everything was planned accordingly. The project therefore represented not only the authority of the architect, but also a wider apparatus in which politics and economics merged as one force. With the advent of capitalism, the project's commanding logic was increasingly driven by the most powerful abstraction ever invented: money. By presupposing the equivalence of all things, money is the ultimate social abstraction that translates everything into economic value. Within this ubiquitous condition, architecture ceased to be valued only for its use and was instead—and especially—valued for its potential to generate profit. In the age of capitalism, a house is not only a space to inhabit but a financial asset. The sharpest definition of this predicament was perhaps given by Manfredo Tafuri: the modern city is nothing more than a machine for the extraction of surplus value.[9] With the commodification and financialization of building processes, architecture was transformed into a built register of economic interests. Superstudio's Histograms of Architecture are perhaps the crudest allegory of this fate, completely subsumed by the abstract logic of financialization. Their gridlike form, which expands ad infinitum and takes myriad shapes, aptly represents a world where everything that exists can be quantified into measurable assets. This understanding of abstraction, which I'll disentangle in the chapters of this book, offers a completely different perspective from that of abstraction as a modern "style." Yet even an art-based conception of abstraction originates in the same sources briefly outlined above.

The Nature of Abstract Art

The beginning of abstraction in the arts is customarily identified with breakthroughs such as the first seven of Wassily Kandinsky's *Composition* series painted between 1910 and 1913, Kazimir Malevich's *Black Square* in 1915, and more recently with the paintings of Hilma af Klint, such as her stunning *Swan* completed in 1915.

Yet the belief that abstraction emerged as an instant epiphany obscures its long incubation in theories and discussions about art since the nineteenth century. With the application of Immanuel Kant's aesthetics to the arts, art theorists, art historians, and artists were increasingly focused on the formal properties of the work of art (and architecture, as discussed in chapter 5), which were interpreted independently of any symbolic or social meaning. To put it simply, by reducing the artwork to its sensible perception, the *aesthetic* approach implied a process of abstraction in which artworks were voided of any symbolic allusion and treated as mere perceptual data. This essentializing attitude emerged in the first discussion of abstraction in the visual arts in Friedrich Faber, Lorenz Clasen, and Johannes Andreas Romberg's influential *Conversations-Lexicon für Bildende Kunst* (1845). The *Lexicon* defines abstraction as the mental activity through which artists reach the essential aspects of a work of art. From the outset abstraction is understood in the arts as the act of *essentializing* or clearing out in order to arrive at the essence of artworks. This tendency compelled artists to comprehend their medium not as a means of representation but as something in itself. Indeed, the transition from impressionist to fauve and cubist painting reflects a gradual process of abstraction in which the depiction of reality was simplified, inevitably leaving nothing more than a composition of colors on a flat surface. Freed from the burden of representation and subject, artists were able to conceive art in mere formal terms. However, this idealist and essentialist understanding of abstraction as focused on the formal properties of art conceals the fact that abstraction was also the consequence of the historical context in which it emerged.

In his seminal essay "Nature of Abstract Art" (1937), Meyer Shapiro argued that abstraction in painting was not the consequence of the artist's will to turn art into a pure aesthetic activity, but of a new way of seeing reality, influenced by the rise of capitalist industrialization.[10] According to Shapiro, in the early twentieth century, under the pressure of the industrial mode of production, artists looked at the world differently: "The older categories of art were translated into the language of modern technology; the essential was identified with the efficient, the unit with standardized element, texture with new materials, representation with photography, drawing with the ruled or mechanically traced line, color with the flat coat of paint."[11]

Piet Mondrian, perhaps more than anyone else, connected the idea of abstraction in painting with the world in which he was living. In his first contribution to the journal *De Stijl* he argued that "today the life of people is moving away from the natural: life becomes increasingly abstract."[12] Mondrian evoked a world so dominated by science and calculations that abstraction becomes not just an aesthetic experience but a way of life. In his text "Nieuwe Beelding" he went further and declared that the abstract was not produced by simplification or purification but was the manifestation of what he called the *universal*, or the *general* as such.[13] But what is the universal in Mondrian's terms? The Dutch painter remained elusive about this term, but he suggested that the universal was a social and cultural condition produced by the urban environment of the metropolis. With his evocative prose, Mondrian wrote: "In the reality of our environment, we see the predominantly natural gradually disappearing through necessity. The capricious forms of rural nature become tautened in the metropolis."[14] Even within his deeply formalist and idealist perspective, Mondrian made clear that he saw a link between abstraction and the industrial age.

Mondrian practiced abstract painting in two ways: initially by abstracting formal motives from real objects (think of his paintings of trees, where he gradually moved from a naturalistic to a stylized representation of vertical and horizontal lines); and then as the creation of abstract paintings completely devoid of any reference outside themselves (think of his compositions of lines and rectangles of color). In the first approach, abstraction was a process of essentializing what exists, and thus can be understood as continuing and heightening to an extreme limit the idea of abstraction that emerged in the nineteenth century. In the second approach, abstraction is no longer a process, but a condition that represents relationships between plastic elements such as color and lines that do not refer to anything beyond themselves. For Mondrian, it was this second approach that manifested the universal and the general, rather than the first, which was still tied to sensible reality. Yet the gridlike form of Mondrian's paintings and the sharp contrast of primary colors can also be perceived as evoking the experience of the metropolis, which he often alluded to in the titles of his paintings and in his writings as the inspiration to his art. In his text "House—Street—City" (1927) he argued that abstraction takes place in the landscape of the street with its artificial lights, advertisements, and utilitarian architectures.[15] For Mondrian, abstract painting was a fragment of a whole *abstract* environment of which modern architecture, with its straight lines and new materials such as reinforced concrete, was a forerunner. He shared the aspiration toward the integration of painting, sculpture, and architecture within an environmental totality with the artists gathered around the journal *De Stijl*, edited by Theo van Doesburg. For both Mondrian and Van Doesburg, architecture—especially modern "utilitarian" architecture with its bare structure and unadorned walls—offered an example of a realm in which abstraction was already realized. As noted by Yve-Alain Bois, for Van Doesburg the idea of planarity was the common denominator of painting and architecture.[16] In his famous axonometric drawings and models for a Maison Particulière (done in collaboration with Cornelis van Eesteren), Van Doesburg intensified the coincidence of planarity in painting and architecture by devising a house as a simple assemblage of slabs and walls rendered as neutral supports for color. This radical abstraction, which reduced both painting and architecture to compositions of surfaces, was not a self-reflexive, inward-looking meditation on art, but rather a formal sublimation of a built environment defined by standardization and elementarization of building components. Felicia Rappe identified the kinship between De Stijl's impetus toward abstraction and J. J. P. Oud's projects such as the Tusschendijken housing blocks in Rotterdam built in 1920, where the Dutch architect worked with the prefabrication of building elements.[17] Although De Stijl artists rejected repetition in favor of composition, as is visible in Van Doesburg and Van Eesteren's Maison, their pursuit of abstraction resonated with an architecture reduced to its planar datum of unadorned walls pierced by unadorned openings—as in Oud's housing blocks. De Stijl's art demonstrates the constitutive ambivalence of artistic abstraction as something where the "perfectly pure" of art evokes the "raw real" of a world increasingly dominated by the social abstraction of capitalist industrialization. This ambivalence was reflected in the role of De Stijl artists as exemplars of twentieth-century avant-garde cultural producers. Indeed, these artists were both aestheticians of capitalist abstraction and freelance workers whose professional precarity was, ironically, the consequence of the system they were trying to aestheticize.

Abstraction: Three Interpretations

One of the most penetrating interpretations of abstraction as a social condition is Henri Lefebvre's concept of *abstract space*[18] which he elaborates in his influential book *The Production of Space* (1974). Lefebvre's theory is known for its concern with the everyday experience of space, and yet, as Japhy Wilson has remarked, Lefebvre's interest in everyday space was focused on its alienation and abstraction within capitalist modernity.[19] Influenced by Marx's 1844 *Manuscripts*, in which the German thinker explored the alienation of capitalist society as a consequence of the separation of producers from their means of production, Lefebvre defined abstract space as the spatialization of capitalist alienation in all aspects of modern life. For the French philosopher, this expression is the product of a deep interaction between physical conditions and representations, between materiality and ideology. Thus abstract space was the outcome of a historical development that proceeded from nature to abstraction, which Lefebvre conceptualized as the transition from absolute to abstract space.[20] Absolute space emerged in ancient civilizations, where the consecration of natural features like mountains, caves, and springs gave origin to ceremonial complexes, quickly appropriated by priestly castes as the locus of their political and religious power. Lefebvre argued that, within absolute space, symbolic significance played a crucial role.[21] There was a prolonged transition between the absolute and the abstract, and it consists of the incipient urban system of trade and commerce established in medieval Europe—a system in which the market and other civil institutions became sites of social interaction.[22] Abstract space emerged from the commodification of land and labor which generated a vast network of banks, productive places, and transportation and information systems that were established with the aid of the modern state to serve the interests of capitalist accumulation. Lefebvre detected this condition in the hegemony of a Euclidean space which subjected everything to geometric commensurability. This space included cartographic representations of entire territories as well as the spatial architectonics of the industrial metropolis such as mass housing, factories, motorways, and railways lines.

The planning and standardization of the city and its infrastructure were, according to Lefebvre, not simply a process of rationalization but a way to gear social organization to the logic of production and profit.[23] While abstract space tended toward the infinite, this condition would never be achieved because its unfolding was deterred by frictional forces that produced "contradictory space," a spatial condition where fragments of previous social constructs survived amid the ubiquity of social abstraction. Importantly, Lefebvre's critique of abstract space particularly addressed large-scale planning as it emerged from welfare state capitalism, which powerfully manifested in postwar France.[24] Lefebvre observed abstract space in the way the state forcefully reorganized society by planning all of human life to strengthen the relationship between production and reproduction. In this process, capitalist social relations and reductive technocratic representation were concretized in lived material reality, of which the standardized forms of welfare architecture—especially mass housing—were the most prominent. It is ironic that Lefebvre advanced this critique of abstract space as embodied in the welfare state just before it was dismantled by neoliberal governance, within which the authority of the state was drastically undermined. Nonetheless, the criticality of Lefebvre's abstract space remains intact, because abstraction is ultimately the outcome not only of technocratic organization but also of the hegemony of exchange value: a process in which everything that exists is subjected to a system of representation that allows quantification and calculation of profit.

As Łukasz Stanek has remarked, Lefebvre's idea of space, and especially of abstract space, is deeply indebted to Marx's theorization of concrete abstraction, which held that, far from being an escape from reality, abstractions were the driving force of capitalist accumulation.[25]

Indeed, coming to terms with abstraction was one of the most pressing methodological issues for Marx.[26] Following Hegel, he was convinced that the correct methodology for grasping concrete reality was to proceed from the abstract to the concrete. For Marx, reality could only be recomposed within thought by taking seriously the most general and simple abstractions—that is to say, abstract categories—as real embodiments of existing processes. For Marx, an example of concrete abstraction is the notion of labor not as a specific activity but as *labor in general*. Marx noted that Adam Smith discovered labor as a general *abstract* category that designated a wealth-creating activity because the advent of industrialization reduced labor to its barest features, stripped of the individuality of the worker. Unlike the physiocratic economists who identified labor with agricultural labor, for Smith labor *as such* was not reducible to any activity such as manufacturing, agriculture, or commerce. However, while Smith hypostatized labor as a timeless category applicable throughout the entire course of history, Marx recognized that labor as a general category could only exist as the result of the historical development of capitalism. As Marx wrote, "As a rule, the most general abstractions arise only in the midst of the richest possible concrete development, where one thing appears as common to many, to all."[27] In an advanced capitalist society, *reasoning*—that is, the reconstitution of a multiplicity of things and events within a coherent "scientific" system of thought—is not a simple depiction of reality, but in fact what makes reality work. Notably, Marx saw abstraction not only as a methodological category but also as a form of life under capitalism. Marx concluded that in advanced industrial societies—such as the United States in Marx's time—abstraction flourished as an ethos. As he wrote in a crucial passage of the introduction to the *Grundrisse*:

> On the other side, this abstraction of labour as such is not merely the mental product of a concrete totality of labours. Indifference towards specific labours corresponds to a form of society in which individuals can with ease transfer from one labour to another, and where the specific kind is a matter of chance for them, hence of indifference. Not only the category, labour, but labour in reality has here become the means of creating wealth in general, and has ceased to be organically linked with particular individuals in any specific

form. Such a state of affairs is at its most developed in the most modern form of existence of bourgeois society—in the United States. Here, then, for the first time, the point of departure of modern economics, namely the abstraction of the category "labour," "labour as such," labour pure and simple, becomes true in practice.[28]

Here Marx described the way in which modern forms of production, such as the mechanized labor in the factory, gutted specialized skill from human labor, reducing it to its generic form of mere physical and mental effort. With its extensive division of labor deconstructing the process of production into myriad simple and repetitive actions coordinated by machines, the factory system de facto created a new ethos in which the *impersonal* became the nomos of society.

In architecture, the rise of the impersonal occurred in the advent of modern construction techniques. For example, reinforced concrete was applied to a wider spectrum of buildings not solely for the purpose of efficiency but also—and especially—as a way to deskill builders by regimenting their work into a strict managerial order. This logic was at work in many forms of standardization and prefabrication of building elements which, to this day, defines the practice of building in architecture. Recently, the logic of abstract labor "that becomes true in practice" entered the world of the architectural project by way of computers and their suite of programs, which play a role analogous to the machines of the industrial age.

This labor is abstract not only because labor in general is the synthesis of the myriad forms of production, but also because in itself labor is a *commodity*, that is, a thing measurable in terms of the ultimate abstract system of universal equivalence: money.

Money is a commodity whose purpose is to function as the universal equivalent for all commodities. With different quantities of the same money anyone can buy anything, including human labor. Money is thus the locus within which disparate things find their common measure in terms of value. This value rules not only human life but also the space in which life unfolds. Money assuredly represents the most powerful abstraction invented by humankind, because money holds the power to measure everything, thus homogenizing what is heterogeneous. Consequently, the multiplicity of uses embedded in a multitude of disparate things is quantifiable and exchangeable.

In his seminal book *Intellectual and Manual Labor* (1978), Alfred Sohn-Rethel studied "commodity form" as the main source of abstraction. Within the condition of *use*, time and space are inseparably linked with nature and the material activities of humans, while within the activity of *exchange*, time and space are emptied of their qualities and become mere quantities that are the measure of value.

As Sohn-Rethel notes, within the practice of exchange, the temporality of commodities is suspended as they travel great distances, making space and time completely homogeneous and continuous so as not to upset the exchange equation. As Sohn-Rethel writes:

> Time and space rendered abstract under the impact of commodity exchange are marked by homogeneity, continuity and emptiness of all natural and material content, visible or invisible (e.g. air). The exchange abstraction excludes everything that makes up history, human and even natural history. The entire empirical reality of facts, events and description by which one moment and locality of time and space is distinguishable from another is wiped out. Time and space assume thereby that character of absolute historical timelessness and universality which must mark the exchange abstraction as a whole and each of its features.[29]

When a commodity is sold and bought, it must adhere to a system of equivalence—that is, the monetary system within which all commodities can be exchanged. For this reason, according to Sohn-Rethel, the form of commodities is abstract, and abstractness is the character of the economic process that produces the commodity form. In the West, starting in the fourteenth century, the practice of exchange fostered a radically different way of experiencing the world. With the increased use of money, abstractions such as measure and calculation played a ubiquitous role in everyday life. Sohn-Rethel identifies the rise of scientific knowledge as the cause of the separation between manual and intellectual labor, since the latter becomes decisive in establishing the scientific parameters for production and exchange. From Sohn-Rethel's perspective, Marx was unable to link the abstract form of the commodity as it emerged from the apparatus of exchange and the disciplines of knowledge that produced all cognitive abstractions necessary for exchange to work.[30] Sohn-Rethel therefore traced the division of mental and manual labor back to its earliest manifestations in history—such as meticulous calendars or even astronomy, which he stripped of their religious aura and portrayed as instrumental in empowering the measuring prerogatives of the ruling class, made of state functionaries and priests. With the rise of private property and the exchange of products for money, the abstractness of geometry and mathematics became a major social force. However, while in antiquity this social force was limited to the exchange of commodities as objects, with the rise of modernity the abstraction of exchange and the equivalence of value begin to include human labor, no longer slave labor devoid of wage, but rather labor sold and purchased as a commodity among "free" citizens. Here, labor is not a direct material interchange but depends on capital. It is at this point that labor becomes what Marx defined as *abstract labor*.

A fundamental result of the advent of abstract labor is the transition from artisanal to industrial labor. While artisanal workers mastered their production by practical know-how and the expertise of their hands, the industrial worker is tied to a means of production where technological sophistication and calculations become crucial. Here we see the *raison d'être* of abstraction as a way to enhance the division of labor and to downgrade manual labor as apparently unable to comprehend the way production works. Needless to say, the division between manual and intellectual labor is the very disciplinary foundation of our modern conception of architecture. To understand architecture within the terms of abstraction thus means to put forward a critique of this foundational disciplinary status.

Architecture, Abstraction, and the Project

The aim of this book is to read the rise and the power of abstraction through the material relations that make possible the design and building of architecture. My intention is to demonstrate how architecture is abstract not because it lacks ornamentation and is reduced to its bare structure (which is a consequence of abstraction, not the cause), but because *any* form of architecture that is designed and built according to a project is in itself an abstraction that becomes concrete. Concreteness here refers not only to the materiality of a building but also—and especially—to its process of production. The nexus between labor, measure, drawing, and calculations is the source of architecture's abstraction. This nexus existed before the rise of the money economy and capitalism, thus the book begins its narrative of abstraction from what I call "the prehistory of the project." Any form of large-scale monumental architecture requires a project, an initial idea, however approximate, of how the building is going to be built and how it is going to look. In this book the focus is mainly on what is known as Western architecture, because it is in this lineage that the idea of architecture as we know it today found its origin. This tradition became hegemonic because of the imperial and colonial politics of many European empires and nation-states, although we should keep in mind that analogous processes of abstraction also happened in other cultures (such as the ancient Indian subcontinent and classical China).[31] In the genealogy of the Western idea of architecture, the term "project" plays a very important role. I argue in this book that project is understood as the main locus of abstraction because its working presupposes the reduction of reality to the exactitude of measure, geometry, and later the relentless quantifying logic of money. For this reason, it may be useful to define this term that is so important for the discipline of architecture and whose use emerged at the dawn of modernity.

The etymological root of the word is the Latin *projectus*—the past participle of a verb which means to throw forward. "Project" often addresses a strategy in which something must be produced or brought out. Now ubiquitous, the word is used to describe undertakings of any kind. The present is so impregnated with entrepreneurial ideology that our own life must be invested as a "project." This word is consequently understood as an individual pursuit, an existential commitment to a life-fulfilling goal. If in the 1960s "everything [was] architecture,"[32] today everything is a project: everything that exists is potentially exploitable and conceivable as a form of entrepreneurial investment.

As Vera Keller and Ted McCormick have noted, however,[33] the original use of the word "project" was not quite so elastic. The term emerged in sixteenth-century Italy and France in the context of building, and specifically related to architectural drafting. With the increased use of firearms, fortification design became a paramount sector of building activity.[34] Compared to previous architectural works, the planning and construction of fortifications—discussed in chapter 2—required unprecedented speed and precision in terms of planning. This prompted architects to rely on rigorous drawing techniques such as the use of orthogonal projections. In this context, words like the Italian *progetto* and the French *projet* acquired a double meaning: they referred to the careful advance planning of labor and resources, while also indicating the technique of drafting by means of projection.

In the seventeenth century the word "project" migrated from military design to economic policy. With the rise of colonialism and capitalism, the terms "project" and "projector" became popular in England when—as Joan Thirsk noted—"everyone with a scheme, whether to make money, to employ the poor, or to explore the far corners of the earth had a 'project.'"[35] The first and most comprehensive theory of the project was put forward by Daniel Defoe in his book *An Essay upon Projects*, written in 1693 and published in 1697. For Defoe, a project is a "vast undertaking" which, due to its complexity, requires more than just the projector's skills and initiative. A proper context of laws and policies is necessary, and in fact essential, to facilitate the entrepreneur's initiative and reduce the risk of failure.[36] Two mythical works of architecture are exemplary as projects for Defoe: Noah's Ark and the Tower of Babel. In both cases the difficulty of the undertaking is emphasized. Noah faced the jibes of his "wiser" peers, who were skeptical of his effort to build the Ark. Likewise, the failure to construct the Tower of Babel was not due to God confounding the language of the builders, but to their inability to calculate the distance from Earth to Heaven.

In describing this genealogy of the project, Defoe emphasized that the activity of projecting involved not just the anticipation of risk, but also a dependence on institutional support. For Defoe, "project" is nearly synonymous with "institution"—a body which has enough social and economic power to promote vast undertakings. Thus the idea of the project is expanded from mere individual creativity to a matter of state policy. On an institutional scale, a project can include banking, wagering, insuring, and even a major public work such as a national highway to facilitate the circulation of people and goods.

Defoe's characterization of the project also contradicts the myth of liberal individual initiative that he himself later celebrated in his novel *The Life and Strange Surprizing Adventures of Robinson Crusoe, of York, Mariner* (1719). Shipwrecked on a deserted island, Crusoe methodically builds a shelter that ensures his survival. His efforts became a vivid ideological projection of capitalist entrepreneurialism, famously ridiculed by Marx as "robinsonade."[37] Against the myth of individuality, the younger Defoe, in *An Essay upon Projects*, presented the project not as a solitary venture but as a vast social and infrastructural reform that combines state and private enterprise for the reorganization of the social order. Defoe stressed that this understanding of project was unique to the early eighteenth century—the "age of projecting."[38] In an age of colonial expansion, marked by the gentry's appropriation of common land for purposes of "improvement" and the intensification of trade and manufacturing, Defoe conceived the project as a form of "civil policy" that could unite state and private interests toward the "benefit of the Publik, and Imploying the poor."[39]

In discussing the predicament of the project, it is crucial to stress the colonial nature of projecting. Command and exploitation on a vast scale are made possible through the concerted effort of finance, logistics, and manpower. Surprisingly, the author responsible for the myth of liberal individuality also, at the beginning of his career, challenged it by arguing that a project's success is dependent on state support. Defoe's early essay has little to do with individual creativity. Instead, "project" is specifically understood as the possibility of an institutional plan—as demonstrated by the fact that the word "project" entered common usage in conjunction with the rise of military engineering.

Within this context, in the first chapter I offer a prehistory of the project in relationship to architecture. In contrast to the typical interpretation of the architectural project as either the preliminary drafting of a structure for construction or as a (delusional) ideological projection—a "vision"—I propose to investigate the project as a technical apparatus that evolved out of the experience of building grand structures. Going beyond project as mere "ideology," I intend to highlight how the rise of the politics and technics of the architectural project reflects the power relations that emerged and evolved through the division of labor in certain societies. The first chapter looks at the building of large-scale structures such as temples and cathedrals—the epicenters of what Lefebvre called "absolute space"—through a form of planning that coordinated labor under an increasingly managerial form of power. This genealogy of the project aims to advance an interpretation of the project as an apparatus of control and valorization, against the more romantic idea of the project as mere ideological manifestation of the architect's will to form. Following this first chapter—which also puts forward a definition of the terms "plan" and "planning"—I explore how abstraction arose in the foundational tropes of architecture such as drawing and design (chapter 2), the grid (chapter 3), "rationalization" (chapter 4), and form (chapter 5). These tropes are persistently understood as autonomous properties of architecture. I analyze their material basis, arguing that they emerged neither from the theoretical mind of architects nor from some autonomous disciplinary tradition, but from the concrete abstractions that ruled the production of architecture. After all, categories such as drawing, design, and form played a major role in creating a divide between intellectual and manual labor in architecture. Since the sixteenth century, the building of architecture can be seen as a site of primitive accumulation of capital where the rationalization of both design and building was dedicated to the extraction of surplus value from every aspect of design and construction. As described in chapter 4 this is particularly evident in the early forms of standardization and industrialization of architecture—from the English terraced house to the factory—caused by the imperatives of profit and accumulation of capital. In the last chapter—which functions as an epilogue—I discuss how abstraction as a social force informed modern architecture not so much in terms of style but more as a condition. Confronted with the uprooting forces of capital and its power to abstract everything for the sake of mass production, certain instances of architecture—from Le Corbusier's Maison Dom-ino to data centers—make the consequences of abstraction in architecture immediately legible. These precedents are described through the lens of Walter Benjamin's essay "Experience and Poverty," which describes how the uprooting forces of the industrial age undermined "experience"—that is to say, the wisdom through which past generations were able to elaborate coherent and epic images of the world. Benjamin noted that poverty of experience paradoxically pushed people to take refuge in the nostalgia of authenticity. This is especially true today when architects oppose the consequences of real abstraction for architecture with a longing for an idyllic idea of craft and references to past traditions. Against such traditionalism, Benjamin argued for the deliberate appropriation of poverty of experience as a way to live at the height of the deeply compromised conditions imposed by capital. Consequently, in the last chapter I map architectural projects that wittingly and unwittingly engaged poverty of experience by turning to abstraction as the main datum of architecture. In doing so these projects became merciless and yet useful cartographies of what architecture is really about in our present social and political predicament.

I close with the way the extreme commodification of architecture now undermines the role of architects, reserving for them the same fate as builders at the dawn of modernity. Yet it is precisely such proletarianization of architectural work that can offer the possibility of rethinking the entire institution of architecture apart from its asymmetrical organization and its subservience to profit. Once abstraction is disconnected from its purpose of furthering the division of labor, it can be appropriated as a general framework to radically rethink architecture and its use. Whether we are going to remain a capitalist society or move away from it, abstraction is going to be a fundamental modus operandi of our world. The question is how to appropriate its legacy toward different ends. Architects should reconsider their practice in radical materialist terms and seek, together with all those involved in design and construction, novel forms of cooperating and producing architecture that are attuned to use value rather than the exchange value of buildings.

But this possibility can be grasped only by rigorously mapping the institutional and technical apparatus that produced architecture. Thus any critique of architecture should descend from its philosophical pedestal and seriously consider the production of architecture as a material and concrete process, because it is here that the arcane of power often lies, what in architectural terms we can call the *arché*.

1 Architecture, Abstraction, and the Prehistory of the Project

Karl Marx famously said that the worst of architects are distinguished from the best of bees—whose geometrically perfect hives would put many architects to shame—because the architect raises a structure as an idea before it is erected in reality.[1] Marx used the architect as an example to highlight the fundamental capacity of human nature to construct, in the *imagination*, a model or blueprint of the task to be performed. As a driver of human labor, this proactive will found one of its earliest manifestations in the manufacturing of utensils. Humans needed to imagine these utilitarian objects in terms of use and making prior to their production. Utensils are thus "concrete concepts" because they link abstractions of the human mind to the physical reality of things. The merging of abstraction and concreteness becomes even more crucial with architecture due to its labor-intensive character. Seldom carried out by a single person, the imagination of architecture as an *idea* operates as a "plan" to be shared by those involved in the construction of the tangible object. The "plan" is thus an abstraction of the building—first as a mental image, then as a set of instructions and notations to be followed by builders. Following this logic, the plan is not only an abstraction as an idea but also an algorithm in the original sense of the word: step-by-step instructions to be carried out mechanically. As such, the plan embodies a vector of command that informs and organizes the whole practice of building, reducing all actions and human participants to a clearly defined process. The millennia-long global history of architecture can consequently be understood as a history of planning in which people and resources are mobilized to undertake the building of physical structures. Until the nineteenth century it was very rare that a building in all its details was planned before being built. Building has, however, always worked through an idea and a plan of what is going to be built. Naturally, an increase in size, complexity, and permanence of these historical structures demanded a higher degree of planning and coordination of labor and resources. Yet planning and coordination should not simply be understood as a consequence of large-scale architecture. Given that the faculty to organize large masses of workers and mobilize resources represents—to this day—the clearest manifestation of power, the capacity to plan is architecture's political precondition.

Power, Planning, and Labor

Natufian settlements and dwellings are among the oldest known examples of building which bear the marks of an aptitude for planning. The Natufians, an Epipaleolithic culture which existed in the eastern Mediterranean area approximately 11,500 to 15,000 years ago, occupy a unique intermediate position between two distinct forms of life: nomadic hunter-gatherers and sedentary farming communities. Their settlements—such as the one discovered at 'Ain Mallaha—appear to have been carefully planned in parallel rows that follow the site topography. This organization reflects an effort to build the settlement following a coherent plan, which defined the layout of the spaces and prescribed the specific location of activities.

Archaeologists Juan José Ibáñez, Jesús Emilio González Urquijo, and Xavier Terradas argue that the carefully planned Natufian hamlets manifest the emergence of a nascent institutionalized communal authority of a political and ritual nature.[2] A remarkable example of such authority is Shelter 131/51 at 'Ain Mallaha. As it is larger than neighboring structures and its form fig. 1.1 is more geometrically precise, this shelter may have been a communal gathering space. Characterized by a circular floor plan dug approximately a meter deep, Shelter 131/51 is framed by a low stone wall that would have enclosed a timber structure. Still legible on the ground are the postholes of this timber structure. The accuracy of the curved wall, the fairly regular rhythm of the postholes, and the exact concentricity of the entire shelter reflect the intention to produce a circular space and the use of techniques such as a compass arm. Tracing the circle with such precision suggests the desire to reinforce the symbolic authority of the building. It is therefore plausible to interpret Shelter 131/51 as one of the earliest surviving executions of a well-defined plan. Here the plan emerges in the most essential of terms: a drawing traced on the ground that defines the relationships between building elements. Even in this early example, the plan ultimately aimed to create a structure in which the position of each element is consistent with the whole. The Natufians were likely familiar with the geometrical concepts of circle and center, and were therefore able to establish stable and communicable representations of architectural forms.[3]

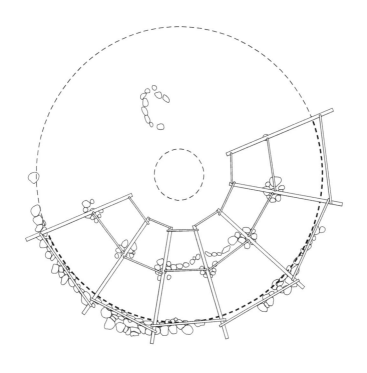

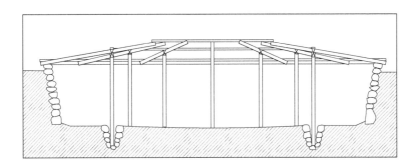

1.1 Shelter 51 at 'Ain Mallaha, Israel, plan and section. © Dogma, adapted from Gil Harklay and Avi Gopher.

These forms allowed them not only to give formal definition to their structures, but also to "design" in advance of building: they are the index of an early attempt to put forward architecture *as a preconceived plan*.

Because they are linked to specific processes, circles and other simple geometric forms can be interpreted as more than mere abstract shapes. They can also be conceived as abstractions of ritual behavior. Lewis Mumford emphasized the role of ritualistic behavior in the origins of human technics.[4] He argued that the "proto-language" of ritual laid down a pattern of order that impacted many other expressions of human culture, such as language and architecture.[5] Repeated ritualistic performances such as feasting or commemorating ancestors were crystallized in the certainty of a permanent structure through the practice of building. Moreover, the act of building itself was a ritualistic activity. Often performed to reinforce the social bonds of a community, the ritual of building was reflected not only in exceptional scale but also and especially in regularity of form.

Deliberately designed to stand out from other dwellings, Shelter 131/51 is also noteworthy as anticipating the transformation of the house into a monumental temple. In many ancient cultures, houses were also places of worship; cultic activities were therefore not centralized but performed within each dispersed household. The emergence of temples as designated spaces for worship divorced from the everyday life of the house—a phenomenon that can be observed in many cultures—is often the consequence of the centralization of power in the hands of an elite or ruler. For this reason, the building of detached temples prompted an increase in scale and the regularization of building form. Such a process of regularization is evident in the geometrically precise layout and in the uniformity of architectural and decorative features such as openings and ornamental patterns. This regimentation is visible in the so-called Terrazzo Building built at Çayönü, Turkey, 8,700 years ago. Here the symmetry of the layout is emphasized by the alignment of the building's corners with the cardinal points of the compass and by flat columns placed at equal intervals along the interior of the enclosing wall. These features support the hypothesis that prior to construction, the building was defined by a premeditated "project."

fig. 1.2

The shift toward geometric regularity gave rise to an increasing monumentalization of architecture, which served the emerging elites' control of religious practice and reinforced their authority over villages and later cities.[6] The building of what archaeologists Kent Flannery and Joyce Marcus call "temples of inequality" required large amounts of resources and manpower and thus made a priori design an inevitable method of work.[7] We must be careful, however, not to generalize the idea of large-scale architectural complexes as an indication of inequality. In their provocative book *The Dawn of Everything*, anthropologist David Graeber and archaeologist David Wengrow have emphasized how the building of large-scale temple complexes need not imply asymmetrical power relationships and could also occur within egalitarian societies.[8] Yet when we analyze monumental complexes in regions such as Mesopotamia we can see a seminal trend in which increasing geometric precision and standardization of building elements in construction of large-scale complexes coincides with the emergence of a more hierarchical organization of society.

Exemplary of this condition is the North Temple found at the ancient Mesopotamian settlement of Tepe Gawra.[9] Its architecture is characterized by a symmetrical plan and by brickwork with a subtle formal play that transforms the walls into a sequence of protruding and recessed vertical strips. The regular cadence of these strips enhances the perceived modularity of the structure. The brickwork appears not just to play a decorative role but also to define the principle through which the temple was conceived. On site, archaeologists have found hundreds of miniature mud bricks, scaled to one-tenth the size of the bricks used to build the temple.[10] These excavations suggest that the North Temple of Tepe Gawra was carefully planned by the builders, using the standardized brick as a modular unit.

In ancient construction, the geometric resolution of architectural form was greatly enhanced by the introduction of mud and clay masonry bricks. Molded in wooden frames, standardized bricks ensured the regularity of building material and strengthened the authority's control over the building process. Specialization and routinization of labor likely played an important role in the production of standardized construction

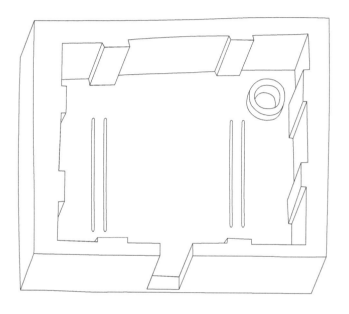

1.2 Reconstruction of the Terrazzo Building, Çayönü, Turkey. © Dogma, adapted from Kent Flannery and Joyce Marcus.

materials, since large quantities of bricks were produced over a short amount of time by the same individuals, who retained the templates of the composition and dimensions of bricks.[11] Historian of mathematics Morris Kline notes that numerous arithmetic and geometric problems are raised in the use of bricks in large-scale architecture such as temples, granaries, and dams.[12] The volume of buildings—especially in the case of granaries—has to be determined with precision in order to estimate the labor power and the time needed for construction. Due to their uniform size, bricks proved ideal for these operations. Brickwork can therefore be considered one of the earliest and most important forms of abstraction in architecture. Simultaneously, a brick is approximately proportioned to the size of a laborer's hand, thus the geometric and standardized form of the brick unit made building a quantifiable activity in terms of both material and labor.

When early cities appeared in Mesopotamia in the fourth millennium BCE, the concurrent emergence of writing, calculation, and geometry was mirrored by the increasing monumentality of architecture on an unprecedented scale. This confluence was caused by the intensification of agriculture, which enabled urban elites to manage the labor of many people, extract surplus, and store excess supply in temples or granaries.[13] Writing, calculation, and geometry were necessary for the elite to record the increasing number of economic transactions as well as to precisely plan public works such as large-scale irrigation systems, dams, and temples.[14] This technical development is apparent in one of the earliest known cities, Uruk. Driven by the relatively rapid rise of intensive agriculture, the development of Uruk was marked by gigantic complexes such as the White Temple and the Eanna Acropolis[15]—structures that are impressive in sheer size and also in their regularity of form. The repetition of flat columns, regular openings, and chapels in both the White Temple complex and the temples that form the Eanna Acropolis articulated an orderly composition that presupposes a clear modular template. Excavators estimated that the building of the White Temple complex likely required 1,500 laborers working an average of ten hours a day for about five years.[16] The city elite clearly held the political power to mobilize people and resources and the managerial ability to coordinate such large-scale undertakings. The same aptitude for engineering is manifested in the production of irrigation systems that allowed the Sumerians to multiply their agricultural output. Regularity of form, in which every element—whether structural or ornamental—fits into an all-encompassing order, cannot simply be interpreted in terms of symbolism. It is necessary to equate the formal uniformity with the capacity to coordinate masses of workers in a state-driven *project*.

Here it is critical to stress the difference between plan and project. By plan I mean simple instructions on how to build a structure. Often this operation was initiated by tracing a geometric layout directly on the ground. A project refers to the complex management of people and resources needed to accomplish vast building programs. Unlike the plan, which is common to structures built with a minumum of formal logic, a project is necessary when the complexity of a task cannot rely on ad hoc solutions. While the Natufian culture employed plans, only in large-scale societies does architecture become the outcome of a project. It is possible to argue that a project entails both the devising of a plan and, especially, the careful planning of the involved logistics.

The requisite of planning in the building of large-scale architectural complexes is legible in a statue of the Sumerian king Gudea, who ruled the state of Lagash in the third millennium BCE. The statue portrays the ruler holding a tablet bearing the plan of an architectural complex, most likely the wall of the temple of Ningirsu. The inclusion of the tablet in Gudea's statue confirms that the symbolic power of monuments rested not only on their built form but also on the effort in planning them as coherent, large-scale enterprises. Accordingly, the building of temples elicited what Lewis Mumford defined as a "megamachine,"[17] the mobilization of a large body of people achieved by rigorously coordinating their activities in both time and space for a predetermined, clearly envisaged and calculated purpose.[18] The megamachine was not simply a technical apparatus but the convergence of science, economy, technics, and political power into a unified system of government. Mumford interpreted such an apparatus of government as "an invisible structure composed of living, but rigidly commanded, human parts, each assigned to their special office, role or task to make possible the immense work-output and grand designs."[19] This mechanical organization served to make human effort subservient to a single rule, which aimed to achieve a well-defined goal with an explicit method. Control at this extreme level required the hierarchical transmission of instructions through a series of intermediate functionaries until it reached the smallest unit of society. As Mumford remarked, "Exact reproduction of the message and absolute compliance were both essential."[20] Mumford's concept of the megamachine implies not just a top-down organization of building work, but a top-down organization of society at large. Here we should be careful not to deduce too linear a hierarchical organization of society from a hierarchical organization of work. Graeber and Wengrow have advanced the interesting—but not fully proved—hypothesis that cultures that built large-scale architectural complexes, such as the monumental mounds built by foragers at Poverty Point in Louisiana or the massive urban structures built by Indus civilizations, were not necessarily societies ruled by elites.[21] And yet even in the case of egalitarian societies the building of such large-scale complexes implied that they had to act as a megamachine, because the logistics of such an enterprise required a maximum coordination of efforts under one rule. In this effort of coordination—made possible through calculation and geometric templates—lies the origin of the architectural project as the prefiguration of a structure yet to be built.

Among large-scale monumental complexes, the pyramids built in antiquity by the Egyptian civilization are perhaps the most radical incarnation of the architectural project at a highly impressive scale. Pyramids not only commemorated the pharaohs; they also mobilized a large number of people in a collective enterprise that in itself provided a tangible representation of state power. Contrary to popular belief, pyramids were not built by slaves[22] but by rotating cohorts of conscripted workers whose laboring activities included quarrying, transportation, building, and supervision. In total, this type of project could require over 15,000 workers, or one percent of the entire population of ancient Egypt.[23] Workers were organized in teams that were coordinated by supervisors who were controlled by the vizier, the pharaoh's prime minister. One of the earliest known "architects," the Egyptian Imhotep, was responsible for the funerary complex of Djoser in Saqqara, built in the twenty-seventh century BCE during the

Third Dynasty. Imhotep was a state official whose role combined priesthood, state administration, and mastery of science, particularly geometry. Even though they were constantly supervised by the representatives of the vizier, the pyramids' builders were highly skilled. Expertise was needed not only in the quarrying and cutting of stone, but also in transportation and the carpentry of the immense ramps necessary to move materials vertically. This work required both physical effort and an unprecedented degree of precision and focus in every moment of the building process.[24] The state therefore cared for workers by providing them with well-organized sleeping barracks, food, laundry, and other forms of sustenance.

The abstracting logic at work in the making of an Egyptian pyramid is comprehensible as a centrifugal force that radiates outward from the singularity of the built artifact to the whole state, its territory, its population, and its bureaucracy. At the same time, the pyramid is the hinge of a centripetal movement in which the diffused managerial power of the Egyptian territory converged toward one discrete monumental artifact. Herein lies the baffling paradox of the pyramid: its image is both symbolic and abstract. As a succession of platforms, it operates as the ultimate symbol of the ruler's absolute power. Concurrently, the pyramid's geometric form and precision of execution are the ultimate abstraction of the state as the governing megamachine that wields an extensive use of geometry for the purpose of planning.

Architecture, Geometry, and Money

For the Egyptians, geometry was not a theoretical corpus but rather the arithmetic breakdown of problems regarding area and volume. Even if their knowledge of mathematics and geometry was rudimentary and exclusively concerned with problem-solving, it was sufficient for them to achieve an unprecedented precision in calculations. This numeric mastery dictated the shift from brick to stone in the building of monumental complexes. On the construction sites of pyramids and temples, the skill and accuracy needed to level the ground and cut stone was not just a matter of individual craftsmanship, but a result of the state's capacity to subjugate every aspect of reality to geometric commensurability. According to Herodotus, the origins of geometry emerged from the practice of stretching rope.[25] In ancient Egypt, stretched rope was used to lay out the land, to build dams, granaries, and temples, and most importantly, to parcel the soil in order to assess the peasants' tributes to the pharaoh after the annual flood of the Nile.[26] If geometry is considered the core of architectural knowledge, such knowledge has been inseparable for millennia, and even today, from the fundamental prerogative of governing powers to measure and quantify. Before the ancient Greeks made it axiomatic, geometry was affirmed as a knowledge of unassailable self-evidence by civilizations like the Egyptians'.

As Alfred Sohn-Rethel noted, it is precisely the mastery of geometry for governing land and building large-scale infrastructure that widened the gap between intellectual and manual labor, and subordinated the latter to the former.[27] Yet Sohn-Rethel also notes that civilizations such as ancient Egypt and ancient China were governed by political systems of lordships and bondage where direct coercion played a decisive role.[28] In these civilizations, the division of labor—and particularly the separation of manual labor from intellectual labor—was the outcome of the centralization of power. A decisive though subtler step toward a deeper chasm between "head" and "hand" occurred, however, not through coercion and concentration of power but thanks to the rise of trade and commodity exchange.[29] When Egypt entered the Assyrian sphere of influence and gradually lost its hegemonic standing, the eastern Mediterranean witnessed an unprecedented intensification of trade. Greek-speaking populations were so profoundly impacted by this acceleration of commerce that in the last quarter of the seventh century BCE, Lydian and Ionian cities introduced the use of coins as a coping mechanism to facilitate and expedite payments.[30] Coinage spread quickly in all Greek city-states, and for the first time in history a transnational money economy matured. Suddenly, all economic transactions were ruled by the numeric logic of exchange value. Quantitative precision arrived with the proliferation of money and its power to reduce everything to the universal law of general equivalence. Money enabled the quantification of goods according to the measuring logic of financial compensation. Sohn-Rethel argues that within the milieu of an abstract money economy, speculative disciplines that instrumentalized the abstracting powers of the mind, like mathematics, geometry, and even philosophy, became the dominant ways of understanding society and the world.[31] While the Egyptians used mathematics and geometry to efficiently solve practical problems like measuring land and building large-scale structures, the Greeks hypostatized these disciplines as forms of abstract thinking, completely independent of any practical purpose. Nonetheless, the "pure reasoning" of the Greeks—in which all of existence is reduced to the abstract logic of numbers—could only arise in a social milieu dominated by the monetary commensuration of commodity values promoted by coinage.

According to conventional historiography, at the moment when the money economy, mathematics, and geometry were solidifying, Greek architecture supposedly transformed in a manner that is considered decisive for the entire history of Western architecture: the passage from timber to stone construction. In his theorization of the Greek temple, Vitruvius argued that the form of the temple gradually evolved from wooden carpentry into stone masonry without a change in tectonic logic.[32] Yet, as archaeological evidence demonstrates, economic wealth acquired by the Greek *poleis* between the seventh and sixth centuries BCE spawned the relatively quick appearance of Doric temples built in stone.[33] It is further necessary to remember that the building of monumental structures like Greek temples—even when financially backed by private donors—was always a state initiative, and it usually signaled the will of the Greek *poleis* to raise their political status. Building in stone would ensure not only permanence but also prestige, as stone monuments could compete with the architecture of the Egyptians, whose formal resolution and geometric precision were an inspiration for the Greeks. Moreover, to build in stone required a more organized workforce, which inevitably reinforced the commanding role of the state—or, in the Greek case, of the city-state.

The advent of stone construction completely changed both building processes and construction techniques. Carpentry relies on a simpler and more flexible supply chain and its operations happen at a smaller scale than those of stone masonry. Further, the very know-how of carpentry does not rely on a radical division

1.3 Propylaea at Athens, east façade, circa 437–432 BCE, exploded isometric view.
© Dogma, adapted from J. J. Coulton.

of design and execution. On the other hand, stone construction is labor-intensive and requires a vast logistical apparatus. The need for careful planning inevitably widens the division of tasks, which include quarrying, transporting, dressing, and planning. From this vantage, stone construction confronted similar issues in both ancient Egypt and ancient Greece. However, the predominance of the money economy distinguished the Greek-speaking world and prompted city authorities to appoint a supervisor—the architect—to plan monumental stone buildings in advance and oversee the building site.[34] In the Egyptian examples discussed earlier, the role of the architect was a complex layering of ritual, political, and technical mandates. In the Greek context the role of the architect became somewhat more specialized and geared to the organization of the construction site. The Greek architect did not just take care of design but also managed labor, from the distribution of tasks to remunerations. Unlike builders, architects were expected to be experts in a wide range of craft and construction approaches and technologies. Moreover, they had to possess a certain knowledge of calculation and geometry; their skills in these fields determined their social status and distinguished them clearly from craftsmen.[35] It was precisely within this framework that the word "architecture" emerged and its meaning was defined.

"Architecture" is a compound of two Greek terms: *arché* and *tekton*. *Arché* comes from *archein*, meaning to initiate or begin, but also to rule. *Tekton* means craftsman. Architecture addresses building *commanded* by a rule or principle, the *arché*. Architecture concerns both the principle, the conception of building, and its faithful execution—thus, in ancient Greece the figure of the architect was often used as the metaphor for a ruling authority.[36] It is in this historical conjuncture that the architectural project emerges as a bridge between institutional authority and technical knowledge.

In the fourth century BCE, Plato wrote that architects differ from builders in that they do not build with their hands but give orders to builders so as to achieve construction. Plato thus addressed the architect as *architekton*, or chief craftsman.[37] Unlike the modern architect, who emerged during the Renaissance, the ancient *architekton* worked on the construction site and interacted directly with the builders. Despite being the chief craftsman, the

fig. 1.3

architekton's contribution did not rely on craftsmanship but on theoretical knowledge.[38] The form of Greek temples was based on customary motives: a plinth, columns topped by capitals, an entablature with a frieze and a pediment. Authorial originality was not expected of the architect. Instead, the role of the architect was to focus on the design of details and the careful control of building execution. Devoid of any urge for formal "invention," the planning and building of Greek temples was produced through the application of a generally regularized protocol. The unprecedented refinement of the components of Greek temples—a stylobate that appeared perfectly flat, the orthostatic logic of the masonry, and the unparalleled smoothness of the stone dressing—was produced through a system of geometry that ensured maximum precision in the design, cutting, and finishing of the stone elements.

The application of geometry bestowed design control that was paramount not only for the sake of beauty but also for cost. By carefully measuring and standardizing building components, the architect could estimate the time and labor power the building process required. In a money-driven economy, such as that of the ancient Greek world, quantification became increasingly relevant, and the architect was expected to plan the work in advance and make reliable estimations. Of course, there was still a high degree of improvisation on the building site, and many features were introduced when the building was under construction. Even so, with the pressure of budgets scrupulously controlled by city authorities,[39] building specifications became increasingly stringent and made planning a precondition to construction. The demands of the money economy and the need to stay on budget made the precise definition and measurement of building components a necessary practice. Building templates and specimens were used by architects to ensure that builders perfectly executed ornamental features. Symmetry and uniformity in architectural features were desired for their aesthetic effect, but also—and especially—because they confirmed and demonstrated subordination to a planned design.

The architecture of the Greek temple is not in itself abstract. On the contrary, its physical form represents the archetypical features of a monumentalized *megaron*, the ancient one-room dwelling that served to house the divinity. As in the Egyptian pyramids, abstraction is evident in the power of the precision employed to build a Greek temple. Beyond defining the formal properties of the building, immense calculating precision extended to every domain entailed in the enterprise of building monumental architecture, including geometric speculation, logistics, budget control, proportional systems, labor management, and building techniques. Such all-encompassing calculating precision—as we have seen—was made possible by a culture driven by the abstraction of both mathematical and geometric rigor and the pervasive role of a money economy with a quantifying attitude that made everything susceptible to and reducible to the logic of numbers.

A belief in the governing logic of numbers—among other things—prompted architects to refine the proportional and syntactic order of temples. Specific geometric ratios determine the dimension of every element in a Doric temple—from the column shaft to the metope and triglyph, to all the moldings of the entablature and the pediment. Further, the position of elements is established by a syntactic order that encompasses the entire building. Ultimately, the harmonic proportions that rule monumental Greek architecture were the outcome of the stringent logic necessitated by a complex construction process.

The historian Richard Seaford traced the emergence of money in ancient Greece in relation to the symbolic and redistributive character of public sacrifices intended to strengthen a sense of communality within the *polis*.[40] The need to fairly divide the bodies of sacrificed animals between men and gods spurred worshipers to create a system of measurement using cuts, essentially abstracting the sacrificial body into a geometric equivalence. According to Seaford, like the communality cultivated by sacrifices, money—with a greater degree of abstraction—eased relationships between people and strengthened their confidence in the all-encompassing order of the community.[41] Money facilitated trade between buyers and sellers, building confidence in the political authority of the *polis* and its responsibility to mint currency. As such, the money economy provided *harmonia*, an abstract equalizing principle that united all things. It is hence possible to argue that the harmonic forms of the Doric temple, its very system of proportion, were both the direct outcome and the subtle sublimation of a society marked by a social synthesis increasingly determined by the abstractions of a money-driven economy.

As chief builders of prestigious undertakings and pressed by public authority, architects consolidated their professional mandate by writing treatises. The circulation of architectural treatises coincided with the development of the first stone temples. In writing *De architectura libri decem*, the oldest extant Western treatise on architecture, Vitruvius developed the legacy of ancient Greek architects as "theorists" whose forerunners came from Ionian cities, where both the money economy and mathematical thinking were conceived. Vitruvius highlighted architects such as Silenus and Theodorus of Samos who started the tradition of architectural writing in the sixth century BCE. In his book Theodorus described his major achievement, the Heraion of Samos, one of the largest and most refined temples built in the archaic period.[42] Today, Theodorus might be considered an "archistar," given that his writing consolidated not just a reputation but also the very authority of the architect as *author*. This authority clearly distinguished the sixth-century BCE architect from builders, for whom intellectual speculation was precluded.

In *De architectura*, Vitruvius reinforced the division between intellectual and manual work by dividing the production of architecture into two moments: *fabrica* and *ratiocinatio*. While *fabrica* refers to the practice of building, *ratiocinatio* refers to reasoning, the ideation of the building before its realization. Unquestionably *ratiocinatio* was the responsibility of the architect.[43] Within this reasoning, geometry played a crucial role. A mastery of geometric computation further distanced the architect from the builder, whose know-how was more empirical than theoretical, more practical than discursive. Through reasoning, architecture becomes a way of contemplating the world, where—as in rhetoric—what is created is not simply an object but discourse itself. This is why Vitruvius (and later Leon Battista Alberti) consistently borrowed categories from rhetoric such as *ordinatio* (ordering) and *dispositio* (arrangement). Here, authority is not only expressed through building knowledge, but also through that which *signifies* built matter, the *idea*—the project—that transforms matter into a geometrically organized form. The locus of this transformation is geometric drawing, and thus Vitruvius considered its expert practice essential for an architect. While the evolution of geometric drawing will be explored in the next chapter, for now it suffices to say that its mastery is a fundamental factor in the expanding gap between intellectual and manual labor. Indeed, following his predecessors, Vitruvius theorizes an architecture whose realization as an artifact could only happen through the prefiguration of geometric drawing, the exactitude of which governs all the details of a building.

The Becoming-Diagram of Architecture

In the beginning of the Middle Ages in Europe, two building traditions confronted each other: building *more germanico*, based on timber construction and customary among northern European populations, and *more romano*, which followed the precisely cut stone and standardized brick building legacy of the Romans. With the weakening of the western portion of the Roman Empire, building *more romano* rapidly declined, and monumental buildings—mostly churches—were built poorly, often by recycling the spolia of ancient structures. But building *more romano* was resuscitated with the rise of new, powerful political actors, such as the Carolingian empire between the eighth and ninth century CE, and their desire to build large-scale projects in masonry to establish a link between the authority of the emerging empire and its ancient predecessor. As in the past, building on a large scale required architects to act as supervisors, or prelates, whose role—similar to Egyptian viziers—combined skills in theology, philosophy, geometry, and management. Architectural historian Carlo Tosco calls these prelates "architect-patrons," because they not only directed work at the building site, often suggesting specific building solutions, but also fundraised and initiated the building itself.[44] This phenomenon was particularly widespread within the monastic tradition, which became one of the most organized and powerful social institutions in medieval Western Europe.

Although inaugurated in the third century CE as a loose movement of hermits, Christian monasticism gradually evolved into communities where monks adopted a highly formalized way

19

of living in which not just worship but the entirety of life—in all its mundane aspects—became an incessant *opus dei*. Adherence to a strict way of life was the purpose of monasticism, so the very existence of the monk was conceived as a project whose unfolding followed a well-defined plan—the rule. Accordingly, from the onset of monastic life, space needed to be carefully planned in all its details, including the act of building the monastery.

Under the Rule of St. Benedict, the collective nature of monasticism was reinforced by further regulating the monks' relationship to both time and space. The cultural and political influence of Benedictine monasticism was greatly bolstered by reforms undertaken by Carolingian rulers; in particular, Charlemagne advanced the dissemination of the Rule, making it a model for communities throughout the empire. Instrumentalizing the monks' skills in planning and organization, Charlemagne's political strategy supported ecclesiastical power in order to strengthen the Carolingian dynasty's governance over its territories. At this time, monasteries became epicenters of political and economic power, and their purpose exceeded the renunciation of worldly life and spiritual contemplation that had originally inspired early monastic communities. From their secluded locations, monasteries functioned as large compounds that included productive, administrative, and educational premises.[45]

The programmatic complexity and managerial logic of post-Carolingian Benedictine monasteries are distinguishable in the ideal plan of a monastery preserved in the library of St. Gall,

fig. 1.4

Switzerland.[46] Drawn in the ninth century CE on five sheets of parchment sewn together, the plan was drafted in the monastery of Reichenau under the supervision of its abbot Haito and sent to Gozbert, the abbot of St. Gall. Addressing Gozbert, Haito states his intention that, in the plan, the abbot of St. Gall should "exercise ... ingenuity and recognize my devotion."[47] It is here suggested that the plan was not meant to be the blueprint for a specific building, but rather a diagram (complete with an extensive text and legend on its back) to help the abbot define the disposition of different spaces and their uses.

The plan shows a complete monastic complex made up of approximately forty buildings, including churches, houses, stables, kitchens, workshops, a brewery, an infirmary, storage, and

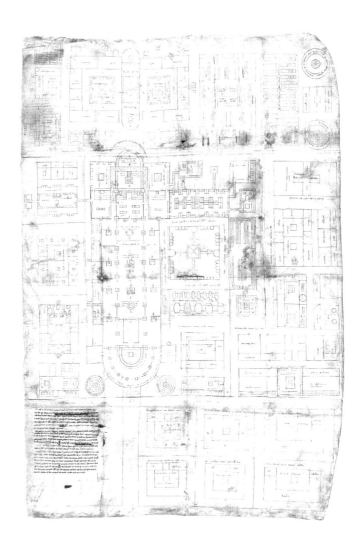

1.4 Ideal plan of the monastery preserved in the library of St. Gall, Switzerland, ninth century CE. © Stiftsbibliothek Sankt Gallen. © Stiftsbibliothek Sankt Gallen.

even a special house for bloodletting. Remarkable emphasis is put on the compound's functional aspects, such as circulation and storage of goods. Use of a grid allows for the efficient organization of a wide range of activities. An architectural plan for the management of life is delineated, within which everything is carefully mapped in terms of a stringent economy of space. This planning effort can be understood not only in relationship to the organization of a vast building complex and its many activities, but also as the embodiment of the most important aspect of monasticism—to live according to the Rule. Within the monastery, *life* became the content of architecture. Each moment of the monk's daily life is translated into a typical space: dormitory (sleeping), refectory (eating), library (studying), workshops (working), chapel (praying). The building is at once a schedule and the embodiment of a form of life. As such, the St. Gall plan should be discerned as an abstraction that represents not the built form of the monastery but its organizational and programmatic logic.

The St. Gall plan anticipates one of the fundamental tendencies of modernity: the becoming-diagram of architecture. A diagram is commonly understood as a means to convey information through a simplified figure; as such, it is used to synthetically represent both concept and form. In contrast to this definition, Michel Foucault, Gilles Deleuze, and Félix Guattari conceived the diagram as a machine that *directly* produces effects of power.[48] For these twentieth-century philosophers, the diagram has nothing to do with representation; rather, the diagram *is what it does*: it makes an instance of power not only legible, but *effective*. The organization of medieval monasteries is an early example of the translation of a diagrammatic abstraction directly into an architecture reduced to its simplest form: a composition of walls defining intervals of space. Actual monasteries were far from the functional perfection of the St. Gall plan. Still, a tendency toward standardization of both plan and architectural features is displayed in many of the monastic complexes built during and after the Carolingian reform. In these projects, abstraction worked to organize discrete and specific moments into more generalizable and repeatable patterns. This operation is further evident in the most important and influential contribution to Western monastic space: the architecture of the Cistercian order.

Building and Abstraction

Seceding from the Benedictine order at the end of the tenth century, the Cistercians sought to return to the basics of the Benedictine Rule—and in particular to the key principles of *ora et labora*, pray and work. Early Cistercian communities settled in extremely remote locations, prompting them to become highly skilled and self-sufficient farmers and builders. These skills would eventually undermine their theological pursuits, eroding their initial ideals of poverty and simplicity and allowing the order to become a proto-industrial enterprise. In a short time, between the twelfth and thirteenth centuries, the Cistercians became sophisticated craftsmen in the fields of metallurgy and construction, as well as excellent engineers with unparalleled experience in hydraulics.[49] Such technological knowledge clearly manifested in their capacity to build ground-up monastic complexes and their adjacent estates by assembling a vast range of know-how that included stonemasons, carpenters, plumbers, brickmakers, joiners, lime burners, tilers, smiths, and other workers. The centralized structure and aggressively expansionist politics of the order allowed it to disseminate specialized knowledge to a multitude of communities settling across Europe. From Poland to Portugal and from England to Italy, Cistercians solidified a unified and systematic approach in not only building but also design.

Indeed, the Cistercians were the first monastic order to elaborate a specific design approach for their monastic premises, based on four principles deduced by historians by analyzing extant Cistercian complexes.[50] The first principle conceived an architecture without *affectus*, that is, without any superfluous ornament that distracted the monks from their focus on ascetic practice. The second principle categorized the monastery as an *officina*, a place devoted only to spiritual and manual work. In adherence to this principle the spatial organization of the monastery was based on a standard disposition of programs within buildings—such as the church, the chapter, the dormitory, the refectory—arranged around a cloister. The third principle stipulated that the monastery was to be built with only one material, usually stone, in order to strengthen its uniformity and solidity. Finally, the fourth principle prescribed the modular logic of the monastery. Defined as "ad quadratum," the measure of the basic square module was derived from the crossing between the nave and transept of the church, which would therefore become a key spatial element endowing the whole complex with rhythm and measure.

fig. 1.5

Visible in numerous Cistercian abbeys built in the eleventh and twelfth centuries, these principles were used by Bernard of Clairvaux himself to found Fontenay in Marmagne in 1118. This unprecedented uniform and standardized way of building defined the architecture of the Cistercian tradition because all new monasteries were built according to plans—*schemata*—sent by the mother abbey. Presumably, these plans acted as simple diagrams that helped monks organize the disposition of different programs and above all the modular logic of the whole complex. None of these documents have survived, but a possible echo of this tradition is found in the plan of a Cistercian church drawn in the first half of the thirteenth century by Villard de Honnecourt in his famous

fig. 1.6

sketchbook.[51] In this drawing, architectural form is abstracted into a grid of pillars and piers that form bays with a proportional relationship of one to two. With an X centered on the pillars, Villard alluded to the structural motive of cross vaulting, which was extensively used and perfected by the Cistercians and allowed them to build their structures—from foundations to ceiling—entirely in stone. The *schemata* were modified and adapted to existing site conditions, resources, and skills, and yet their extensive use produced a highly uniform approach to design and construction for the first time in medieval Europe. As in the case of Greek temples, this process of standardization was enabled by the use of stone, of which Cistercians became expert cutters. Requiring more attention to planning and geometry, the use of stone allowed the Cistercians to resurrect the ancient practice of building orthostatic masonry, that is, perfectly horizontal courses of stones.[52] It was this desire for precision and economy of construction that prompted Cistercian builders to standardize building components and achieve an architecture in which the syntactic relationships between elements gradually replaced the additive and ad hoc way of building of early Romanesque architecture. The result was an architecture based on regular sequences of precisely delineated features like pillars, buttresses, arches, and ribs.

The consequences of this architectural language were not merely aesthetic: in fact, the Cistercian language dramatically

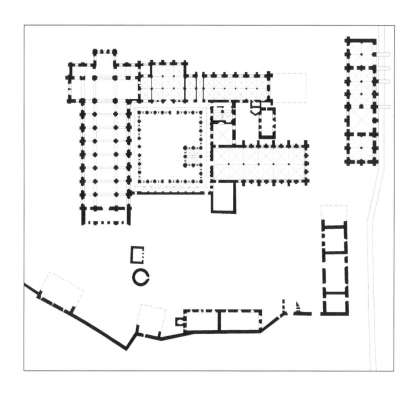

1.5 Cistercian Abbey of Fontenay in Marmagne, founded in the twelfth century. © Dogma.

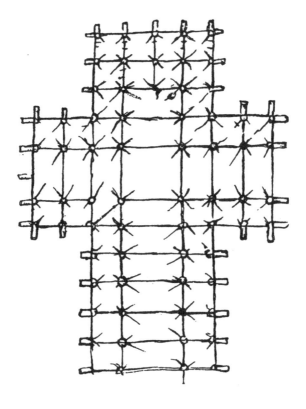

1.6 Plan of a Cistercian church, from Villard de Honnecourt's sketchbook, 1230s. From Villard de Honnecourt, *Album* (Paris: Hachette, 2013).

influenced the rationalization of building practices. By standardizing building components, it made construction faster and costs controllable.

At a monumental scale with no existing precedent in Europe, the Cistercian way of building inspired an even more impressive way of producing stone architecture that materialized in the so-called "Gothic" cathedral. These artifacts represent the culmination of medieval building knowledge, but they are also the locus where the *project* acquired a renewed urgency.

If in ancient times the purpose of the project was the command and coordination of numerous laborers for building large-scale artifacts, during the Middle Ages this purpose was reinforced to counter the political and contractual power of builders. It is possible to argue that, from the Middle Ages onward, the project became a mechanism of "dispossession" of the products that builders produced with their hands and knowledge. The role of the project in this process of class construction was not theorized until the Renaissance and was put into practice even later, and it must be understood in regard to the ever-evolving social meaning of labor. In Roman culture, *labor* originally described the servile activity of the slave in contrast to *negotia*, the political and professional activity of the free citizen. With the diffusion of Christianity, laboring activities acquired a positive meaning. To labor was not simply a form of subsistence; it also pertained to a life of Christian *dignitas* and contributed to the wealth of communities.[53] It was the medieval reevaluation of labor as an active form of citizenship that prompted artisans to acquire a strong ideological self-confidence which, especially in the building trades, resulted in their political emancipation. Significantly, in many medieval cities, stone and wood cutters organized the first guilds, which allowed them to leverage a collective political pressure that secured unprecedented power for builders on the building site.[54] Due to their scale and importance in medieval cities, cathedrals were a place where builders' agency coalesced and, conversely, where patrons and financial donors made early attempts to tame, counter, and gain command of such agency.

Cathedrals were the seat of bishops whose spiritual leadership was paralleled, if not exceeded, by their political and administrative prestige. After the fall of the Roman Empire and the collapse of its vast administrative system, bishops assumed uncontested and longstanding political authority in European cities.[55] While periodically challenged, the authority of bishops was often confirmed and even enhanced by kings and emperors who leveraged alliances with episcopal power to reinforce their rule. For ruling sovereigns, stewarding the construction of large-scale cathedrals was an important aspect of state-making.[56] This strategy underscored the rise of cathedrals built between the twelfth and fourteenth centuries in the Île-de-France and beyond. In cities such as Amiens, Laon, Chartres, and Reims, cathedrals were built to help consolidate the authority of the Capetian kingdom as the first embodiment of the French nation. In light of its significant physical and economic impact on a locale, the erection of a cathedral demanded the agreement of many stakeholders including the monarchy, the episcopate, and the emerging class of merchants needed for financial backing. In fact, apart from embodying theological principles, the scale and structural coherence of these monuments represented the coalescing of multiple political and economic forces into a unified public work. Not simply places for worship, cathedrals were also multifunctional halls for all kinds of public gatherings.[57]

fig. 1.7

The prototype of the twelfth-century Gothic cathedral was the reconstruction and expansion of the abbey church of Saint-Denis into a royal basilica. This considerable undertaking, started in 1135 and supervised by the powerful abbot Suger, introduced major formal and structural innovations in the building of large-scale churches. Most notably the cathedral contains a complex ambulatory with radiating chapels, clustered columns supporting pointed arches, and cross vaulting that allows for large glass expanses in the windows. Advances in architectural elements were made possible by builders' capacity to cut and lay stone with increased geometric precision, but also because in undertakings that involved prominent stakeholders, many workers, and substantial funding, planning again became an unavoidable requisite to the production of architecture. As argued by the architectural historian Dieter Kimpel, the building of Gothic cathedrals in Île-de-France represented a significant step in the rationalization of architecture both formally and especially in terms of

1.7 Basilica of Saint-Denis, Paris, twelfth century, interior of the ambulatory built under Abbot Suger's direction. © Bildarchiv Monheim GmbH / Alamy Stock Photo.

production.[58] The integration of larger stone blocks required the use of complex machinery like pulleys and cranes on the construction site; moreover, the daunting scale of these buildings required perfect geometric regularization of each masonry component. This mandated symmetry of all the architectural elements and increased coordination of the labor force.[59]

Literature and popular culture have commonly promoted the narrative that cathedrals were built by the collective effort of builders without the guidance of a singular architect.[60] This is partly true, given that the building process endured for a long time (often for centuries). Yet the scale and increasing geometric precision of cathedrals yielded a more stringent division of labor and asymmetrical relationships among workers. On the building site of a cathedral, for every skilled stonecutter there were two or more unskilled workers attending to menial activities like cleaning or moving materials.[61] Moreover, the coordination of vast numbers of workers required administrative hierarchy and, increasingly, a separation between those who decided and those who executed. From the twelfth century onward, the construction process of cathedrals became the impetus for the progressive splintering of the workforce. Specialized professional figures were identified as the workers at the quarry, the movers of materials, the stonecutters, the master builder who was addressed as the "architect," and the *parler*, a unique figure who mediated between architects and stonecutters by translating the design of the architect into verbal instructions for the builders.[62] Compared to previous medieval building endeavors, the material exactitude evident in cathedrals engendered a surplus of mediation in terms of graphic and verbal instructions. The precision executed in the manifestation of a cathedral reflects a marked tendency across medieval Europe toward the radical rationalization of time and space, augmented by calculations and accentuated by a society dominated by the ethos of commerce.

Although not yet under the pressure of clearly defined budgets and schedules, it is not an exaggeration to say that cathedral building sites anticipated Fordist factories where the division of labor, standardization of materials and tasks, and heightened worker dependence on a wage became major issues of both design and building.[63] Above all, the building of cathedrals imposed, rather dramatically, a split between intellectual and manual labor. This split is well rendered in a sermon by the Dominican friar Nicolas de Biart in which the masters of the masons are exemplary of bad conduct because, "with gloves on their hands," they command builders and, not unlike corrupt bishops, receive higher pay despite not working.[64] This anecdote demonstrates the pertinence of the division of labor and that cathedral builders recognized and sometimes even resisted their place within this division. The medieval building site inevitably became a place of conflict between two competing interests: the increasing financialization of construction work, which required an expedited working arrangement, and the desire of builders to methodically carry out their craftsmanship.[65]

From this conflict the modern architect emerged. The abstraction of the architectural drawing was the weapon used by architects to control builders. With the building of Gothic cathedrals, the practice of drawing once again became widespread. The thirteenth-century Reims Palimpsest[66] is one of the oldest extant drawings on parchment belonging to the so-called "Gothic" tradition. Remarkably, this drawing renders the elevation of the façade of Reims cathedral in a canonical orthogonal projection. The drawing makes the features of the cathedral easily measurable in scale[67] and was presumably used by the chief architect to set the overall framework and direct the work of crews of stonecutters. Although the Palimpsest does not represent the actual thickness of architectural elements—leaving room for improvisation by the craftsmen of the masons' guild—it determined a stringent compositional armature used to dictate the direction of the work. Such drawings, created by means of compass and rule, allowed architects to test proportional schemes. Additionally, patrons reviewed drawings to control and agree upon a preliminary design and accordingly arrange work and funds. In the production of layouts, the compass-and-rule method favored the use of squares and equilateral triangles; when translated into stone, these figures generate proportions governed by irrational numbers (respectively, $\sqrt{2}$ and $\sqrt{3}/2$). For this reason, "Gothic" drawings reached a significant level of idealized abstraction in layout. Their execution, however, still necessitated adjustments as the resultant proportional relationships made calculations very difficult.[68] By

fig. 1.8

1.8 Reims Palimpsest, redrawing of geometrical overlay. © Dogma.

contrast, as will become evident in following chapters, the modular logic adopted during the Renaissance granted architects full control over material quantities, making calculations much easier. In the thirteenth century, abstraction in drawings like the Reims Palimpsest mediated idea and execution, and started to play a fundamental role in the intellectualization of architecture and to emancipate the architect from the master builder.

It could be argued that when, in the fifteenth century, Leon Battista Alberti articulated the authority of architects over builders, he was simply theorizing a trend that had been under way since the beginning of the twelfth century. In this view, Alberti's theory was not novel but rather plainly enunciated the unfolding reality that labor-intensive building sites required a hierarchically organized division of labor in which the architect was no longer the master builder but the "architect theorist." When describing the role of the architect, Alberti emphasized the split between intellectual and manual skills:

> Before I go any farther, I should explain whom I mean by an architect; for it is no carpenter that I would have you to compare to the greatest exponents of other disciplines: the carpenter is but an instrument in the hands of the architect. Him I consider the architect, who by sure and wonderful reason and method, knows how to devise through his own mind and energy, and to realize by construction, whatever can be most beautifully fitted out for the noble needs, by the movement of weights and the joining and massing of bodies. To do this he must have an understanding and knowledge of all the highest and most noble disciplines. This is then the architect.[69]

Alberti's definition of the architect *per via negativa*, in opposition to the carpenter, implies the downgrading of manual work in relation to ideation. For Alberti, builders are important, but their agency must be surrendered to the will of the architect. In this argument, Alberti subordinated building to the architect's abstract *idea*, the source of the architect's power, but also—and especially—a tool of the patron to command architecture. Alberti's theory is thus the first explicit attempt to theorize and valorize the architect's act of ideation. Yet it should not be understood as a plea for an ideal condition, but rather as an interpretation of the economic context of European cities. While building was an important public expenditure in many powerful cities that garnered economic success in the thirteenth century (such as Florence or Siena), the financing of large-scale projects often depended on private support. In the course of the 1300s, the conflict between labor and finance was exacerbated by several factors that generally transformed the condition of work. Most decisive was the spread of the Black Plague in 1347 and 1348, which killed nearly one-third of the European population, thus increasing the cost of labor. Labor conflicts escalated in the aftermath of the plague because the scarcity of manpower enabled workers to bargain for better working conditions.[70] Moreover, the emergence of early forms of financial capitalism, such as moneylending, forcefully changed the prevailing cultural attitude toward *time*. Although the precise timing of human activities was introduced by monastic orders,[71] the advent of public mechanical clocks in the thirteenth century allowed city dwellers to coordinate their activities to precise schedules, giving the economy its specific temporal structure.[72] In regard to investment of capital and control of production, timing became a stringent discipline, especially in relation to building sites. Attention to time as a financial criterion made it incumbent to carefully plan the design process ahead of construction. Planning in advance of construction was also obligatory in the drawing of contracts, which served to estimate building costs and stipulate remunerations. Often considered a tool for artistic representation, the act of drawing in preparation for construction in fact evolved out of the contractual relationship between builders and patrons. This reality is exemplified in the famous elevation drawing for Palazzo Sansedoni in Siena.[73] One of the oldest known measured drawings of a building façade, the elevation was drafted as a contract between client and master builder, with the contract terms written directly below the drawing itself. This document is further evidence that, as early as the middle of the thirteenth century, the project, in its essence, concerned planning with intent to finance a substantial undertaking. The subordination of building to planning de facto made the architect responsible not solely

34

for the supervision of work but also, and more significantly, for the ideation of the building's design. Planning, building, and finance have a close affiliation, and, as is clearly evident in the Sansedoni elevation, this tripartite relationship is fundamentally mediated by the project in the form of measurable drawing. Yet the author of the Sansedoni drawing is not yet an architect whose status is completely emancipated from the role of builder. The Albertian architect is born only during the political counterrevolution of the fifteenth century, when guild power was countered by an emerging capitalist elite who approached architecture as a fundamental political investment, and through their patronage anointed Filippo Brunelleschi as the charismatic archetype of the emerging professional architect.

Project and Counterrevolution

Born in Florence in 1377 and trained as a goldsmith and sculptor, Brunelleschi participated in the most important architectural undertakings of the Florentine Republic in the first decades of the fifteenth century. Although his career was mythologized by his followers as that of the "exemplary" architect, historian Marvin Trachtenberg warns against uncritically accepting such narratives. Trachtenberg contends that Brunelleschi's biographer Antonio di Tuccio Manetti was more interested in celebrating Brunelleschi as prototype of the Albertian architect than considering the real aspects of his work.[74] Trachtenberg further argues that Brunelleschi's work is situated in the middle of a paradigm shift between two temporalities of architectural practice.[75] The first of these Trachtenberg defines as "Building-in-time": a practice of building in which continuous redesign was accepted and even celebrated as a fundamental condition of architecture. Building-in-time, Trachtenberg notes, was not the outcome of ad hoc self-organization, but rather of the "principle of *concatenation*," or concatenate design.[76] Concatenate design consisted of a chainlike linkage of design events that manifested while building progressed. This process required every design phase to be consistent with the previous step, but such consistency was not governed by a comprehensive plan. Design and building, therefore, are not diachronic but synchronic in concatenate design: indeed, they happen almost at the same time, as in the building of cathedrals, where foundations could be laid well before façades were designed.

The second temporality was what Trachtenberg defines as "Building-outside-time," which consisted of a temporal separation between design and building, making the latter subordinate to the former.[77] In Building-outside-time the temporality of building as something that necessarily happens *in time* was suppressed by the imposition of a design that conceived the building in its entirety before the start of construction. Within this temporality design is meant to be immutable; change or *adaptation during construction* was categorically prohibited.

As Trachtenberg notes, Building-outside-time became possible only in the nineteenth century when detailed specifications ensured that buildings were executed according to the architect's design. Yet the theory of Building-outside-time was advanced in the fifteenth century by Alberti in his *De re aedificatoria*, when he theorized the architect as the unequivocal *author* of architecture. For Alberti, the architect imagines an abstract idea of construction that is completely subsumed by the all-encompassing order of design. As discussed above, Alberti accepted that the architect's design depended on consultation and discussion with experts and even builders; however, once defined, the design could not be altered during its execution.

According to Trachtenberg, Brunelleschi's work represents a cohabitation of both temporalities.[78] On the one hand, he engaged with the tradition of Building-in-time by revising his architectural ideas while they were tested through building. On the other hand, he composed representations of the building process that benefited his authority over the construction site and made him the *author* of the realized buildings. Trachtenberg rightly argues that political connections aided Brunelleschi's ability to self-fashion himself as the unquestionable author of his buildings, and influential contacts helped him secure crucial supervising roles in major public works, among which the cupola of Santa Maria del Fiore, initiated in 1418, is perhaps the most illustrious example. Beyond this, however, a decisive factor in making Brunelleschi the embodiment of the architect as author—despite his dependence on Building-in-time—was the use of a specific approach to architectural form that resonated with contemporary Florentine politics.[79]

Brunelleschi's architecture is one of the earliest consequences of a counterrevolution led by an oligarchic elite of wealthy families who rose to power as a reaction to the turmoil of fourteenth-century political life in Florence. During that century, guilds had countered and successfully limited wealthy families' control of city governance. Yet guild politics were ambivalent, as they defended the rights of merchants and artisans against the *magnati* but precluded political representation for workers, especially the wage workers of large artisanal enterprises.[80] In 1378, this lack of representation provoked textile workers, known as *ciompi*, to lead a major revolution and establish a short-lived revolutionary government. Although immediately repressed, the *tumulto dei ciompi* and the fear of political instability prompted, over time, an elite group of wealthy families to persuade merchants and artisans to support political reforms that ultimately, in the early fifteenth century, moved the Florentine Republic toward oligarchic rule.[81] The subsequent decline of guild power is clearly reflected in Brunelleschi's political emancipation from the guild's professional structure. The political support for Brunelleschi's career needs to be understood in this context.

The success of Brunelleschi can also be ascribed to his refinement and radicalization of what Arnaldo Bruschi has defined as "syntactical architecture,"[82] a formal language in which every architectural element is a syntagma, a constituent segment of a coherently ordered whole. While developed by Brunelleschi, this language was already nascent in several medieval church interiors, where the formal and spatial coherence was often reinforced by ornamental features such as frames and entablatures. In Brunelleschi's architecture this approach reached an apex of formal abstraction, because he subjected building parts to a "rational" whole. With this approach, Brunelleschi introduced an architectural language in which any building was dominated by an overall *disegno*. For example, in the Ospedale degli Innocenti— started in 1418—the module of the loggia coordinates every architectural element and becomes legible through ornamentation which emphasizes the syntactical logic of the building. In the loggia, the agent of coordination is the systematic use of columns and arches, the latter of which are further inscribed within a half-square. Moreover, Brunelleschi's use of standardized decorative

fig. 1.9

37

elements, carved out of gray, textureless, "abstract" *pietra serena*, deprived builders of their artistic autonomy by prohibiting interpretation of decorative elements, thus granting total control to the architect. Brunelleschi, who may have been familiar with Vitruvius and examples of ancient Roman architecture, adopted the use of a design grammar. Yet his understanding of the systematic nature of Roman architecture was overly idealized. Apart from a few canonical buildings such as the Colosseum, which shows a coherent stacking of different orders, the ruins of ancient Roman architecture are varied in their syntax and irreducible to the logic of the "classical" orders. Brunelleschi's architectural language, in contrast, is based on a strict modularity within which ornament becomes a device used to visually confirm the relationship between each element and the whole. In this way the entire building process becomes subsumed within the architect's design control.

Crucially, Brunelleschi's control was not limited to the formal qualities of the building but extended to construction techniques and the organization of the building site. This authority is palpable in his most important and celebrated undertaking: the cupola of Florence's cathedral, commenced under his supervision in 1418. It is well documented that Brunelleschi ingeniously constructed the dome by developing a revolutionary method based on a scaffolding system that rested on the in-progress structure, thus allowing it to rise as construction advanced.[83] As Trachtenberg reminds us,[84] in the design of the dome Brunelleschi exploited the Building-in-time technique by elaborating and revising his solution while building was in progress. Additionally, Brunelleschi's organization of the building site and its labor force was decisive in the success of the project. Not only did he devise sophisticated machinery for lifting materials, he also enforced precise shifts to minimize the time needed for workers to climb up and down the scaffolding, rigorous safety checks, and schedules for meal breaks.[85]

To ensure the builders submitted to his leadership he refused to reveal his design, giving instruction only as work progressed. Further, Brunelleschi would occasionally not show up on site, thus sowing confusion as builders would not know how to proceed without his guidance.[86] Above all, his supremacy on the building site was sealed by the geometric precision

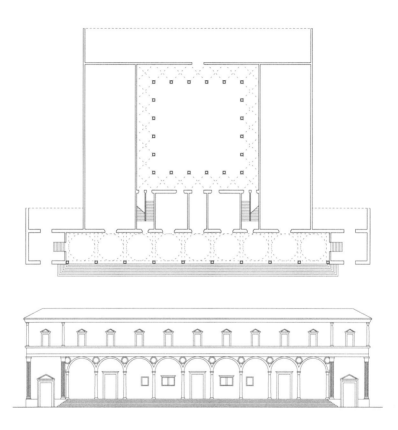

1.9   Filippo Brunelleschi, Ospedale degli Innocenti, Florence, started in 1418, plan and façade.
© Dogma, adapted from Amir Djalali.

of the structure, where one misplaced brick would compromise everything. Brunelleschi's attitude was clearly subsumed in the unprecedented geometric precision of the dome. The dome's stark silhouette, augmented by contrasting cloves clad with red tiles and crests made of white marble, violently conflicted with the urban chaos of the medieval city.

Brunelleschi's authority did not remain unchallenged. First, he was arrested for failing to pay his annual subscription to the stonemasons' and carpenters' guild while practicing as a master builder. Second, workers on the building site went on strike, bargaining for better working conditions.[87] Both events allowed Brunelleschi to reinforce his role as a freelance architect. Because work could not proceed on the building site without his supervision, guild and city authorities were forced to release him from jail, thus recognizing his role as architect outside the guild system. In dealing with the strike, Brunelleschi hired another team of builders, breaking the strike and forcing the original workers to surrender to lower wages. These conflicts were indicative of a crucial transition in Renaissance culture in which manual work was increasingly subordinated to intellectual work. The breach had begun with the hierarchical organization of labor at large-scale undertakings like cathedrals; in the fifteenth century, the division was theorized, propagating the idea that the author and authority of building was the architect. Although it would take time before the architect's design project took full command of building practice, starting with Alberti the theorization of architecture established the architect as sole author of a building, despite the truth that building is a collaborative enterprise that involves, today more than ever, many actors, from experts to builders.

The basis of Alberti's architectural theory with regard to building is precisely that the authority of the project is *unquestionable* and cannot be challenged by those who build. Therefore, the task of the architect as *author* is to provide a project with what Alberti defines in a passage of *De re aedificatoria* as *modo et ratione* (method and purpose).[88] In her Italian translation of Alberti's book, the philologist Valeria Giontella translates these two terms as "progetto."[89] For Alberti, the project addresses not just the creative inception of architecture but the control of the building process. Therefore, the project is essentially *planning*: not an act of pure will, but a careful consideration of means toward an end. Enter the architectural project.

Notably, while writing *De re aedificatoria*, Alberti was also working on *Del governo della famiglia*, a book that established his centuries-long reputation as a humanist. The latter, a treatise on domestic economy, addressed the management of the family as a successful enterprise. Werner Sombart identifies *Del governo della famiglia* as the manifesto of a nascent bourgeois "spirit of undertaking" in early capitalism.[90] According to Sombart, the core of Alberti's teachings is that beyond thrift, success in business requires proper coordination of actions and the profitable administration of time. Here Alberti equates economy of time with economy of money. From this perspective, entrepreneurialism is not cast as individual bravura, but instead as a concerted plan in which—more than individual leadership—organization and coordination play a decisive role. For Sombart, Alberti's spirit of undertaking anticipates the projecting age described and advocated by Defoe: a theory of the project as an institutional framework invoked to facilitate economic ventures.

It is now necessary to exit the prehistory of the project and enter its history proper. In the next chapters the project will be discussed as a vessel of a new organization of building labor, in which the work of construction is subordinated to the regulating force of financial capital.

2   From *Disegno* to Design

Since the Renaissance, the architect, unlike the builder, *draws*. As became clear in the previous chapter, drawing as an antecedent to building was practiced in antiquity and later recuperated by medieval master builders when undertaking large-scale ventures like cathedrals. However, it was not customary to draw every detail of a building, even for prominent works, and builders were not accustomed to following graphic notations. Many design decisions were made *in situ* by master builders in direct discussion with builders. For this reason, until the Renaissance, drawing was limited to the production of a few general documents, often plans and elevations needed to describe the overall appearance of a building. This situation changed toward the end of the fifteenth century, when a more comprehensive and thorough approach to architectural drawing became a widespread practice. Less motivated by pragmatism, the increased preparation of drawings in advance of building developed in response to the categorization of art and architecture as liberal professions fundamentally defined by reasoning. In this light, drawing was not just a medium but a practice that expressed the *conceptual* origin of the work of art. Distinct from manual craft, *disegno* involved the mental effort to conceive.

Disegno comes from the Latin *designare*, which means "to mark out, to point out, to devise."[1] In sixteenth-century Italian artistic parlance, the Latin word gave origin to *disegnare*, which addressed both cognition and the gesture of tracing lines on a sheet of paper. The term *disegno* was used simultaneously in painting, sculpture, and architecture to suggest a universal form of artistic ideation. This meaning made *disegno* a buzz word in the Renaissance realm of art and beyond.[2] As art historian Michael Baxandall noted, the English word *design*, which emerged in the late sixteenth century, originated from the Italian *disegno* via the Middle French term *desseing*, which referred to a project, a plot, or a purpose, something more general than the graphic aspect of drawing (*dessin*).[3] According to Baxandall, the writer John Evelyn argued in his 1662 book *Sculptura* that while *drawing* refers to the act of copying things, *design* refers to the imagination of things that do not yet exist.[4] Design, which modernity unleashed as a widespread concept, reinforced the ideational and projective aspect of *disegno* in relation to the manual aspects of drawing. Yet this "expanded" understanding of *disegno* as ideation was already embryonic in sixteenth-century Italy, when it became not just a word but the ideological banner of a new class of practitioners eager to distinguish themselves from artisans. In *The Lives of the Artists*, Giorgio Vasari identifies the intellect as the origin of drawing.[5] As an *idea*, *disegno* was perceived as a conceptual activity that could both transcend and give form to any material or situation. It was precisely this transcendental status that elevated the artistic practice of *disegno* from manual to intellectual work. The unity of head and hand typical of medieval craftsmanship was undermined by both the concept and practice of drawing. Further weakening the hold of craftsmanship on building was the governmental subversion of guild power[6] and the fragmentation of artisanal production into specialized activities coordinated by investors and entrepreneurs. However, most deleterious to guild power was the institutionalization of geometric drawing as the precondition for not just making but thinking architecture.

Here, Alberti's theory of the project as the architect's capacity for authority over builders augments not only the architect's position but also—and especially—the patron's ability to subordinate builders' agency to patron's will. It is not surprising that he wrote *De re aedificatoria* in Latin, explicitly addressing patrons rather than builders. Not simply a means of representation, drawing, as an accomplice to planning and in service of the patron, is the device that translates the anticipated building into measurable data. Preparatory drawings were particularly needed to guide artisanal activities that required precise execution, particularly in cases where such activities required massive financial investment. Not by chance, early manifestations of design, in correlation with the suppression of handicraft, related to the manufacture of firearms. With the introduction of gunpowder in the fourteenth century in Europe, fabrication of weaponry became unprecedentedly complex and required specialized craftsmen. Known as master gunmakers, these craftsmen maintained artisanal practices but had a specific knowledge of metallurgy, ballistics, and chemistry, and could communicate their expertise on paper.[7] Notable as an early form of design, sketches made by master gunmakers were increasingly necessary because manufacturing guns—artifacts composed of many pieces that demanded accurate fabrication—required an unprecedented division of labor. This work could not be left to the individual agency of craftsmen. Drawings such as those in Johannes Formschneider's *Master Gunmaker's Book*[8] highlight the difficulties inherent in the representation of complex forms on a flat sheet of paper. Not yet ruled by scale or measure, or disciplined by orthogonal projection, the drawings of gunmakers were merely pictorial impressions; and yet their rudimentary representational qualities were sufficient for gunmakers to memorize production processes.

The manufacture of firearms is a radical example of the need for ideation prior to production in assembling complex artifacts under the pressure of economic constraints. The evolution of drawing into design, as both a practice and an ideology, needs to be understood within a political and economic context increasingly dominated by the pressure of war and its financial interests. Although drawing is a manual activity, its "ideational" role reinforced a split between thinking and making, head and hand, intellectual and manual labor; as such, its practice played a significant role in downgrading the preeminence of craftsmanship, starting in the fifteenth century.[9]

Making Drawing Difficult

The supremacy of drawing over handicraft presupposes that drawing as a practice is not accessible to everyone, especially artisans. For this reason, theorists of art and architecture, like Alberti, deleted spontaneity from drawing and codified it as a discipline. Drawing acquired its utmost role as status signifier in the realm of geometric drawing, the mastery of which became the prerogative of both the intellectualized artist and the "professional" architect. Unlike the more empirical and accessible graphic language of master gunmakers, architectural drawing, in the fifteenth and sixteenth centuries, underwent a process of codification that made it increasingly difficult both to execute and to understand. The first attempt to codify geometric drawing was presented by Alberti in two books: *Elementa picturae* and *De pictura*, both composed in 1435.[10] Alberti did not define drawing in these books, but he made it distinctly clear that conception and design before execution were crucial for painters.

Unlike previous textbooks on painting,[11] which solely gave painters practical advice, Alberti's books addressed painting as an intellectual pursuit grounded in geometry. While geometry's importance is emphasized in both texts, its primary role is made clear in the title of the first manuscript. *Elementa picturae* unequivocally refers to Euclid's *magnum opus*, the *Elements*, the seminal text, composed in the fourth century BCE, that systematized geometry and mathematics and was rediscovered in the Middle Ages. With its axiomatic clarity and systematic approach, Euclid's text became a model of pure theoretical speculation during the Renaissance. The Greek mathematician made geometry and mathematics forms of pure logical thinking, severing them from any material implications.[12] Although Alberti's theory of painting offered an application and not a philosophy of geometry and mathematics, its reference to Euclid disclosed that pure intellectual reasoning had priority over manual execution in painting. In order to prioritize intellectual work, Alberti posited mathematically constructed perspective as the core of pictorial representation. For him, "legitimate" construction of perspective presupposed the measurability of space. Consequently, by providing a rigorous method for rendering objects and space in perspective, Alberti implied that every aspect of human visual experience was quantifiable and geometrically describable. This assumption made drawing not just a means of depiction, but also a tool that could mathematically and geometrically evaluate any spatial relationship.

The belief in the geometricization of space and form anchors one of the most important concepts of Alberti's theory of architecture: the *lineament*.[13] As developed in *De re aedificatoria*, this word is key to Alberti's conception of architecture and can be interpreted as "shape defined by lines." Alberti argues that buildings are made of lineaments and matter. The purpose of lineaments, he writes,

> lies in finding the correct, infallible way of joining and fitting together those lines and angles which define and enclose the surfaces of the building. It is the function and duty of lineaments, then, to prescribe an appropriate place, exact numbers, a proper scale, and a graceful order for whole buildings and for each of their constituent parts, so that the

whole form and appearance of the building may depend on the lineaments alone.[14]

Lineaments are thus a template made of measurable lines, independent of yet giving form to matter. As historian Branko Mitrović argued, Alberti's lineaments are a *prescribing* datum that originates in the architect's rational mind.[15] Lineaments assume the architect's total control of building form.

Alberti further argued that conventions of orthogonality, not the pictorial illusionism of artistic representation, should define architectural drawing.[16] This attitude echoed Vitruvius's famous classification of architectural representation in three genres: *ichnographia*, that is, the plan; *orthographia*, or the elevation; and *scaenographia*, or the drawing that shows the relationship between the "front" and the "side" of buildings. While *scaenographia* is a rather pictorial form of representation of architecture, *ichnographia* and *orthographia* abstracted the building into its orthogonal projections, thus reducing architecture to a system of notations. With the expulsion of illusion, architectural drawing could render the true measures of what it represents. Orthogonal projections were already well known before Alberti's treatises. For example, the medieval stonecutters of Central Europe used them extensively as a method for both representation and design.[17] Preceding the protected status of perspective drawing in the Renaissance, mastery of "how to derive the elevation from the plan" was the stonecutter's privileged knowledge, a trade secret of the guild.[18]

In Italy, Alberti's theory clashed with the widespread custom of drawing architecture in an illusionistic manner. As in gunmakers' drawings, architects used illusion to augment the accessibility of information. Not until the sixteenth century would it be possible for architects to embrace the abstraction of orthogonal projections. For Alberti, however, orthogonality exclusively guaranteed design precision and thus was critical to the architect's authorship of architecture.

What is the epistemological implication of orthogonal projection? As is well known, Alberti's plea for designing architecture orthogonally initiated a three-centuries-long narrative that culminated with Gaspard Monge's systematization of descriptive geometry. Using a specific set of procedures, descriptive geometry permits the representation of three-dimensional objects in two dimensions. As theorized by Alberti, mathematically constructed perspective operated as an incipient manifestation of descriptive geometry by implying the use of measured plans in concert with elevations. Perhaps unintuitively, the advent of a technical approach to perspective drawing provoked, and made conceivable, the use of orthogonal projection to produce measured plans. While Alberti favored orthogonal notations and deemed perspectival representations of architecture deceptive, his theory of perspective in painting established a relationship between plan and elevation that triggered a scientific methodology for the representation of architecture.[19] This methodology was perfected and further theorized by Raphael in his famous 1519 letter to Pope Leo X. Historians consider Raphael's letter the first exhaustive theory of orthogonal projection in the history of architectural drawing, but it can also be considered a further elaboration of Alberti's teachings.[20] The premise of the letter is the survey of ancient buildings in Rome, but its most significant consequence was the codification of a rigorous drawing method that allowed architects to draw plans, sections, and elevations as separate documents that operated in reciprocal geometric coordination. In his seminal essay on the representation of interiors in Renaissance architecture, Wolfgang Lotz argued[21] that Raphael's theory of orthogonal drawing was developed in response to the increasing geometric complexity of architectural form that arose between the late fifteenth and early sixteenth century in Italy. Architects such as Bramante and Raphael used the compenetrating of geometric forms such as domes, arches, and vaults to conceive complex interiors.[22] At that time, most architects generally drew a plan and left a wooden model at the building site for reference. It was the unprecedented formal complexity and large size of buildings, exemplified in the reconstruction of the basilica of St. Peter, that prompted Raphael to establish a drawing methodology that allowed him and his collaborators to coordinate their design efforts and strengthen the supervision of the construction process. Antonio da Sangallo the Younger, originally one of Raphael's collaborators at St. Peter's and later the main architect of the basilica, was the first architect to consistently employ not just orthogonal sections and elevations but also their rigorous coordination with plans. Unlike many Renaissance architects, Sangallo the Younger's training was not in the visual arts but in carpentry and construction, thus his understanding of architecture was more technical than pictorial. Lotz suggests that it was Sangallo the Younger who helped Raphael systematize architectural drawing, in stark contrast to the illusionistic style of other Renaissance architects.[23] Importantly, while orthogonal drawing became more and more popular among architects, it was not circulated among builders, who did not know how to read graphic notation apart from 1:1 specimens of details.[24] Yet, due to the flattened appearance of this type of drawing, orthogonal architectural elevations and sections remained challenging for architects. It may seem counterintuitive that architects who were capable of drawing in perspective found it difficult to draw orthogonally, but this is precisely the point: perspectival representation approximates our own vision, while orthogonal projections are a flat depiction of reality, an abstraction that poses problems both in terms of execution and comprehension. The creation of orthogonal elevations and sections is closer to the practice of the surveyor than that of the painter, making these techniques foreign to the fine arts background of many Renaissance architects.

The heightened abstraction of drawing as a measurable notation divided head and hand in the formation of architecture, and imposed a design mentality rooted in methods of geometry and mathematics. Even if architects were forced to use direct communication to convey their designs to builders, the conception and design of architecture became increasingly ruled by the abstracting logic of projections.

Drawings of Sangallo the Younger's chapel project, or Baldassare Peruzzi's elevation for the interior of the church of San Domenico in Siena, demonstrate the ability of some architects to render complex architectural forms through the use of orthogonal projections. Sangallo's and Peruzzi's many drawings are moreover noteworthy for their use of Indo-Arabic numbers in annotations and calculations. Mastery of the Indo-Arabic system, which spread in central Italy prior to the rest of Europe, allowed these architects unprecedented precision in calculating surfaces and volumes.

fig. 2.1

2.1 Antonio da Sangallo the Younger, project for a chapel, 1535.
© Gabinetto Disegni e Stampe, Florence.

Along with its use as a means of invention, orthogonality was a preferred tool for estimating material and financial resources. The use of drawing as an instrument of ideation and appraisal was at odds with the methods of builders who—as Alfred Sohn-Rethel argued—mastered their production not through abstract knowledge but through practical know-how and the expertise of touch.[25] A deep cleft was cut between designers and builders when the work of designers, grounded in geometric prescription, became the vessel that mathematized form. "It is no exaggeration," wrote Sohn-Rethel, "that one can measure the extent of division of head and hand by the inroad of mathematics in any particular task."[26]

However, Sohn-Rethel also noted that artists like Albrecht Dürer attempted to bridge the gap between intellectual and manual labor by refashioning the mathematical and geometric implications of drawing to accommodate artisanry.[27] Dürer was not an architect, but his theoretical interests, especially in the fields of measurement, perspective, and military engineering, pervaded early Renaissance design culture. Dürer's *Instructions for Measuring with Compass and Ruler*, written in 1525, is the first book on mathematics written by a nonmathematician for nonmathematicians. Dürer's intended audience was goldsmiths, carpenters, painters, sculptors, and even architects.

Dürer aimed to instruct craftsmen in the representation of complex geometrical forms using cutting-edge mathematics. As Bernard Cache observed, Dürer's *Instructions* is a treatise that consists not of theoretical propositions but of procedures: algorithms illustrated by geometrical figures. By virtue of their resolute abstraction, these procedures were applicable to a vast range of cases by a multitude of makers in different fields.[28] *Instructions* firmly exhibits the extent to which, at the turn of the sixteenth century, the act of design involved knowledge far beyond the craft of traditional artisanal culture; it was an abstract scientific knowledge procedurally removed from specific material applications. Nevertheless, despite embracing the radical abstraction of mathematics and geometry, Dürer's effort focused on maintaining the unity of head and hand by encouraging artisans to embrace the benefits of mathematical knowledge without themselves becoming mathematically inclined cognitive workers. As

Sohn-Rethel notes, this project failed. Dürer's desired "social utopia," where artisans preserved their sovereignty as independent producers, could not contend with the challenge of learning an advanced body of knowledge that required training in abstract thinking more akin to the great mathematicians and scientists of the day, such as Nicolò Tartaglia and later Galileo Galilei.

Abstracting the World through Plan, Perspective, and Axonometry

Beyond architectural artifacts, the abstracting force of numeric systems was invested in the totality of urban space through the development of a specific methodology of city cartography: *ichnographia*. A compound of two Greek words—*ichnos* (meaning trace or outline) and *graphia* (meaning writing)—*ichnographia* addresses a type of representation in which a ground plan is used to depict urban features such as streets and buildings. As this view of the ground is impossible to truly experience, its representation required a high degree of measuring and recording skills. Fundamental in the history of urban planning and in the imposition of property land rights, *ichnographia* abstracted the building in two dimensions, thus reducing architecture to a system of notations that Greek authors called *schemata*.[29] The Latin translation of this term is *formae*. The Romans called the cadastral tablets produced by *agrimensores* (land measurers) *formae*, which were made to record land use in the empire. The production of *formae* was thus linked to the institutionalization of land as property and its quantification in terms of patrimonial value. There was indeed a close kinship between the orthogonal projections of architectural drawings and land surveys aimed at abstracting land and buildings into quantifiable data. Drawing land and drawing architecture are practices that can be found in many cultures, but within the Mediterranean cultural genealogy that goes from Egypt to Greece to Rome, architectural drawing was deeply implicated in the spread of geometric thinking whose ultimate purpose was to reduce every element to a *measurable* entity. It was precisely under these circumstances that geometric drawing became a fundamental instrument of governance whose managerial logic extended well beyond the art of building. In the Roman Empire, *agrimensores* and *gromatici* (from *groma*, the surveying instrument) played a crucial role in tightening the relationship between land, law, and economy.

With modernity, a new impetus for furthering the precision of land survey stemmed from the development of portolan charts used for navigation.[30] Unlike traditional city maps, which organized urban space around idealized depictions of symbolic features such as monuments, portolan charts were composed through direct observation of the Earth's surface using scientific instruments. Of particular importance was the magnetic compass. Fragments of the sea and coastline were inscribed within a network of wind rose lines that emanated from several compass roses located at various points on the maps. Although portolan charts focused on specific geographic areas, they introduced an initial impression of space as a uniform continuum. Ichnographic maps were additionally informed by intellectuals' rediscovery, during the Renaissance, of Ptolemy's coherent and systematic approach to geography. This precedent inspired Alberti's attempt, as reported in *Descriptio urbis Romae*, to realize the first accurate topographical survey of a city through scientific means.[31] With a radius divided into fifty units and placed on a circle divided into forty-eight degrees—what he called the "horizon"—Alberti was able to measure, locate, and draw any point in the city on a sheet of paper. Because it reduced the three-dimensional view of a place to its mathematical resolution as a plan, this survey technique was the direct inversion of perspective. As argued by historian John Pinto, Alberti's method was not simply a technique for drawing city plans but, following Ptolemaic geography, also a method of description and subsequent representation of people's environment in mathematical terms.[32] The effort to produce scientific orthogonal maps of cities grew out of a culture of perspective, which in turn originated from the practice of measuring distances between objects.

Traditionally, Filippo Brunelleschi is credited with introducing mathematically constructed perspective to the realm of visual arts. With striking perspectival effect, he painted the two most important public buildings of Florence in his time: the baptistery and the Palazzo Pubblico. What was crucial was not the similarity between the painted image and the object itself, but that the resemblance between image and object was mathematically constructed. The convincing perspectival effect of the picture was obtained by measuring the exact dimensions of the baptistery and its surrounding buildings and then using these measurements as the basis for the painted perspective. Brunelleschi demonstrates that perspective is not explicitly the representation of three-dimensional space. More than a technique of mimicry, perspective is a mathematical construct that implies the measurability of three-dimensional space. Indeed, the typical diagram of a perspectival view is an isotropic grid of vanishing lines that renders space geometrically measurable. By making infinite space quantifiable, perspective enabled the architect to simultaneously govern solid bodies and the surrounding world in which those bodies exist. Its affordance of expansive measurability is why perspective was essential to the production of ichnographic plans of cities and territories. Practically, perspective was the outgrowth of the increasing need to measure distant objects throughout medieval cites in Europe and in the Arabic-speaking world.[33] More profoundly, the possibility of mathematically constructed space meant that everything in existence could fall under the rule of measure.

First formulated in theories of vision advanced by Arab mathematicians and astronomers, such as the influential *De aspectibus* by Alhazen, perspective was adopted in medieval Europe through the use of applied geometry, the science of measuring objects at a distance. At the beginning of the fifteenth century in Florence, the rise of mathematically constructed perspective was linked to the theory of mathematical space introduced by the fourteenth-century mathematician, philosopher, and astrologer Biagio Pelacani. For Pelacani, only geometry and mathematics were capable of accurately describing the location of an object in space. Defining "real objects in space" depended on assessing interstitial distances. In Pelacani's conception of mathematical space, once the metrics of an object were known, it was possible to measure the distance to another nearby object and ascertain the measurements of that object. Applied geometry here links the totality of space within one commensurable system. Before the Renaissance, empty space was considered a vacuum, a lacuna that, precisely because of its intangibility and incommensurability, could not be grasped by the human mind. With Pelacani's mathematical space, empty space was no longer an unknowable reality detached from the world of physical objects, but rather became a quantifiable medium that gives measure to the objects it contains. This novel empty, but definable, space is both real and abstract: it is real because it allows viewers to locate their physical position in the world, and abstract in its dependence on mathematical relationships. Space as homogeneous and thus measurable was the epistemological premise of both the invention of perspective and its corollary, orthogonal projection—which, as discussed above, was essential to the ichnographic plan's transformation of real space. Even so, the mathematical conception of space would reach new levels of importance in military design, where exact measurement of distance was paramount, particularly with the introduction of firearms.

fig. 2.2

The early production of ichnographic city plans was motivated by the planning of defensive structures. A case in point is Leonardo da Vinci's survey of the city walls of Cesena, drawn in 1503 as part of the fortification of the Emilian town. Using a sophisticated technique that involved an odometer and a "transit" to record distances on paper, Leonardo was able to meticulously draw the entire irregular circuit of walls. The abstraction of this map is impressive. Cartographic information is delivered only through points, lines, and numbers. With the rise of artillery-based warfare, measuring distances was imperative to ascertain the shooting range of a firearm, making the symbolic function of maps inconsequential. Many ichnographic plans drawn in the sixteenth century, such as Leonardo's plan of Imola, Giuliano da Sangallo's plan of Pisa, and John Rogers's and Richard Lee's plan of Guînes, were executed to buttress the military defense of these cities. The acute precision of the maps is paralleled by their graphic minimalism, in which topography is reduced to thin lines. For the purpose of warfare, what mattered was not the appearance of things on the map but the presence and measure of the space *between* things.

Mathematically constructed perspective and ichnographic plans made mathematical space operative for architects. While nonarchitects longed to use these methods of representation, technical geometric drawings were often too difficult for them to execute. Axonometric drawing, an easier yet effective way of rendering three-dimensional representations, emerged to bypass

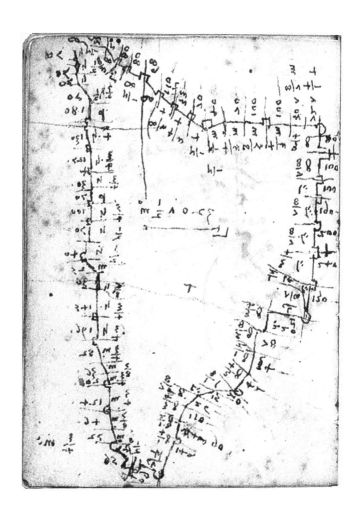

2.2 Leonardo da Vinci, plan of the walls of Cesena, 1502. © Institut de France.

the proprietary and complex nature of mathematically constructed drawing. An axon consists of parallel projections where at least one spatial axis is aligned with the plane of projection. With relative ease, Massimo Scolari charts the application and elaboration of parallel projection in ancient Greek vase painting, Byzantine mosaics, late medieval painting, and beyond.[34] It is less easy to locate the theoretical premise of axonometric drawing, since, unlike perspectival drawing, it has always remained a pragmatic device and resided in the sphere of empirical knowledge. Given the challenging task of reading an ichnographic plan and the belief that perspectival views deformed angles and sidelines and were difficult to draw, soldiers and engineers in the sixteenth century opted for axonometries, or what they called "soldierly perspective."[35] Avoiding the foreshortening effect of perspective, axonometric drawing combined the readability of perspectival rendering and the measurability of the ichnographic plan. Axonometry thus became one of the most effective and easy ways to depict both fortifications and battlefields, as evident in Girolamo Maggi's *Della fortificatione delle città* (1545). Maggi's text is considered the first treatise to explicitly theorize the use of axonometric drawing.

As Scolari demonstrated, the use of parallel projections was not new. Widespread since antiquity, both in the West and in Asia, a version of axonometric drawing was often used not only by artists but also by artisans, most notably in China, to design machines and complex pieces of carpentry. This was also the case for master gunmakers centuries later. Axonometry, based on its representational clarity and measurability, was used in manuals of geometry, such as Luca Pacioli's *De divina proportione*, and for technical design, as in Leonardo's and Francesco di Giorgio's isometric views of machines.[36] For both engineers and scientists in the sixteenth century, this type of drawing was championed as the most scientific form of representation. Ancillary to its accessibility, axonometric representation advantageously made three-dimensional depiction less subjective. Less dependent on the human eye, axonometries avoided pictorial deformation and were therefore more objective—ultimately, considered more in tune with the geometric reality of the objects depicted. While perspective views were organized around the position of a fixed embedded observer, axonometry is conveyed as a projection where the observer's point of view cannot be located and is somehow outside the physical world.

With the diffusion of axonometric projections, the epistemological premise of perspective as the mathematization of space expanded toward a universe of total measurability. Axonometric space, as it emerges from military design in the sixteenth and seventeenth centuries, divorced the perception of space and objects from human sight. Unlike perspective, which mimics eyesight, axonometries exist within the mathematical abstraction of boundless measurability. Accordingly, axonometric drawing is widely used in the field of industrial design, which requires depictions that are intuitively easy to understand for nonexperts, yet reliable for measurements and geometric precision. To a certain extent, axonometric projections made geometric drawing more accessible. Accessibility was still dependent on the inclusion of not just painters and architects but a multitude of professionals—soldiers, engineers, mathematicians, scientists—in design undertakings, from the engineering of firearms to the manufacturing of industrial machines. This inclusiveness was augmented by the condition of "total design," which subsumed everything into the abstraction of mathematical space, and initially surfaced in the architecture of modern fortresses. As will become evident, the planning and building of defensive works in the age of early firearms would decisively transform architecture into design.

Fortress Mentality

It is a well-known fact that traditional forms of defensive architecture in Europe, such as city walls and castles, became obsolete upon the introduction of artillery in the fifteenth century. Less considered—at least within the historiography of architecture—is the fact that the changes brought about by the introduction of artillery had a major impact on both design and building far beyond the ambit of military design. In order to understand why this happened, we need to briefly consider what was really at stake in creating fortifications that could withstand bombardment by novel forms of firearms.

In warfare by artillery, not the height and solidity but the optimized geometry of fortifications was of utmost importance. The main objective of fortress design in projectile-focused warfare was to increase firing range and avoid excessively long perpendicular walls.[37] Angling walls properly was necessary to avoid excessive damage from cannon balls, which were more impactful when meeting a perpendicular surface. In the fifteenth and sixteenth centuries, Europe was ravaged by a succession of wars. For mercenary armies this frequent fighting was lucrative business, but the ongoing wars, together with the introduction of artillery, made fortification design an urgent task for those in power.

The architect most known for his work as a fortification engineer was Francesco di Giorgio Martini. Born in Siena and trained as a painter, he was also well acquainted with solving complex engineering problems: in 1469 he was appointed by the republic of Siena to survey, repair, and expand the city's complex hydraulic system known as the *bottini*.[38] This experience made him proficient in solving design problems where the evaluation of material weight and resistance, in addition to geometry, was of central concern. Moreover, Francesco di Giorgio was raised in an urban context where the centrality of trade made arithmetic a dominant aspect of the education system. Highly efficient in calculation, with a skill set paramount for rapidly estimating costs and time, he was perfectly suited for the prioritization of timing and budgeting within the large economy surrounding warfare. Ultimately, the budgetary and scheduling concerns brought forth by the technological advances of war would come to characterize the modern economy at large.

In the 1470s, Francesco di Giorgio was hired by Federico da Montefeltro. The duke of Urbino, Montefeltro was a celebrated patron of the arts, an exceptionally skilled soldier, and an expert in military strategy. Francesco di Giorgio was allegedly responsible for hundreds of design interventions across Montefeltro's territory, located in the north of the Marche region. Many of these interventions involved not new fortresses but refurbishment and restoration of existing defensive structures. The sheer number of design tasks permitted the Sienese architect to perfect a design methodology that continued to influence military architecture until the nineteenth century.[39]

As architectural historian Francesco Benelli remarks, Francesco di Giorgio's approach to fortress design elaborated the dialectical relationship between construction and destruction in order to carefully calibrate every element to the possibility of attack by firearms.[40] The need to realize this contingency-driven approach prompted him to prioritize the surveying of sites in advance of design. A priori principles, like proportion and symmetry, were not useful in improving the strength of fortifications. Architects were thus faced with a paradoxical condition: heightened scientific accuracy decreased the predictability of outcomes.

Discarding a focus on formal perfection, Francesco di Giorgio procedurally considered context. Scientific parameters such as land surveying, estimates on firing ranges, and structural capacity of masonry construction informed the placement and position of his fortresses. In his work for Montefeltro the scientific and empirical definitively outweighed the representational and symbolic. This was not true of his more classical work outside of fortification design. Tension between the study of classical sources and his research on fortifications is evident in Francesco di Giorgio's theoretical *magnum opus*, the *Trattato di architettura civile e militare*, which was simultaneously influenced by Vitruvius and by engineers such as Konrad Keyser and Mariano Taccola.[41] A striking aspect of the treatise is the author's recurrent and obsessive representation of architectural form as defined by an idealized conception of the human body. In several drawings that historians consider archetypes of the anthropomorphizing tendency of humanism in Renaissance architecture, Francesco di Giorgio drew cities, church plans, and capitals inscribed within idealized human bodies and heads. In contrast, when designing military architecture, this anthropocentrism was replaced by the abstraction of engineering, a discipline irreducible to symbolic form. Abstraction is not only implicit in his scientific way of working, which privileged measured design, but is also visible in the architectural form of his fortification works, in particular Costacciaro, Sassocorvaro, and fig. 2.3 San Leo. Impressively smooth, the walls of these structures have a complex yet bare geometric profile, making them the precursors of bunker architecture.

This approach to fortress design was further developed by Antonio da Sangallo the Younger who, in many fortification

2.3 Francesco di Giorgio Martini, bastion, Costacciaro, Umbria. © Manuel Orazi.

projects in central Italy, perfected the "bastion" typology.[42] Perhaps the most important contribution to modern military architecture, this typology hides cannons within the neck of the bastion in order to protect the exposed zone in front of the fortification wall. Optimization of the bastion position in relation to the context required rigorous calculations of firing range as well as careful planning to eliminate blind spots and dead ground within a cannon's range. Military architects were consequently among the first practitioners to plan, with unquestioned authority, coherent schemes for large-scale projects.

The urgency and expediency with which fortifications were built obligated builders to scrupulously follow the instructions of architects. To a larger degree than any other building type, measured drawing was unquestionably decisive in the conception, but also in the transmission, of fortification designs.

Despite the need for streamlined command of planning, architects were forced to collaborate with a multitude of experts when designing fortresses. Formal innovations, like bastioned fortresses, were the product of a cumulative design process that involved architects and many specialized experts, including soldiers and mathematicians.[43] Exceeding the demands of previous large-scale architectural enterprises like cathedrals, the realization of fortresses and other military architecture was both labor-intensive and design-intensive, and design strategies were constantly evolving alongside firearms technology.[44] The development of modern fortification thus ignited a shift from architecture to *design*.

In architecture, the *arché* is not only the act of commanding the work of builders, but also the cultural and ideological authority embedded in the specific form of columns, entablatures, pediments, and other archetypical motives. During the Renaissance, architectural ideological authority, both professional and intellectual, was largely derived from mastering the language of the classical orders. Thwarting this knowledge base, the design of fortifications was devoid of architectural archetypes and the grammar of the orders. The radical novelty of artillery warfare and its constant evolution eluded the use of fixed principles in the manifestation of architecture. Unlike the architectural project— governed by symmetry and proportion—the practice of fortress design mandated the ceaseless estimation of firing range and structural loads. Furthermore, labor management and budgeting became crucial factors that architects had to account for in the design of fortresses. In their research of design techniques used in Tudor fortifications in England, Anthony Gerbino and Stephen Johnston argued that in bastion fortification "each separate part of the fortress had to serve another," making it necessary to subordinate craftsmen to a single authoritative design.[45] The dual professionalism induced by fortification design distinguished between *architetto* and *ingegnere*: while the architect gives buildings form, the engineer resolves complex design problems that relate to building form but also pertain to the expanded field of logistics and infrastructure.[46] The term *ingegnere* comes from *ingegno*, a word repeatedly used by Renaissance theorists to express the mind's cognitive power to solve any practical issue.[47] In military engineering *disegno* became a totalizing factor: design through the act of drawing and mediated by the scientific parameters of geometry and calculation conclusively replaced the craft approach of artisans and master builders.

In his book *Delle fortificationi* (written 1597), the preeminent sixteenth-century military engineer Bonaiuto Lorini wrote that "on *disegno* depends the true understanding of all things: it enables to show that great perfection which the *ingegno* of a man may have."[48] Lorini exclaimed that drawing should confirm the conception and the illustration of things in their exact measure. He also insisted that drawing, not writing, effectively captured the extreme complexity of military design.[49] This statement was rather confrontational, given that, since Alberti and throughout the Renaissance, the written text was the most secure vessel for architectural knowledge. It is common knowledge that Alberti excluded the use of images from *De re aedificatoria*. Before the diffusion of printing techniques, it was impossible to rely on drawing as a secure means of knowledge transmission due to the difficulty in making a faithful reproduction. Regardless of Alberti's skepticism, printed media would later make drawing the primary means of transmitting scientific content. No amount of literary eloquence could fully describe the many factors and constant evolution of military design. Written architectural descriptions were hence trumped by illustrations such as plans, axonometries, and diagrams.

Preparatory design in advance of construction was so important in military architecture that mathematician and engineer Nicolò Tartaglia, in his seminal book *Nova scientia* (written 1537), argued that the validity of a fortification design, regardless of the materials used, rests solely on its geometric form.[50] This bold statement presumes the autonomy of geometric reasoning from the constraints of the physical world. Yet Tartaglia's geometric theory did not pursue ideal form; rather, his design planning attended to practical problems of estimating distances and material resistance to cannonball strikes. Not conceived as instructions for building, Tartaglia's teachings demonstrated the ability to conceive and judge design using exclusively mathematical and geometric criteria. As engineer Roberto Rossi argues, the novelty of Tartaglia's theory lay in its use of abstract mathematical models to achieve practical outcomes.[51] This fusion of mathematical abstraction and empirical applications anticipates Galileo Galilei's science, in which calculation governs every aspect of reality. For Tartaglia, mathematical disciplines divulge "the reason of things," making things decipherable within any experimental model.[52] In conception, Tartaglia's approach to warfare aimed to advance a science that was axiomatic and deductive, but he also understood the necessity of observation and experience in the field. Forgoing detached geometric analysis, he used a quadrant to measure multiple shots fired at different angles in order to conclude that a cannon raised 45 degrees shoots the greatest distance. Similar deductive reasoning is evident in the design of the fortress town of Palmanova, built in 1593 by the republic of Venice under the supervision of Giulio Savorgnan. The regular placement of bastions around the town's perimeter (planned as a perfect decagon) minimized the length of vulnerable stretches of rectilinear walls and established a system of defense in which every inch of ground around the fortress was protected by a cannon. Although its perfect geometry evokes the layout of an "ideal city," Palmanova's form was the crude result of firing range parameters. Shunning ideal principles, textbooks published in the sixteenth and seventeenth centuries advised engineers to deduce fortification layouts from the appreciable factors of topography, combat strategies, and firing range.[53] Mathematical and geometric calculations were here relied on to solve contingent and practical problems. Being

fig. 2.4

highly provisional, this empirical approach did not presuppose the absolute measurability of all things.

The empirical approach to armament design was finally brought to its radical conclusion by the French marshal Sébastien Le Prestre de Vauban. In 1666 Louis XIV's prime minister Colbert appointed Vauban the general commissioner of fortifications in France. During his life, Vauban supervised the construction and amelioration of 160 fortresses and, most dramatically, directed 53 successful sieges during the many wars waged by Louis XIV.[54] His offensive and defensive military experience allowed him to apprehend a wide range of advanced warfare techniques, and assured him, above all else, of the importance of planning and logistics. In terms of design, Vauban followed the tradition of bastioned fortification but emphasized "defense in depth." Depth here entails the enclosure of fortified compounds with multiple circuits of walls, bastions, ravelins, counterguards, hornworks, and glacises. Devised like the multiple layers of an onion, Vauban's system was deployed following precise measurements gleaned from firing distances and optimized according to topography. Extensive surveying and remodeling of the whole landscape, as demonstrated in the citadels of Lille and Gravelines, was necessary to design and build his concentric structures.[55] Although Vauban did write about fortifications,[56] he was reluctant to impart his knowledge in the form of a theory. Rather than predefined rules, he believed that only direct lived experience could instill an understanding of general military strategy and aid the design of military architecture. The concept of defense in depth was later standardized by his followers[57] in terms of "systems" arranged around levels of complexity in the defensive circuit. Still, Vauban himself never propagated any "system" and even sarcastically titled his own reflections *Oisivetés* (Idle thoughts). Far from improvised, however, his approach to fortress design was guided by rigorous quantitative and rational planning.[58] He took great care in studying precedents, making exact descriptions of the intended work, and drafting accurate drawings of both the site and the proposed construction. Further, by calculating the volume of materials needed and determining the necessary labor force, Vauban made precise prefatory specifications and cost estimations. Besides employing mathematics, geometry, trigonometry,

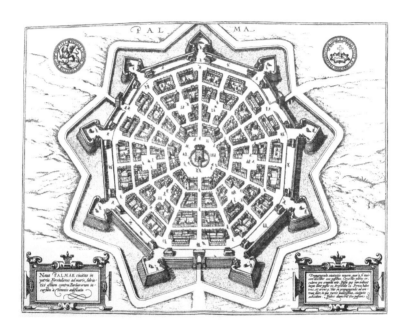

2.4 Georg Braun and Frans Hogenberg, plan of Palmanova, from *Civitates orbis terrarum*, 1598.

surveying, and geography, Vauban also used statistics to optimize design decisions. This managerial and calculating approach was particularly applicable to siegecraft. By hypothesizing the character of enemy forces—such as their manpower and strength of built structures—Vauban could precisely estimate the length of a siege. Marked by an indifference to theoretical speculation, Vauban's strategy focused on matter-of-fact issues like the mechanical and hydraulic performance of built structures and the management of manpower. For Vauban, fortifications were effective only if conceived as part of a large-scale planning operation in which everything was assessed within a general economic policy. With the maturation of fortress design, architecture experienced a process of technological optimization that made its planning more rigorous, comprehensive, and financially sound. This rigor was the outcome of organizational and scientific skills, not an all-encompassing theory. Here we can see how the development of military architecture in the sixteenth and seventeenth centuries and the fortress mentality that arose in this domain had an impact on architecture at large. It forced architects and then engineers to confront for the first time a reality irreducible to any certainty or durable principle. Artillery was something completely new, unprecedented and constantly evolving, that exposed architects to a radically different understanding of the project in which the speed of construction and the solution of specific building problems were more important than adhering to some overreaching building theory. Design thus manifested for the first time as a way of working on building without resorting to any metaphysical conception of architecture but supported by pragmatism and relentless mathematical control. Such control was also provided by the increasing exactitude of cartographic surveys and the use of advanced drawing techniques such as orthogonal projections and axonometric representation. Above all, military design forced the architect to focus on efficiency rather than beauty. Establishing unparalleled standards, examples such as Vauban's emblematic reorganization of the design and construction of fortifications manifested the profound efficiency attainable when the art of building is reduced to scientific and financial parameters.

The growing business of fortification design—and the whole military-industrial complex that began to flourish in

Europe and its colonies in the fifteen century—should be understood as part and parcel of a vast process of dispossession of the craftsman's means of production and the financialization of architecture. By industrializing its design and construction in unprecedented terms, military design was instrumental in preparing architecture for its commodification by capital. This radical reification of architecture by advanced military design was paralleled by developments in architectural theory itself, in which metaphysical conceptions of beauty were displaced by a more pragmatic attitude toward construction.

Design Takes Command

In his seminal study of seventeenth- and eighteenth-century French architecture, Alberto Pérez-Gómez highlights the impact of the so-called Galilean revolution on architecture.[59] Critical in this period was the discovery of the possibility of understanding and explaining empirical phenomena through the abstract means of mathematics.[60] In the wake of scientific enquiry revolutionized by Galilean science, architects, largely in France, questioned the metaphysical assumptions of the classical orders.[61] This reckoning was epitomized by *Ordonnance pour les cinq espèces de colonnes selon la méthode des anciens*, written by Claude Perrault in 1683. In challenging one of the most enduring tropes of architecture, Perrault provoked strong reactions from architects like François Blondel, who still subscribed to the authority of Vitruvius.[62] Against Blondel's resistance, Perrault garnered strong support from the increasing number of architects interested in the more pragmatic aspects of architectural production. Apart from the influence of Galilean science, military design more directly shifted architects' focus away from the conventions of classicism.

The reorientation of design toward more concrete concerns was further a consequence of the inauguration of the Académie Royale d'Architecture and the institutionalization of architectural education by the French state in 1671. The novel royal academy—often considered the first "school of architecture"— was the offspring of the French royal building administration, the Bâtiments du Roi, a public organization founded in the late fourteenth century that shaped architectural practice as we know it today.[63] The building administration was created by the French crown to place master masons under state control. Aspiring to the model of Italian architectural professionalization, kings such as François I and Henri IV used the royal building administration to embolden master masons to adopt more systematic and erudite approaches to design. Really at stake in this effort was the intention to detach building knowledge from artisanal customs. The state aimed to secure a more standardized—and thus controllable—building practice. Aligned with the absolutist state's process of centralization, the founding of the Académie Royale d'Architecture advanced the process of professionalization begun with the Bâtiments du Roi. As a school specialized in architectural design, the academy further codified knowledge across the foundational disciplines, from science to literature. To a certain extent, the Académie Royale d'Architecture was analogous to the Accademia delle Arti del Disegno, founded in Florence in 1553 by Cosimo I de' Medici and inspired by Giorgio Vasari. Ostensibly, the purpose of the Accademia was to promote the arts and organize educational initiatives like lectures. In actuality, the goal was to both supervise artistic production and undermine the already waning power of guilds. The ideological core of the Accademia was *disegno*, which—as discussed earlier—was understood as the conceptual template for all the arts, including architecture. Although the Académie Royale had a similar program, and at the outset was invested in theoretical debates on topics such as beauty, it became increasingly concerned with construction. Here, construction connoted not artisanal craft but administrative and scientific practice. Under the influence of painter, mathematician, astronomer, and architect Philippe de la Hire, the activities and teachings of the Académie became progressively focused on technical issues such as statics and mechanics of construction.[64] Before assuming his role at the Académie, de la Hire was a member of the Académie des Sciences and professor of mathematics at the Collège Royal. With the shift in focus from issues of proportion and beauty to problems of construction and economy, the pedagogical direction of the Académie embodied the French architecture establishment in the seventeenth and eighteenth centuries. This disciplinary transformation was triggered by a major reorganization of the French state's infrastructure to improve circulation of people and goods. Conducted over the course of a century, the initiative was primarily implemented during Colbert's administrative rule.[65] The same planning capacity mobilized in Vauban's vast modernization of defensive structures in France was extended to every aspect of territorial planning, from the civic infrastructure of roads, bridges, and aqueducts to the dissemination of new building types. The French state, French architects, and French engineers together conceived the city and the rural territory as an object of total design, a "machine" with multiple gears that required the utmost degree of rational planning.[66] Dispensing with the intellectual drive of *disegno*, the Académie Royale d'Architecture became a laboratory for a technocratic and managerial approach to design.

More than any other architect, the elusive and enigmatic Pierre Patte embraced the shift from *disegno* to design in architecture and city planning. While he built almost nothing, he composed several treatises. His *Mémoire sur les objets les plus importans de l'architecture*, written in 1769, is perhaps the most important fig. 2.5 book on architectural and urban theory from the age of Enlightenment. Here, Patte described the characteristics of an ideal town, planned according to "rational" criteria. Initially, he seems to describe a town with traditional baroque characteristics, including a regular hexagonal or octagonal plan, regular squares, and a triumphal arch. Upon closer investigation, the baroque nature of the town proves only superficial. In fact, as Antoine Picon states, Patte's ideal town is a "catalogue of urban technology."[67] First, in an unprecedented manner, Patte separated working activities from residential space, anticipating twentieth-century zoning techniques. Second, he conceived both buildings and urban space as mere pieces of infrastructure, prioritizing circulation, water drainage, waste disposal, and ventilation over beauty and proportion. This machine-like understanding of architecture and the city is clearly reflected in the plates of his book, particularly one that illustrates the section of the street. In this drawing, the city is represented as an instrument that regulates flows of water, air, smoke, and traffic. Patte expanded the role of design beyond form. For him, design embraces protocols regarding the height of rooms, the provision of sewers, and the maintenance of the street as a safe and regulated space. The result was the radical

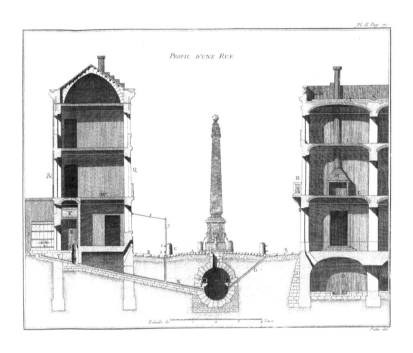

2.5 Pierre Patte, section of a city,
from *Mémoire sur les objets les plus importans de l'architecture*, 1769.

instrumentalization of architecture as a technological apparatus for maintaining urban life.

Patte's "urban design," as Cesare Birignani notes, was clearly influenced by the emergence of policing as the way to control and manage the city.[68] Until the mid-eighteenth century, the term "police" addressed not a specific institution but a way to secure urban order.[69] As Birignani argues, in its formation as a body of knowledge, "police" was transformed into the verb "to police," defined by a set of actions and measures exercised to govern people in accordance with the general interest.[70] This approach was systematized in the *Traité de la police* by Nicolas de La Mare, written in 1705. The treatise was based on La Mare's experience as the lieutenant general of police in Paris. Although it was inspired by architectural treatises such as Vitruvius's *Ten Books on Architecture*, La Mare's unfinished book was not written as a coherent theory. Instead, it compiles an endless collection of observations of and recommendations for urban life, including jurisprudence, religion, morality, public health, food supply, and urban form. Not only a matter of violence and coercion, La Mare's notion of control was uniquely a mode of population management. This concept of control was attainable only if the city's vital infrastructure was maintained and modernized. It is exactly this expanded field of urban design that Patte engaged in his treatise. No longer a coherent body delineated by a unitary project, the city was envisioned as a network of machines—streets, canals, sewers, aqueducts, fountains, bridges—that required constant management and oversight.

The notion of the architect as holistic designer, versed in technical skills but focused on issues of beauty and proportion, was thrown into its final crisis by the epistemological understanding of the city as infrastructure. The fate of this crisis was unequivocally sealed by the rise of the professional engineer as the main designer of the built environment. Engineering became an independent profession, distinct from architecture, with the foundation of the Corps des Ponts et Chaussées in 1715, from which sprang the École Nationale des Ponts et Chaussées, certified as a school in 1756 and known as the École Polytechnique after the Revolution. Unlike architecture, which chiefly transmitted knowledge through treatises and theories, engineering was a profession driven by utilitarian goals and lacking a central doctrine.[71] Setting this mentality was the ideological premise of *homo economicus*: the belief that the urban territory, in its entirety, needed to be reformed to enhance production and circulation.

Exemplary of this approach was the work of the French engineer Jean-Rodolphe Perronet. Trained as an architect, Perronet started his career as the aide to the chief architect of Paris, and was assigned the tasks of checking quantities of materials, settling workers' payments, and supervising building sites.[72] Based on this professional experience, Perronet developed an interest in the production process of building. His concern with built form was surpassed by his concern with the rational planning of the building site and the management of resources and labor. These issues underscored his role as director of the Bureau des Dessinateurs du Roi. A state-led agency founded in 1744, which eventually became part of the Corps des Ponts et Chaussées, the Bureau des Dessinateurs's task was to rationalize state planning policies. Best known for the planning of infrastructure such as bridges (for which he was famous), aqueducts, and roads, Perronet fixated on the science of construction and management of the building site. Economy of construction was the sole focus of his proposals. Any preoccupation with the formal conventions of architecture, such as the use of the classical orders, symmetry, and even composition, was eradicated. Perronet's role in civil engineering is to a certain degree analogous to Vauban's role in military design. For both Vauban and Perronet, calculation was everything and geometry was vacated of any theoretical purpose. His insistence on a hyperrationalized process of construction is apparent in the engravings that illustrate Perronet's design of the bridge of Neuilly, built in 1770. As Picon notes, the main plate represents the bridge not in its final stage but under construction, thus emphasizing the primacy of rational building and manufacturing.[73]

The epistemological exaltation of engineering severely delegitimized the architect's more artistic conception of design and the erudite use of ornamental features. The transition to an architecture made of basic geometric volumes and bare walls, most notable in the mature work of architects Étienne-Louis Boullée and Claude-Nicolas Ledoux, signifies the cultural sublimation of the collapse of classicist ornamentation.

Architecture after Design

At the end of the eighteenth century, for both architects and engineers the driving logic of building design was no longer form but *construction* understood as both a pragmatic and a scientific problem. In postrevolutionary France, the École Polytechnique fully embraced the study of construction, and design methods were applied to every aspect of urban technology. The inquiries of the École Polytechnique embodied the logic of design as it first emerged in fortification structures. Absorbing and fostering the state's machine-like approach to territorial and infrastructure management, the École Polytechnique reified "state reason." Following Napoleon's conquest of Europe in the early nineteenth century, the Polytechnique mentality spread beyond France and became the basis of modern and contemporary forms of engineering. In the tradition of the Corps des Ponts et Chaussées, the École Polytechnique formed expert engineers with the capacity to design anything. A Polytechnique engineer was proficient in machine and building design as well as surveying and urban planning. The aim of the École Polytechnique was to distill an integral approach to design applicable to the pragmatic aspects of constructing machinery and infrastructure, from weapons to ports. The school's design edicts also focused on state administration.[74] At the Polytechnique, engineers were also expected to design architecture. Given their expanded knowledge of design, engineers, not architects, were increasingly in command of building processes. Believed to be more capable than the architect, the engineer administered the financial and managerial apparatus of the building process in addition to the built form. When budget and time were limited, only engineers could guarantee a strict economy of means. This was especially important when it came to public works such as granaries, garrisons, and docks.

Appointed professor at the École Polytechnique in 1795, Jean-Nicolas-Louis Durand was the only architect and theorist who, firmly within the discipline of architecture, responded to the ascent of engineering. His teachings, collected in the famous treatise *Précis des leçons d'architecture* (published beginning in 1802), are in many ways the last attempt to comprehensively theorize architecture in the manner of the great theorists of the Renaissance. Durand's theory effectively erased the legacy of classicism and reduced architecture to the abstract composition of discrete architectural elements. Walls, openings, columns, and other components were independently deployable. Aligned with Perrault's *Ordonnance*, Durand criticized and even ridiculed classicism's mythical interpretation of architecture,[75] scorning, for example, Marc Antoine Laugier's dubious account of the genesis of architecture in the "primitive hut." For Durand, the *raison d'être* of architecture was economy, understood not as "political economy" but as economy of means: to make the most out of minimal resources.

As professor at the École Polytechnique, Durand was explicitly aware that pragmatic aspects of building had superseded "form-making" in architecture. In tune with the expeditious enterprise of engineers, Durand reduced and simplified the process of architectural design.[76] Gone was the formal and graphic virtuosity that distinguished the architect's work in the Renaissance. Against classicism, Durand preferred simplicity and logic in drawing and design. After laying out a few basic elements and principles, Durand's system enabled the architect to rapidly design anything. The lessons of the *Précis* solely pertain to the formal properties of design, given that matters of material, construction, and finance were already theorized by Durand's engineer colleagues. Notably, Jean-Baptiste Rondelet's encyclopedic *Traité théorique et pratique de l'art de bâtir* (also published in 1802) provided an exhaustive overview of all scientific, technological, and economic aspects of building. Rondelet's book insisted on the practice of the *devis*, the need to comprehensively estimate quantities prior to construction in order to avoid negligence on the part of contractors or craftsmen.[77] In concert, Durand's reductive method is the formal counterpart to Rondelet's administrative approach to architecture.

Following the structure of his lectures, Durand divided the *Précis* into three parts: the elements of building, general composition, and primary building types. Part I provided a concise definition of architectural elements, including floors, ceilings, openings, walls, and pavings. Despite his anticlassical stance, Durand included the architectural orders, though they were reduced to abstract shapes, and for ease of design their proportions adhered to an arithmetic gradient. In part II, Durand

fig. 2.6

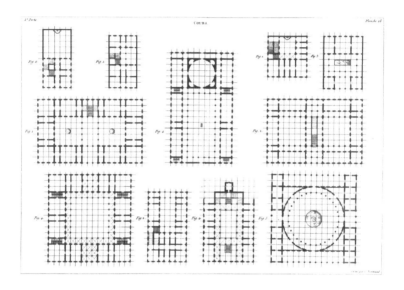

2.6 Jean-Nicolas-Louis Durand, plate 16 from *Précis des leçons d'architecture*, 1802–1805.

illustrated building "parts." Façades, porches, vestibules, stairs, halls, galleries, courtyards, rotundas, and other parts were each the result of the simple combination of building elements. Here Durand introduced the most fundamental concept of his theory: *composition*. Although in the *Précis* he claimed to have invented this concept, composition was an important topic in Renaissance art theory. In fact, Alberti outlines a pivotal theory of composition in *De pictura*.[78] For Alberti, composition determines the organization of a painting so that each element plays its part in the effect of the whole. *Concinnitas* echoes this idea of composition in architecture. With this concept Alberti describes the unification of heterogeneous architectural elements into a plausible and pleasant whole.[79] In contrast, for Durand composition lacked any aesthetic objective. The rational character of composition clinically allocated architectural elements in relation to programmatic requirements. Composition is endorsed by Durand as an alternative to *distribution*, a concept that dominated architectural theory in France through the eighteenth century.[80] The art of distribution prioritized the arrangement of building parts according to established habits and rituals. Teaching in the aftermath of the French Revolution, Durand encountered novel programs that lacked precedent in the repertoire of architecture history. He deemed distribution anachronistic and thus not useful in the design of schools, museums, slaughterhouses, hospitals, and other new public buildings. The combinatory logic of composition was more flexible and therefore suitable when confronting unprecedented programs. Durand reduced his method to a generic set of rules, illustrated on a famous plate in the *Précis*, titled "procedure to be followed in the composition of whatever building." Here, Durand divides composition into four easy steps: (1) trace the building's main *parti*, (2) inscribe symmetry lines on the *parti*, and then place (3) walls and (4) columns along the symmetry lines. To reinforce the validity of this procedure, Durand drew a plate (which only appeared in the first edition of the *Précis*) in which building plans are reduced to their diagrammatic *parti*. In one of the most abstract renderings of architecture ever created, *disegno* is reduced to nothing but the simplest and most generic form, opening the possibility of accommodating almost any program or situation. This methodological abstraction was unlocked by

fig. 2.7

fig. 2.8

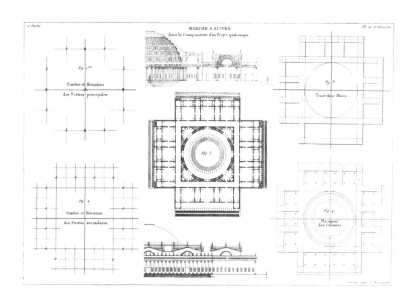

2.7 Jean-Nicolas-Louis Durand, "procedure to be followed in the composition of whatever building," from *Précis des leçons d'architecture*, 1802–1805.

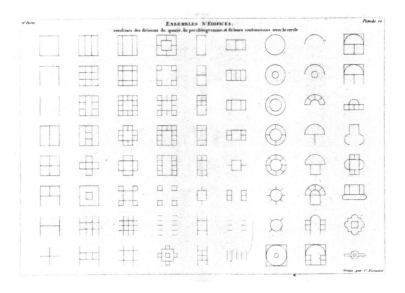

2.8 Jean-Nicolas-Louis Durand, plate 20 from *Précis des leçons d'architecture*, 1802–1805.

Durand's deconstruction of architecture into elements ready to be organized into myriad syntactical combinations.

Developed in a period dominated by the neoclassical style, Durand's theoretical project is unmistakably classicist, but in a reductionist fashion where columns, pediments, and other stereotypical "classical" features are positioned in symmetrical arrangements. Symmetry, however, is not an aspiration of beauty but rather of economy—a tool to accelerate the conception and design of a building. Not the symmetry of antiquity, which implied an all-encompassing harmonic logic, Durand's "impoverished" neoclassical symmetry is limited to the axial arrangement of parts. Incumbent in his design operations is the prioritization of designing in plan. Subsequent elevations simply conform, almost automatically, to the plan. To aid in the composition of plans, Durand uses a modular grid. Throughout the plates in the *Précis* the grid regulates the plans and parts of buildings and anchors the modular nature of his compositions. If the compositions were not bound by classicist symmetry, their arrangement, coaxed by the grid, could take any form.

In part III of the *Précis*, Durand demonstrates the potential of his method to produce a variety of public and private buildings. His typological approach, in which buildings are classified according to their program, is well documented.[81] This classifying method is often understood as the allocation of type to given programs. A closer reading reveals that the radical elementalism of Durand's architecture destabilizes typological classifications through the proposition of an infinite arrangement of programs. The eclipse of type by compositional flexibility is legible in the astonishing "graphic portion" of the *Précis*, where, demonstrating the versatility and adaptability of his method, Durand composes buildings with no program.

Durand further magnifies the programless study of buildings in the final pages of part III. Here, improbable building configurations are displayed, pushing the combinatory logic of the compositional method to the utmost degree of openness: anything goes. Durand's prescriptive method, where architecture is deconstructed into its constituent elements, results in the deskilling of design. What Durand offers is economy of form to professionals who have to design architecture in great quantities.

Efficiency in form-making, in terms of time and skills, was especially important for the engineers who designed the new cities of the French Empire. Following Monge's method of descriptive geometry, Durand represents his design using only orthogonal projection, even though his architecture lacks the formal complexity that first gave rise to projective and orthogonal techniques of representation. This proclivity for orthogonal representation reflects a world increasingly dominated by the calculating reason of engineering. Saturating every aspect of urban life, the pragmatism of engineering reduced buildings to abstract containers with formal properties that conform to construction processes, technology, and economy. If Alberti's geometry made drawing more difficult, and hence privileged knowledge, Durand's geometry made drawing easier and facilitated engineers' cooptation of *disegno*. In Durand's simplified methodology, the mastery of geometry lost its relevance. Evacuating the conceptual virtuosity that underscores mathematized architecture, Durand's system simplifies *disegno* to a rational procedure of composition that marks one moment in the expanded process that is *design*. Here the complexity of design goes far beyond the scope of architectural form. From now on, architecture enter its crisis.

3   Appropriation,
Subdivision, Abstraction:
A Political History of the Urban Grid

In the previous chapters, design first emerged as a mode of thinking architecture in managerial terms. Still operating as a cognitive function, the use of design subsequently shifted from the conceptual to the pragmatic, becoming a means of problem-solving. In both applications of design, drawing was a device of abstraction that distanced laborers from the act of design. Abstraction manifested through drawing initially claimed a stake in the production of buildings, but it later infiltrated the planning of cities and territories. Planning on a large scale requires the reduction of concrete things into measurable increments. In reductive procedures, cartography, statistics, and building codes translate the concrete, lived experience of reality into the certainty of data. Perceived as legible, this data is used to plan the organization of cities and territories.

In many ways the foundational moment of abstraction in planning is the rectangular subdivision of land by ancient cultures to define their habitat. Still functioning today, rectangular subdivision is arguably the most ubiquitous and resilient method of spatial organization in history: from cartography to urbanism to architecture, we see, understand, and construct our world by inscribing it with rectilinear lines.

In certain parts of the world, the phenomenon of rectangular subdivision gave rise to a specific spatial apparatus: the grid. While the grid is well known as a formal, functional, and cultural figure, its political significance remains opaque. Countering this opacity, this chapter will define the grid as the utmost embodiment of abstraction in the material organization of land. A provisional spatial definition of the grid is established by outlining its foremost role in the consolidation and appropriation of land through subdivision. Of course, this general definition does not imply that all grids have a single origin or purpose.[1] The use of the grid can be seen in many different contexts and civilizations, from ancient China to the Teotihuacan Mesoamerican civilization, and in each instance the grid displays very specific characteristics. The focus here is the rectilinear grid as an instrument to spatialize property through the subdivision of land into measurable plots. The aim is to challenge the conventional reading of the grid as a rational system and instead highlight the grid's crucial link to the violence of land appropriation and the transformation of land into abstract property in modern times. The grid's subdividing impulse abstracts the relationships between people and the human relationship to land into a readable and measurable form, immediately recognizable as antithetical to nature. In the course of history, this highly artificial system ultimately naturalized the possession of land. Human acclimation to this system is so all-encompassing that it is now utterly accepted that the urban world is an immense tapestry of rectangular subdivisions that parcels the earth into myriad indoor and outdoor enclosures. Once appropriated and subdivided, land is processed by the grid into the abstraction of measurement, making it a quantifiable item. Ultimately, abstraction is the mechanism that transforms the grid from a physical order imposed on the ground into an ordering social apparatus that invests and orients the totality of human relationships.

Subdivision

In order to understand how rectangular subdivision abstracts the landscape, it is necessary to consider the change in the perception of land as humans transitioned from hunter-gatherers to sedentary life. Of course, this progression happened in different ways, at different times, in different parts of the world, and it is not yet complete. For this reason, it is reductive to narrow the emergence of sedentary life to a linear narrative, yet it is possible to prudently generalize that human action prior to settlement was organized by *points, not lines*. It is important to stress that hunter-gatherers were not adrift over vast spaces: their movements were organized by specific landmarks such as mountains, lakes, river, haunts, waterholes, and other outstanding topographical features. In other words, hunter-gatherers did not conceive of land as a surface but as a constellation of specific marks. Often transformed into sacred sites, these marks served as means of symbolic and physical orientation. As anthropologist Peter J. Wilson has emphasized, hunter-gatherers inhabited space not as lines but as "focuses."[2] In this geography of points, land was not bound but organized as zones of influence, which emitted a power of attraction that was not exclusionary. Wilson argued that this hazy sense of boundary was reflected in the way hunter-gatherers did not think in terms of culturally uniform social categories. Citing the hunter-gatherer people of southern India, specifically the Paliyan and the Hill Pandaram, Wilson explains how nonsedentary people operate with "memorate knowledge," that is, "knowledge derived by individual experience unmodified by any such socially shared or transmitted process as education."[3] This condition, which survives today in what remains of the hunter-gatherer way of life, was radically challenged by the spread of sedentary living and stable communities where the rights of land possession were embodied in physical boundaries. The earliest manifestation of such boundaries were the walls of the sedentary home. As is well known, the beginnings of sedentary life predate the rise of agriculture, which in many cases is the first occurrence of large-scale territorial subdivision. As practices of subdividing space with rectilinear lines become more prevalent, a shift from circular to rectangular house layouts is also evident.[4] The archaeologist Kent V. Flannery suggests that many societies that inhabited circular houses—like the Natufians of Palestine—had little incentive to produce large quantities of food reserves because what was reaped had to be shared.[5] He maintains that where people inhabited circular huts, often storage was shared outside buildings. With the rise of rectangular houses, however, storage was "privatized" inside the dwelling.[6] Thus, inhabiting rectangular enclosures signals the becoming-storage of the house. This is the case of the houses found in Çayönü, in

fig. 3.1

what is now Turkey (6000 BCE), where each house was probably built with mud bricks laid on top of a stone basement subdivided into small cells that archaeologists believe to be storage spaces.[7] In her seminal study of domestic form, archaeologist Rosalind Hunter-Anderson defines the rectangular house as a "warebox" whose form serves to contain its contents in an orderly manner.[8] This warebox is subdivided into rooms, each potentially hosting a different activity or function. With the rise of agriculture, the specialization of labor activities and the storing of surplus required the house to be internally subdivided into rooms that accommodated a more complex household organization. The tripartite houses of Mesopotamia clearly demonstrate this change.

Unlike the circle, the rectangular enclosure eased the process of subdivision and facilitated the addition of new spaces. It also

opened the possibility of further subdividing internal rooms into

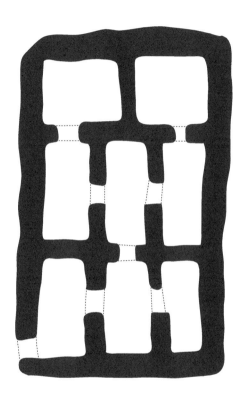

3.1 Houses excavated in Çayönü, Turkey. © Dogma.

smaller ones and externally demarcating the household boundaries in relation to the rest of the community. Before becoming the organizational logic of agricultural fields, rectangular subdivision was the product of defining space through permanent walls. Many sedentary communities around the world used permanent walls to coherently organize their dwelling space based on permanent possession. Nonetheless, it was through the consolidation of agriculture as intensive and large-scale cultivation that the rectangular subdivision expanded from the house to the village to the territory.

Surplus and Colonization

The surplus-creating economy of agriculture first manifested not only through the subdivision of houses and settlements but also through the parceling of rural territory into rectangular fields. This process was documented in Mesopotamia, just before the rise of Uruk.[9] Around 4,000–3,500 BCE, population growth and technological breakthroughs in cultivation led to the parceling of rural territory into long strips of land perpendicular to canals. This system enabled the efficient irrigation of land and aided the animal-drawn plow because it reduced the need to rotate. The making and maintenance of this quasi-rectilinear hydraulic system caused production to skyrocket in Mesopotamia and led to what V. Gordon Childe called the "urban revolution."[10] The rapidity and inevitable impact of this development were calibrated by the subdivision of land into fields as a fundamental unit of measure.[11] Large-scale surplus agriculture and rectilinear subdivision in Mesopotamia invariably became part of the system of geometric regularity that allowed a centralized authority to correlate quantities of labor and product to the extension of land plots. According to archaeologist Mario Liverani, the new scale of economic transactions, fueled by agricultural surplus, required an impersonal system of governance based on counting and measuring, implemented to give value to commodities, labor, time, and land.[12] The definition of surplus as the quantity that remains after the realization of subsistence has always implied a system of measurement capable of giving this excess amount a precise economic value. Not by chance, early forms of writing are tied to cadastral records and to bookkeeping for the production and distribution of agricultural produce. In tablets found in Mesopotamia, the organization of the writing—pictographic signs inscribed in rectilinear strips—seems almost to replicate the linear organization of cultivated fields. In early urban civilizations such as Sumer and the Indus valley, rectilinear subdivision emerges in the spatial organization of society at different scales: from irrigation to domestic space, from monumental architecture to writing. It is also evident that the general principle of rectilinear subdivision marks the rise of societies characterized by a proclivity toward political unification.

In many parts of the world, land subdivision was achieved by directly tracing lines on the soil. This operation requires two consequential conditions: land that is flat, and the intersection of lines at 90-degree angles so that the resulting plots have the same dimensions. By ensuring the regularity of the grid, the latter condition is an effective means not only of subdivision but also of measurement. The grid unveils a sameness of measure that is useful as a concrete, tangible template. Laying out the grid on an extensive area is a complex operation that could be carried out only by powerful institutions with the capacity to accumulate enough power to submit large portions of land to a unifying system. This attempt to impose straight lines on land is precisely the origin of *geometry*. In the parceling of rectangular plots of land, the ancient Egyptians perfected the use of the right angle, a feature that would become dominant in every aspect of Western urbanism, from architecture to settlements. As documented in the first chapter, a measured stretched rope was used in ancient Egypt to delineate areas for the building of dams, granaries, and temples. Most importantly, as described by Herodotus, the stretching of rope was used to parcel out soil when it reemerged from the Nile's seasonal flood.[13] Alfred Sohn-Rethel remarked that techniques of measuring and parceling were invented in Egypt not for the sake of cultivation but to reassess the peasants' tributes to the pharaoh after a flood.[14] Although geometry may predate the Egyptian civilization, Herodotus's description is a reminder that the inception of this mathematical field is linked to quantification and economic valuation.

During the Middle Kingdom the pharaohs and state officials took a deep interest in settling communities along the Nile Valley in places where they would function as colonies of the state.[15]

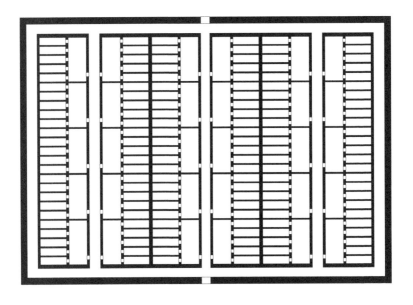

0   20 m

3.2 Reconstruction of the workers' settlement at Qasr el-Sagha, Egypt.
© Maria Shéhérazade Giudici.

These colonies were conceived as towns to house workers for specialized labor, such as cultivating the fields, working at quarries, or building funerary complexes. The most striking feature of these settlements was their strict orthogonal geometry, which was often based on the repetition of a module. In some cases, the module was the household unit, which gave unprecedented geometric consistency to these settlements. Remarkable examples of these planned towns are found at Tell el Dab'a in the Nile delta and Qasr el-Sagha in the northern Fayum region, both built in the second millennium BCE. In these two settlements, orthogonal geometry dominates everything: the use of modular mud bricks, the definition of domestic layout, and the organization of the settlement as a grid of perfectly rectilinear walls. This strict geometric order was motivated not only by a desire for efficiency in building, but also by state officials' need to strictly control the reproduction of the labor force—an extremely important aspect of state governance.[16] In Egyptian urbanism, rectangular subdivision was thus instrumental in defining a form that would integrate workforce and household as a coherent whole, a kind of social factory in which not just work but life itself was rigidly disciplined.[17]

fig. 3.2

For this reason, the planned workers' settlements of ancient Egypt can be interpreted as an early incarnation of an urbanism that is colonial in nature.[18] The word "colony" comes from the Latin *colere*, which means to cultivate. The Latin term also refers to ancient Rome's tendency to encourage veterans to settle on and cultivate newly conquered land as a form of occupation. A colony is thus not just a form of military occupation but also—and especially—a form of civilian appropriation of land mobilized by a state in order to expand its political and economic power. The regularity of form that characterizes colonial settlements is a consequence of the fact that land appropriation—the origin of many state formations—requires planning. Colonization often involves the mobilization of a large number of people in a potentially hostile territory; thus it is only effective when there is efficient and swift management of resources. For this reason, the history of colonial appropriation, from the early gridiron settlements in ancient Egypt to the conquest of the Americas beginning in the sixteenth century, coincides with the history of the grid. The grid provides a spatial template to coordinate operations at different scales, including the household unit, the settlement at large, and the efficient division of land within the abstraction of geometric order.

The colonial logic of the urban grid was perfected in ancient Greece, which, from the first half of the first millennium BCE, made colonization its primary method of founding cities. Even though Greek civilization was a constellation of autonomous city-states that never became an empire, many *poleis* were active in settling colonies across the Mediterranean basin to consolidate trade networks.[19] Unlike mother cities that grew organically over long stretches of time, colonial cities were built in a relatively short time, which required planning. The first act of settlement often involved imposing a grid of paths on the site to divide the land into equal plots. Because establishing colonies was risky, it could only be accomplished by rewarding participants with a plot of land. The Greek colonial gridiron was influenced by the principle of *isonomia*, meaning equality of citizens before the law, which was translated spatially into the even distribution of land tenure to each settler household.[20]

fig. 3.3

In Greek colonial cities, the grid was not just a means of land distribution; it was also a way to regularize, consolidate, and protect private property.[21] Emerging after the seventh century BCE, Greek *poleis* were organized around the distinction between public and private spaces, the latter being the space of the *oikos*, or household, governed by its owner. Thus the perfect gridiron of the planned city reveals how public and private interests—*polis* and *oikos*—were not antagonistic but mutually dependent. This dependency is visible in the plan of cities like Olynthus (fifth century BCE), in which the subdivision of the city into regular blocks is carried into the standardized internal subdivision of the houses.[22] Therefore the spatial order of the colonial Greek city does not consist of public space that defines private space, but rather the latter—in the form of the rectangular house—determines the overall form of the city. For this reason, the common understanding of street grids as a means to ease circulation is questionable, for it completely overlooks the role that rectilinear subdivision played in defining land tenure in the Greek *polis*.

The relationship between the orthogonal grid and city subdivision was theorized (and not invented, as is commonly

3.3 Plan of the colonial city of Naxos. © Dogma.

assumed) in the fifth century BCE by Hippodamus of Miletus, who is depicted in two brief passages in Aristotle's *Politics* as a political philosopher and planner concerned with the organization of the *polis*.[23] Because Aristotle mentioned Hippodamus while discussing constitutional models, his grid should not be understood as a mere topographic template but as a form of political order. According to Aristotle, Hippodamus proposed to divide the population into three classes: artisans, farmers, and soldiers. He then proposed to divide city land into three parts: one sacred, one common, and one private. Sacred land was for the customary offerings to the gods, common land was for providing food for soldiers, and private land was for farmers. Artisans are here presumed landless and thus dependent on farmers for their subsistence. In fact, the novelty of Hippodamus's theory was his use of the grid as a way to distribute land-use profits in service of organizing the *polis* into distinct social classes.

This meant that Hippodamus challenged the isonomic nature of the grid (and *isonomia* itself) by using the grid to discreetly instill hierarchy in the subdivided city rather than equally distribute property.[24] In his theory, the principle of subdivision immediately reflected the relationship between social groupings and land ownership, and thus defined power relations among the citizens. For example, in Hippodamus's *polis*, soldiers were more powerful than artisans: soldiers could count on the use of common land for their subsistence while artisans depended on farmers for products and nourishment. This situation inevitably established a hierarchy that disrupted the seemingly egalitarian order of the grid. At the same time, it was precisely the abstract character of the grid as a means of subdivision that allowed Hippodamus to plan and articulate these subtle social differences in terms of land use. Hippodamus theorized the geometric rigor of the grid in order to objectify social differences, rooting them in the way land was subdivided and distributed.

Res

While the Greeks developed the gridiron as a system of land distribution, the Romans perfected the grid as an effective way to consolidate property rights. Ancient Rome made the grid its preferred urban template when, in the sixth century BCE, it initiated its aggressive politics of conquest. As is well known, Rome ensured its domination in newly conquered territories by establishing colonies and filling them with populations that were often mobilized from elsewhere. Rome's use of the grid was influenced by Greek colonial planning, but unlike the Greeks, the Romans organized the grid around the crossing of two main axes, the *cardo* and the *decumanus*. In this way, they countered the isotropy of the grid with the strong centralizing logic of the cross, a figure favored by the Romans because it evoked the power of the center.[25] The *cardo* and *decumanus* were the organizing axes not only of the town but also of the surrounding territory, thereby forming a coherent whole in which the grid defined land use both inside and outside the walled city. This unification of city and territory became even stronger when the Romans conquered the flat land of northern Italy and reordered this territory through the process of centuriation, a method of subdivision based on the delineation of land into regular squares known as *centuria* (710 by 710 meters).[26] Through centuriation the state distributed and allo-cated newly conquered land as private property.[27] When new land was conquered it was divided and assigned to farmers that the state transported from elsewhere to replace or integrate with the indigenous population. The process of settling new territory was directed and paid for by the army, and as such, it manifested the ideological impetus behind colonial settling based on the strong relationships between war and farming.[28] Accordingly, the Roman army's main pool of recruits was farmers. Moreover, the state was responsible for a great number of veterans who expected some form of welfare after serving in the always belligerent Roman army. On the one hand, land ownership rooted farmers and their families in newly conquered territories, and on the other, it made adult male farmers recruitable, since to serve in the army, one had to own property.[29] Thus the main purpose of centuriation was the efficient control of land and the formation of a class of landowners, however small their parcels might be.

The precedents for centuriation were the methods of land subdivision already practiced by Egyptians, Greeks, and Etrus-cans, but significantly the Roman version systematically applied virtually the same grid across different territories. Whether for military camps or colonial towns, centuriation involved a careful survey of land that only the state could undertake using authorized surveyors known as *finitores* or *agrimensores*.[30] The main feature of this survey was the use of the *groma*, an instrument that allowed a surveyor to ensure that perpendicular lines would meet at right angles. The survey process was immediately followed by the tracing of *limites*, the lines that divided the *centuria* into submodules such as squares or strips of land known as *strigae* and *scamna*. Only when the land was properly divided into modules could it be assigned to its owners as a *sorte*, a plot of land that was clearly measured and contained. To make the subdividing lines permanent and immediately legible to the owners, stone markers were placed where the lines intersected.[31] The centuriation also organized the *ager publicus*, or public land, which was often violently seized or conquered from indigenous inhabitants. Ultimately this land was carefully subdivided into a tapestry of holdings and given to individual owners who—as recipients of property—had no choice but to remain loyal to the state.

Centuriation was the most radical, but not the sole, embodiment of Roman private property, and it demonstrated the Romans' precise ability to impose lines on large portions of land. Beyond this physical act of subdivision, the Romans uniquely conceptualized private property through *res*, the most important category of Roman law. *Res* refers to the process where objects, places, and human relationships become objectified as "things" or commeasurable entities. For the Romans, the designation of something *as res publica* or *res privata* indicated not the thing in itself or its concrete use, but its ownership status. For example, a building as *res publica* meant that it was owned by the state, while a house or a plot of land as *res privata* was owned by individual citizens. Although *res* defined the totality of things that could be owned, it primarily referred to land ownership.[32] Once designated as *res*, land was understood primarily in terms of its patrimonial value.[33] The Egyptians' and the Greeks' use of geometry to measure the earth was instrumental in developing land surveys. For the Romans, the relationship between geometry, ownership, and monetary value was even tighter because it was mandated by the universalizing force of law itself. As legal historian Yan Thomas points out, Roman law was essentially a process in which the contingent properties of an object or a person were abstracted in order to fit generalizable cases.[34] Objects and land were intelligible entities under law only if they were considered purely in terms of the economic quantities of ownership. This means that everything that was *res*—and land especially—was subjected to immediate translation into financial value. The grid of Roman centuriation, with its potentially infinite extensive logic, is the ultimate embodiment of the economic implications of *res* as a spatial datum. With its standardized system of measurement realized in the orderly placement of stone markers, roads, canals, lines of trees, walls, and fences, centuriation abstracted land not simply as a geometric figure but as patrimonial assets. The deployment of the grid is thus the clearest example of how geometry supported ownership by allowing not only the neat subdivision of land as measurable parcels, but also the abstraction of land into monetary value underscored by the law. While the expansion of the Roman Empire is typically thought of as the ongoing spread of troops and infrastructure, the very core of this expansion was the *res extensa* of property as a legal framework in which domination was exerted through the force not only of soldiers but also—and especially—of law.

Civilian Occupation

It is now evident that geometry is the crucial link between land and property. Discussing the art of geometry, Cicero made clear that its utility was in the measuring of land.[35]

The rebirth of urbanization in Europe after the eleventh century was paralleled by a renewed capacity to map and measure land. With the increasing importance of agricultural production, Greek geometry and Roman *planimetria* (the art of measuring fields) again became fundamental sources of knowledge for abbots, lords, and kings seeking to master their own territories. During the thirteenth century, in the context of the increasing appropriation and systematic exploitation of rural land by monastic enterprises and other institutions, bastides, the prototype of colonial planning in modern Europe, took form in southwest France. Neither villages nor cities but towns, the main purpose of these settlements was economic. Coinciding with a large

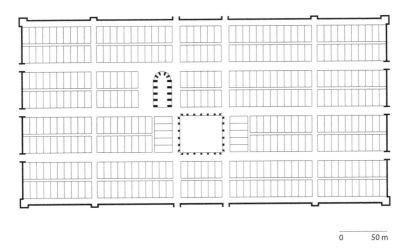

0   50 m

3.4 Plan of the bastide of Monpazier in Dordogne. © Maria Shéhérazade Giudici.

population surge, bastides emerged during the Hundred Years' War when the French region of Aquitaine was under English rule and quickly became an influential model of town-making across Europe, from Italy to Portugal.[36] The French and English monarchs both consolidated their holdings in France by establishing gridded towns that attracted people, developed agriculture and commerce, and provided military support in case of conflict. The bastides were unique due to their entrepreneurial nature. Their foundation was defined by a contract, known in France as *paréage*. A legal agreement between the crown and a local authority such as a lord or abbot, *paréage* ensured that the crown received a share of land in return for the maintenance of order and security.[37] Once a bastide was founded, the king and local landowners attracted settlers to it by granting them property both inside and outside the town. For this reason, many bastides were planned as compact rectangular settlements defined by a uniform grid of streets. The initial investors of bastides made money by taxing the property and trade of residents. Today, extant bastides like Monpazier in fig. 3.4 Dordogne may look like picturesque medieval villages, but when planned and built in the thirteenth century they were conceived as the mere subdivision of saleable plots of land—a model sustained in the sale of suburban estates today. Apart from facilitating the sale and taxation of private property, the grids' regularity helped to expedite construction and prevent conflict among settlers. Because these features recur in many bastides, the grid plan was arguably the product of a centralized form of planning directly initiated by monarchies.[38] Therefore, the bastides, like Roman colonial cities, were the result of a repeatable urban template mutable enough to allow local authorities to introduce any necessary adjustments. Moreover, bastides proved to be an efficient form of urbanization because their simple form required minimal investment at the outset and building was the responsibility of inhabitants. For this reason, the towns were important antecedents (and perhaps a direct source) for colonial urbanism in the Americas and in Asia, where speed and efficiency in establishing a city became a crucial goal. In his important study *Town Planning in Frontier America*, John W. Reps notes that before the English began colonizing America, the plans of thirteenth-century towns established in England by King Edward I appeared in William Camden's

1587 book *Britannia*.[39] Edward I was behind the building of many bastides in France, and the towns he established in England and Wales, such as Flint, Hull, Carnarvon, and Winchelsea, also had rectangular plans with straight streets intersecting at right angles. Reps also argues that the siege town of Santa Fe, built in 1490 near Granada—the last Moorish stronghold in Spain—is likely a main source for the Law of the Indies, the body of laws issued by the Spanish crown in 1573 for governing the empire's American and Philippine possessions.[40] Even though the law was an amalgam of ancient Roman and Renaissance planning principles, its rationalizing impetus was certainly informed by the tradition of the standardized bastides, which, beginning in the fourteenth century, became a model for many planned towns, from the Terre Nuove in Tuscany to Dutch colonial cities in Asia.[41] The prevalence of the bastides and colonial settlements in the Americas and Asia was largely a consequence of their minimal planning requirements, which allowed anyone with a rudimentary knowledge of surveying land to immediately start a city. Plans of colonial towns in the Americas were often simple diagrams traced on the ground where the only information recorded was the outlines of plots of land and the occasional name of a location. This rudimentary approach is evident in cities established under the laws of Virginia, such as Yorktown, founded in 1691, where the drawn plan provides only minimal topographic information about the settlement.

fig. 3.5

Despite the expedience with which they were planned and built, the defining aspect of the bastides and of many colonial cities in the Americas and Asia was the way regular subdivision concealed the asymmetry of power behind their making. The equality suggested by these town grids is only convincing when considered from a morphological point of view. Not the result of a local agreement among settlers, the regular distribution of property was wholly determined by a sovereign's control of social and spatial assets.

Grids are also deceptive in another way: their apparent uniformity often articulates hidden forms of spatial hierarchy. For example, in the French bastides, public buildings such as the church, the town hall, and the market square were inconspicuous and aligned with the order of the grid, yet their positions affected

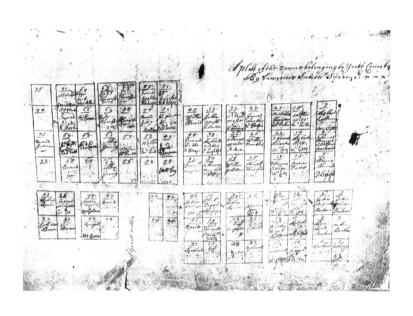

3.5 Plan of Yorktown, founded in 1691. From John W. Reps, *The Making of Urban America: A History of City Planning in the United States* (Princeton: Princeton University Press, 1965). Drawn by Lawrence Smith.

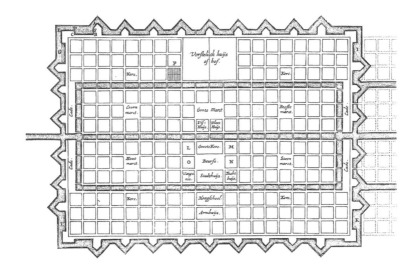

3.6 Simon Stevin, ideal plan for a city. From Simon Stevin, *Materiae politicae*, 1649.

the commercial value of nearby properties. Inequality was also easily achieved by applying different uses to different zones within the grid, making some areas more valuable than others. This logic was at work in most colonial cities built by European powers in the Americas and in Asia. A remarkable example of the grid's instrumental role in allocating inequality is the colonial town of Batavia, built in Indonesia by the Dutch East India Company as a trading post to facilitate the region's spice trade.[42] The plan of Batavia adapts an abstract town model drawn by the Flemish mathematician Simon Stevin in 1650.[43] In his plan, which strongly resembles a French bastide, Stevin complements the grid of rectilinear streets with canals. While canals are a main urban feature for drainage and transportation in the Netherlands, their deployment in Stevin's abstract model serves a more subtle purpose: the subdivision of the rectangular town into four sectors. Moreover, as in the bastides, the placement of public squares and buildings introduces hierarchies into the isotropic order of the grid. Additionally, the continuation of plots of land beyond the town's perimeter wall suggests that part of the population is kept outside of, but close to, the city. Stevin's plan is thus a subdivision strategy that allowed the planner to calibrate hierarchies and proximities without disrupting the seemingly egalitarian form of the grid. A version of this logic is apparent in Batavia. Since very few bridges crossed the city's canals, movement from sector to sector was controllable. Further, as was suggested in Stevin's plan, part of the population—mostly the indigenous people who worked for the Dutch East India Company—inhabited the area outside of, but close to, the city walls. They could therefore work in the town but were kept outside to avoid revolts. The plan of Batavia and Stevin's ideal plan exemplify how the geometric order of the grid fostered segregation and inequality in colonial cities. Yet the root of inequality was not the grid in itself, but the legal framework the grid enforced, which was centered on the principle of private property.

fig. 3.6

Lawfare

Property is not appropriation *sic et simpliciter*. Property is defined by a legal apparatus enforced by the state that gives people the right to use or benefit from something they own. If someone has the right to own something, it means that the use of that thing by others is not possible without the owner's consent. As Nicholas Blomley puts it, "Property's 'bundle' of rights includes the power to exclude others, to use, and to transfer. Such rights are enforceable, whether by custom or the law."[44] Even if today property takes myriad forms both material and immaterial, the most important form of property is arguably still land. To legally own land allows owners to enclose it and regulate its use and the life that unfolds upon it. This is why, as geographer Gary Fields has argued, the ultimate weapon of conquest in the Americas by European colonizers was not warfare but *lawfare*—the imposition of land ownership defined by law against possession of land defined by custom.[45] Indeed, as argued by Brenna Bhandar, the modern concept of property emerged from colonial modes of appropriation.[46]

In Spanish colonization, often settlers did not receive an absolute title to land but rather were given land in perpetuity according to prescribed duties of cultivation. A similar ethic of cultivation is evident in New England Puritan communities. In towns such as New Haven, the use of the grid to subdivide land had a more symbolic than economic purpose. Here the nine-square grid replicated the plan of Solomon's Temple in Jerusalem as reconstructed by the Jesuit priest Juan Bautista Villalpando in his *Ezechielem explanationes* (1596).[47] The intention behind this city plan, with its symmetric form and large town common at the center, was the realization of the *Civitas Dei* on earth. The situation was different in other English possessions of North America where the grid was the main tool for appropriating land under the discipline of individual property.[48] In these cases, however, private property was not introduced simply as a right to own land, but as the "virtuous" act of cultivating land that the colonizers perceived—or wanted to perceive—as land previously *without* owners.

The settlement and cultivation of land on a vast scale required surveying and parceling. To make the measured and subdivided land productive, not just for subsistence but for profit, required intense labor. For this reason, the English made the virtues of cultivating and thus "improving" land the main ideological basis for the exclusionary right to own property.[49]

While Spanish and Portuguese colonization was justified based on the duty to convert natives to Christianity, English colonization was motivated explicitly by the idea of settling a territory by improving its productivity.[50] The orderly grid of cultivated fields was a fundamental "imaginary landscape" that both British and, later, other white American colonizers projected on the land that they violently appropriated from the native populations. Instrumental to this appropriation was the idea, promoted by liberal thinkers such as John Locke, that unbound and untilled land could not properly be cultivated and thus was akin to lying waste.[51] For Locke, only private ownership by individuals could guarantee cultivation and thus economic growth. Indeed, he believed land improvement and land ownership were two faces of the same coin. This idea was echoed by the colonizers' belief in *res nullius*, one of the forms of *res* introduced by the ancient Romans. For the Romans, *res nullius* described ownerless objects that were available for appropriation. In the colonizer's imagination, *res nullius* became *terra nullius*—that is, ownerless land that could be appropriated without committing an act of dispossession. Such a juridical apparatus could only be supported by representing North America as a wide "empty space" populated by indigenous people who, in the words of Locke, knew no enclosure.[52] It is here that we fully understand how the British—like the ancient Romans—imposed a grid of boundaries on the land to make the theft of land from indigenous communities lawful.

The walls and boundaries of different civilizations have a long tradition as political territorial markers. Boundaries often embodied rights of occupation, yet—with the exceptions of ancient Rome and, later, modern Europe—this kind of occupation was seldom enforced legally, only justified by custom. As Fields writes, native populations of North America had developed a sophisticated system of land tenure manifested by a dense network of boundaries demarcating areas of possession, access, and trespass alongside rules for rights of use, occupancy, and circulation.[53] With the colonists' introduction of private property as an individual right to land ownership, the tracing of boundaries was invested with a completely different meaning. The boundary that encloses land as property is not simply a physical element. It is also the embodiment of an abstract legal right with the power to exclude that is far stronger than any physical barrier. The English tradition of building drystone walls to enclose property is a remarkable example of a legal and physical boundary working in concert.[54] From a material standpoint, these walls look like archaic boundaries, more symbolic than functional; in fact, their building technique was inspired by ancient drystone walls built to define the boundaries of common pastureland. Yet the purpose of these walls was not only to contain animals but also—and especially—to physicalize the legal power by which landowners had removed this land from common tenure. The laying of stone walls materialized a careful survey through which landowners ultimately had their acquired property legalized by Parliamentary bills. It is this kind of legal approach to boundaries that the English colonizers brought to the New World, continuing the theft of common land that they had initiated in the fifteenth century in their home country. Marx called this method of appropriation "primitive accumulation," which he defined as the process through which possessors accumulated the initial wealth that formed the backbone of their investment.[55] Classical political economy represented this process as the virtuous labor of one select group within society, but Marx emphasized that primitive accumulation was essentially a form of legal (i.e., state-promoted) *theft* effected by the enclosure of land and the ensuing appropriation of resources that deprived large segments of the population of their livelihood. As a legalized process, forceful appropriation led to a surge in land surveys and cartographic representations in which scientific mapping replaced the more idealized and pictographic representation of land. Estate maps became the precondition for knowing one's own land. This cadastral vision of the rural world was soon translated into a landscape in which property took the form of an all-encompassing grid of lines made by fences, shrubbery, canals, and rows of trees.[56] These innocent landscape features physicalized the abstraction of the cadastral property line which first existed in the vacuum of geometric reasoning.

"Landscape," in the form of the composition of lines and fields, is the very product of the exclusionary violence of enclosure by way of the abstraction of cadastral geometry.[57] It is important not to forget that the British colonization of North America

3.7 Thomas Jefferson's proposal to parcel out the western territory in squares.
© Maria Shéhérazade Giudici, adapted from William D. Pattison.

occurred according to the method of enclosing common land that was first pursued in the home territory. Enclosure and colonization are parts of the same process of appropriation that monetizes landed property.

A Nation in the Form of a Grid

When the British colonies along the east coast of America gained independence from the British Empire, the new nation continued the process of dispossession initiated by the British at the expense of indigenous people. Against native collective land tenure, the colonizers mobilized an imagined landscape subdivided by legal boundaries and sold to new owners.[58] It was precisely this territorial concept that prompted the leaders of the newly formed United States government to choose the rectilinear grid as the proper spatial template for land appropriation. While traditional colonial gridiron settlements—including early colonial cities in the Americas—were finite settlements surrounded by land for cultivation, the United States' colonization of the West transformed the grid into a potentially infinite extension of property rights. The same grid still underlies the prevailing American tendency toward geometrically regular roads and fields. The origin of this grid was the Land Ordinance of 1785, which established a standardized system for settlers to buy legal title to farmland west of the Appalachian Mountains and north of the Ohio River. As is well known, this system was adapted from Thomas Jefferson's proposal

fig. 3.7 to parcel out the western territory in squares. Jefferson's initial grid subdivided land into what he called *hundreds*—a ten-by-ten-mile unit enclosing 100 square miles. In his vision, the hundred was also made of 100 individuals and their families, who would form a self-governing township. The strict roundness of these figures was based on Jefferson's attempt to introduce the decimal system into American life.[59] Whether for his architecture or for measuring or coinage, Jefferson adamantly advocated the use of the decimal system for its ease of calculation. It is interesting to note that his design of the rectangular survey system paralleled his proposal to divide the dollar into tenths and hundredths.[60] The resulting grid was an all-encompassing system that coalesced

110 geometrical order, surveying, and financial value into one efficient

apparatus. To make the grid an absolute system not determined by any local condition, Jefferson also adopted an unprecedented unit of measure for land, the geographical mile, which was derived from sea navigation. Such an operation implied the projection of the sea's "emptiness" on a territory that was far from empty. Another striking aspect of Jefferson's land survey system was its alignment with the global grid of longitude and latitude, giving the nationwide survey the "objectivity" of scientific fact.

The Jeffersonian grid allowed any settler using rudimentary instruments to survey property.[61] In this way, Jefferson rooted his republican agrarianism to the individual's ability to own and quantify a plot of land. The implementation of the Land Ordinance of 1785 ultimately stripped Jefferson's land survey system of many of its features, including the hundreds and decimal divisions, but the rectilinear grid remained the basic principle of its organization. The hundred was replaced by the concept of a township measuring six miles per side and subdivided into 36 squares of land, which were sold through government auction to private owners in order to repay public debt. Parcels were identified only by numbers, but this relentless abstraction was the product of a far-from-peaceful survey campaign. Between 1785 and 1788, a team surveying the notorious Seven Ranges—a tract of land in eastern Ohio—met resistance from natives who understood that the surveyor's simple act of leaving marks on the ground and on trees was intended to dispossess them of their land.[62] While on a map the Seven Ranges looks like a supremely serene gridded landscape, on the ground this landscape was fiercely contested and required the US government to deploy troops and build forts to protect the survey operation.

Although the survey of the Seven Ranges failed to meet the government's primary goal of paying down the national debt through land sales, it represented an important step for surveying methodology in the appropriation of the American West. Above all, the 1785 Land Ordinance demonstrates that gridding of a territory was not primarily about circulation—although infrastructural systems, such as railways, played a fundamental role in the colonization of the West—but about the violent act of appropriation and the consolidation of that appropriation through subdivision.

fig. 3.8

The grid plays an ambivalent role in urbanization. At first its geometry is ostensibly artificial, which makes clear that it is anything but a natural order. Neither the Law of the Indies nor Jefferson's grid hide their overt political mission of bringing civilization to a land believed to be populated by people incapable of such spatial mastery. In addition to enforcing the idea of property, the grid was an ideological tool used to impress and overwhelm indigenous populations with the colonizers' unlimited power to master the land. But when grids became the rule of colonial settlement, this ostensible geometry became so ubiquitous that it appeared almost natural, hiding its actual instrumentality in the appropriation and commodification of land.

Urbanization

Even though Jefferson's grids and those of the Land Ordinance of 1785 were aligned with the global system of meridians and parallels, their scope was limited to one country. With the rise of long-distance navigation and industrialization in the eighteenth century, the idea of a gridiron encompassing the entire world took the form of imaginary lines known as meridians and longitudes. Establishment of these global lines aimed to overcome the rather fragmentary and disorganized patchwork of nautical maps and replace it with a uniform geographic system. In a visual manner, parallels and longitudes symbolize the ethos of unlimited urbanization as a condition in which everything that exists is subsumed within the logic of capitalist accumulation. Today, the word "urban" is casually used to address something "related to cities" as distinct from rural areas. When Spanish engineer Ildefons Cerdà coined the term "urbanization" in the second half of the nineteenth century, he meant something very specific.[63] In his book *Teoría general de la urbanización* (General theory of urbanization), published in 1867, Cerdà defined urbanization as a "vast swirling ocean of persons, of things, of interest of every sort, of a thousand diverse elements" that work reciprocally and thus form a totality that cannot be contained by any previous finite territorial formation such as the old walled city.[64] For Cerdà, the urban condition implied a completely new kind of design, called *urbanism*, the focus of which was no longer just city form

3.8 Map of the United States showing areas covered by the land survey system.
© Dogma, adapted from William D. Pattison.

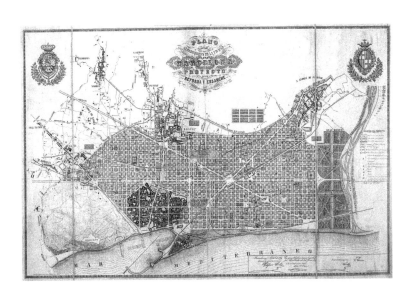

3.9 Extension of the city of Barcelona in 1859. © Museu d'Historia de la Ciutat.

but the whole functioning of the inhabited territory as a large-scale infrastructural system. His theorization of urbanization expanded urban design to involve the use of statistical data, diagrams of circulation, and mappings of natural resources—in short, a variety of information that allowed for the comprehensive understanding of human dwelling beyond the physical character of the city as built form.

Cerdà's theory of urbanization built upon his plan for the extension of the city of Barcelona in 1859. With the large influx of immigrants attracted by the growing industrialization of the city in the first half of nineteenth century, unprecedented numbers of people, epidemics, and social unrest plagued Barcelona.[65] These conditions prompted city authorities to implement a plan to expand the city far beyond its medieval limits. Cerdà believed that industrialization required an altogether new model of living and working, and he was critical of traditional city-making and its focus on the design of urban form.[66] Moreover, he opposed structuring the city with monumental buildings and squares connected by large avenues, considering this approach obsolete because it reflected a hierarchical organization of society that was prone to foment class antagonism. To overcome these issues and to introduce more efficient management of circulation, Cerdà proposed to expand Barcelona through a grid of 133-by-133-meter blocks that allowed the even distribution of services and roads throughout the city. Blocks were distributed to achieve a density of 250 inhabitants per hectare, the standard he recommended to guarantee maximum hygienic social order. The ordering of urban space as a potentially limitless tapestry of housing, workplaces, and public services linked by efficient circulation routes constituted the core of Cerdà's urbanism. Crucially, this model eclipsed the perception of the city as a finite urban artifact and advanced a new entity that was neither city nor countryside.

In the making for centuries, the urban world was not the sudden revelation of Cerdà. Indeed it may be argued that Cerdà's idea of urbanization was the culmination of centuries of colonization. Not by chance, the historical model on which he based the neologism *urbanization* is the Latin *urbs*.[67] For the ancient Romans, *urbs* designated the city less as a political entity—that is to say, the *civitas*, or congregation of *cives*, citizens—and more as the material

fig. 3.9

artifact made of buildings and infrastructure. Cerdà proposed to replace the Spanish word *ciudad* (city) with *urbs*. This manipulation of words implied that he was abandoning the idea of the city as a political entity in favor of an all-encompassing technocratic system of houses, mobility, and industry. With *urbs*, Cerdà addressed a prepolitical generic condition of cohabitation whose structural principle he termed *vialidad*, or circulation.[68] Suspicious of politics, which he saw as unnecessary, he had great faith in technology as a means of social amelioration. We should not forget that Cerdà wrote his theory in the midst of a century of working-class revolutions; against the threat of class conflict, he believed that technically efficient planning, not politics, would allow workers and capital to peacefully coexist, and that new technologies such as automated locomotion and mass communication would lead to the disappearance of limits and boundaries, ultimately making the world a single, peaceful global entity.

The core of Cerdà's urbanism and grid plan for Barcelona was his concept of *intervia*, a spatial template that included both block and street and, in if his intentions were realized, would bring together multiple stakeholders such as the state, the municipal council, landowners, and tenants. In other words, the uniform grid was not intended to ease property subdivision but to integrate private and public interests in a coherent and legible governmental apparatus. Cerdà also made innovative and extensive use of statistics, which he presented in a graph format, reflecting the abstract representation of the entire plan. Yet the abstraction of his planning system was not the result of an a priori measure, as in the case of Jefferson's grid, but of the extreme synthesis of data inputs. Everything in Cerdà's plan was reduced to elements whose measure and quantity were optimized according to empirical data obtained from the extensive surveys he conducted on behalf of the city. The grid allowed him not only to evenly distribute population and public facilities but also to correlate predefined elements such as streets sections, housing types, and land use schemes with economic opportunities and population conditions. Thus his plan was informed by an unprecedented abstraction in which every architectural or urban fact was planned following a strictly economic logic. In both his plan for Barcelona and his *Teoría general de la urbanización*, city-making was no longer focused on a specific form. Decisions about form were decreased as much as possible by the ever-present template of the grid. In Cerdà's schemes and diagrams, the grid ruled everything, from planning to architectural details. Every aspect of human life—from living to working, culture to healthcare, retail to parks—was abstracted according to the relentless rectilinear logic of the grid so that the urban became manageable as a gigantic and all-encompassing *oikos*.

The key factors of Cerdà's urban grid were its low density and profuse integration of public amenities. As a reformist planner, Cerdà firmly believed that for the social good, everybody, from workers to capitalists, would willingly take part in the social equilibrium of the *intervia*. But insufficient public funding forced the city to turn to private investors to fund the city expansion, and landowners' eagerness to profit from their holdings radically altered Cerdà's egalitarian urban field. With their large capital investment in the extension, they were de facto empowered to drive the realization of the plan.[69] In some cases, cartels of investors and developers acquired entire blocks or even groups of blocks, thus privatizing parts of the grid. Moreover, in order to speed up development, city authorities allowed municipal taxes to benefit public space adjacent to the property of landowners who were invested in the urbanization effort. This special treatment of landed individuals directed funds away from a municipal fund established for the development of the entire plan.[70] For Cerdà, the grid was a way to equally distribute capital and resources, but in reality it was used to subdivide land in a way that helped developers and landowners capitalize on the building of the new plan. For example, the famous chamfered corners of the typical block—which Cerdà designed to ease circulation at intersections—garnered premium rents for ground-floor commercial space located at the quasi squares opened by these corners. Ultimately, utilization of Cerdà's grid was not that different from the implementation of the American Land Ordinance. In both cases, the government was the great legal appropriator working for the benefit of private owners who then charged tenants for land and building use. It is precisely under those terms that the total urbanization of the world was achieved. The contemporary urban grid is the enforcement of a total regime of property. Cerdà attempted to make circulation the most important datum of urbanism, but it was the idea of property, with its relentless appetite for the appropriation of resources and economic valorization, that took over his rational grid.

Grid as Diagram

The North American city grid is perhaps best exemplified by Philadelphia. Founded in 1682 by William Penn, Philadelphia was a critical settlement venture in the British colonies promoted by King Charles II, who gave Penn land patents to lead the initiative. The city plan was designed in 1683 by surveyor Thomas Holme, who, at Penn's request, also drew a detailed map of the city's surroundings in order to prepare the territory for potential settlers, or "first purchasers." The remarkable feature of Holme's map is the city grid. It becomes the figure that organizes property rights both inside and outside the city and presents the urban territory as plots of land to be sold.

fig. 3.10

Nearly 300 years later, between 1952 and 1953, Louis Kahn was working as a consulting architect for the Philadelphia Redevelopment Authority, drawing a series of urban plans related to the organization of automobile traffic.[71] Kahn made these drawings when Philadelphia was undergoing urban renewal, a kind of transformation that was taking place in all major cities in the United States. The urban renewal program sought to maintain the dominant economic position of city centers in the face of suburban growth in the decades following World War II. But its most implicit (and effective) agenda was the takeover of city centers by private capital, an operation actively supported by local authorities and the federal government. The ultimate goal of urban renewal was to raise the commercial value of downtown areas, which consequently led to displacing local populations, especially African Americans. With the excuse of improving dilapidated housing districts mostly inhabited by minorities, urban renewal agencies gave city land to private investors to rebuild and accelerate profits. Even though Philadelphia's urban renewal program was less aggressive than that in other cities, its main objectives remained the same, and the city was largely taken over by private developers who transformed the city by dispossessing minorities of their neighborhoods.[72]

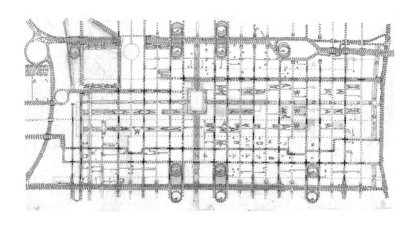

3.10 Louis I. Kahn, traffic study, Philadelphia, 1952. Ink, graphite, and cut-and-pasted papers on paper, 24½ by 43¾ inches. © The Museum of Modern Art / Licensed by SCALA / Art Resource, NY.

It is precisely the context of urban renewal—typical of the postwar American city—that makes Kahn's 1950s drawings for Philadelphia noteworthy. Kahn abstracted the existing city as a series of symbols, using dots to indicate what he called slow "staccato" circulation, arrows for fast "go" circulation, spirals for parking, and crosses for intersections. With everything else omitted, Kahn's Philadelphia is nothing but symbols indicating traffic flow. Kahn observed that the city's many intersections were the main cause of traffic.[73] Anyone with experience driving in a grid city knows that an excess of crossroads slows traffic and makes driving an ordeal. To solve this problem, he proposed reordering traffic by establishing a hierarchy of speeds, ranging from express-ways to pedestrian streets, and dramatically reducing the number of crossroads. A key architectural element in his proposal was the strategic positioning of parking structures to encourage the use of private transportation to reach the city center. This conceptualized the city as the orchestration of vehicular movement through the organization of expressways as "rivers" and parking structures as "harbors." Once drivers reached the harbors, they were freed from the need for cars and circulated on pedestrian paths, most of which, in Kahn's conception, supported retail activities. Such an idyllic image of "civic life" conveyed the idea that downtown was not a hostile territory for driving and shopping, activities that, starting in the 1950s, investors deemed sine qua non to successful urbanity. Although Kahn's proposal was never realized, its logic epitomized the philosophy of the urban renewal project. If a chief goal of urban renewal was to upgrade city infrastructure to make it more hospitable to greater numbers of private vehicles, such a goal was ultimately instrumental in leveraging private capital, which sought to consolidate its hold on the city. Again, the urban grid played an important role in this process, since it allowed city authorities to easily and clearly subdivide the city into neatly bounded sectors available for purchase by private investors. Once priority areas had been established, the major concern of urban renewal agencies was traffic, because they understood that the key to increasing land value was rapid access by car. While the explicit goal of Kahn's traffic studies was the smooth orchestration of movement, its implicit goal was to make the city a more prof-
120   itable ground for investment. Kahn's elegantly abstracted traffic

studies are the unwitting image of the appropriation of the city by postwar capital. Even if Kahn's urban form seems to be detached from property, his proposal shows the strategic role played by traffic "improvement" in waging war against urban minorities determined to fight displacement.

It is here that the affinity between Holme's 1683 map and Kahn's 1952 traffic studies becomes clear. In both cases the urban territory is reduced to a diagrammatic grid. In the first instance, the diagram defines property lines; in the second, it consists of lines of movement. The concept of the diagram is key to understanding these representations of gridded urban territories. A diagram, as discussed in chapter 1, is here understood as a machine that directly produces the effects of power, not as a synthetic representation of concept and form.[74] The grids devised by Holme and Kahn—in which the city is abstracted as thin lines, dots, or arrows, thereby shifting attention away from physical structure toward functional and spatial organization—are not representations but instances in which power is legible and effective. In Holme's map, power is effective in clearly delineating the landscape as a tapestry of properties, while in Kahn's traffic studies power is effective in directing traffic in ways that make downtown more enticing for land speculation. Here the historic logic of urban grids becomes legible: the grid is not just a form; it is also the abstraction of material and social relationships as property. The urban grid reduces the city to a composition of properties, and everything that exists within the grid is forced to comply with the asymmetric power relations that property, backed by the force of the law, implies. From this perspective, urbanization is nothing other than the realization of space as a diagram of "lawful" property.

In his book *The Nomos of the Earth*, Carl Schmitt argues that when the mythic understanding of the earth was supplanted by science, agents of appropriation began to trace lines at a global scale.[75] These lines were instrumental in the subdivision of the world by European powers into the large geographical domains of north, south, east, and west. The grid of meridians and parallels through which the world was made scientifically intelligible were lines traced not only as a system of geographical orientation but also as a vast subdivision of land to be conquered and exploited. The geographic exploration and cartographic representation that reinforced these lines constitute the ultimate scale of colonial appropriation, which is continually reproduced in the myriad lines that still subdivide the world into endless enclosures: the fields, streets, squares, houses, and rooms we presently inhabit.

4   Without Architecture:
The Townhouse, the Factory, and the Abstraction of Building Form

In 1826 architect Karl Friedrich Schinkel traveled to England to visit museums, warehouses, bridges, and factories on behalf of the Prussian state. One of the highlights of this visit was a trip to Manchester, which, at that time, was the epicenter of industrial manufacturing.[1] Describing what is perhaps the first encounter of a classically trained continental architect with a factory, Schinkel wrote in his diary that Manchester made "a dreadful and dismal impression: monstrous shapeless buildings put up only by foremen *without architecture*, only the least that was necessary and out of red brick."[2] Schinkel's written impressions were accompanied by

fig. 4.1

several sketches: a view of the stark rectangular factory buildings pierced by monotonous fenestration, details of roof construction, a section of an industrial building, and a typical residential doorway which, as the Prussian architect noted with irritation, "is reproduced here as it is in the rest of England many thousand times over."[3] Schinkel's notes on Manchester encapsulate the disgust that architects felt toward early industrial buildings. This sentiment was especially strong because industrial buildings left no room for the ornament and composition that for centuries had characterized architecture. Yet Schinkel's sketches of technical details show that, beyond the disgust, there was also keen interest in learning from these buildings "without architecture." It was during the so-called industrial revolution in England, between the eighteenth and nineteenth centuries, that architecture experienced one of its most radical processes of formal and spatial transformation. The main driver of this transformation was not the stylistic choice of a few architects and patrons (if there was ever such a thing as "stylistic choice") but the pressure of industrial manufacturing—a realm where architectural form followed the logic of the mode of production.

In reviewing the projects Schinkel built after his trip to England, it becomes clear that the stark simplicity of factory buildings with their boxlike form, uniform fenestration, and load-bearing column grids influenced his "modern" architectural language. This is apparent in the Packhof built in 1835 and the Bauakademie built between 1832 and 1836. Perhaps a more informative aspect of Schinkel's visual and written impressions of Manchester is the inadvertent link he draws between the architecture of the factory and the typical English residential doorway.

4.1 Karl Friedrich Schinkel, "Die Baumwollspinnereien von Manchester—Tagebucheintrag von der Reise nach Manchester," from the manuscript (1826) of Schinkel's diary of his journey to England, Inventar-Nr.: NL Schinkel 5, Reisen III. © bpk / Zentralarchiv, SMB.

The stereotypical classicism of English doorways was a thin veil covering what was otherwise one of the most abstracted forms of housing ever produced: the English terraced house. Built cheaply and efficiently in rows, this housing model, which proliferated in England starting in the seventeenth century, reduced domestic architecture to its bare essentials: floors supported by party walls, with usually two rooms per floor. The development of this kind of architecture set in motion a radically commercialized building trade whose modus operandi quickly expanded to every utilitarian building—above all, factories. What Schinkel called "building without architecture" found its origin in a new way of conceiving and building architecture as commodity. Yet this utility-driven architecture casts a much longer shadow that goes back to the late Middle Ages when the emergence of the bourgeoisie in Europe manifested a new building type—the townhouse.

Exchange Value:
The Birth of Generic Architecture

Beginning in the Middle Ages the townhouse became a habitation for middle-class households that combined living and working premises. It proliferated in cities such as Pisa, Venice, and Bruges where manufacturing and commerce drove the economy. The architecture of the townhouse was the direct extrusion of the rectangular parcels inscribed by city authorities to carefully subdivide the city's land. Compared to previous housing models, the townhouse was differentiated by a great deal of standardization due to building codes that often regulated the height of floors and the fenestration.[4] An early response to this housing typology in terms of architectural design came from the Italian architect and theorist Sebastiano Serlio. In the mid sixteenth century Serlio drafted the first architectural textbook on housing for "all grades of men" as part of his seven-volume architectural treatise. In this book—which remained unpublished but was nonetheless extremely influential, especially among French architects—Serlio proposed a catalogue of houses conceived according to a social hierarchy that ranged from the poor peasant and artisan to the prince. The most compelling section of this catalogue was devoted to houses for the class in the "middle": artisans, merchants, professionals

such as lawyers, or what Serlio called "citizens."[5] The houses in
this section are marked by a deliberate restraint in ornament. Further, Serlio's houses for "citizens" are distinct in their careful and
rational planning: interiors are subdivided by simple partitions,
and infrastructural elements such as fireplaces, wells, and latrines
are conveniently grouped along the party wall that divides two
houses. The result is an architecture without quality, a standardized form that is easily replicable.

fig. 4.2

Serlio's middle-class houses had a profound influence on
the development of urban architecture in seventeenth-century
Europe, especially in France, where state bureaucracy had a keen
interest in the promotion of standardized housing models. As
previously discussed, in the late fourteenth century, the French
crown established the Bâtiments du Roi to control the work of
stonemasons and carpenters. In the seventeenth century, with the
reorganization of the state administration following the Wars of
Religion between Catholics and Protestants, King Henri IV issued
a building code for Paris which established a uniform body of
regulations for safe, fireproof construction throughout the city.
Moreover, in 1608 a royal decree stated that supervising architects
were obligated to check that masons executed their work according to the *rules of art*.[6] Within this context, the Bâtiments du Roi
promoted books like Pierre Le Muet's treatise *Manière de bien bastir
pour toutes sortes de personnes* (1623), which followed and expanded
on Serlio's thinking on middle-class households. As Maria S. Giudici observes, Le Muet's treatise was developed subsequent to the
building of the first Parisian "royal squares," such as Place Royale
built between 1605 and 1612 and Place Dauphine built between
1607 and 1616.[7]

fig. 4.3

Both squares were promoted by Henri IV as the starting
point for a general urban reform of the capital city of France.[8]
The architecture of these squares was conspicuous for the absence
of any outstanding monument. Instead, their form was defined
by rows of townhouses in which the interior layout was left to the
owner's initiative while the exterior was standardized, thereby
forming a uniform urban façade. This architecture made of plain
façades, minimally marked by simplified stringcourses and uniform fenestration, became known as *architecture d'accompagnement*,
because of its implicit role in city-making. The Parisian royal

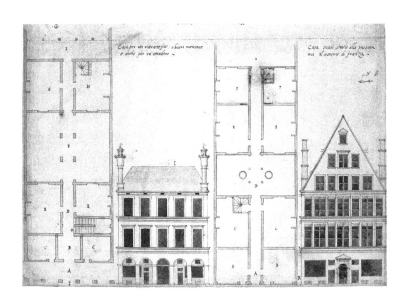

4.2 Sebastiano Serlio, houses for wealthy craftsmen,
from *Sesto libro d'architettura. Delle habitationi fuori e dentro delle città.*

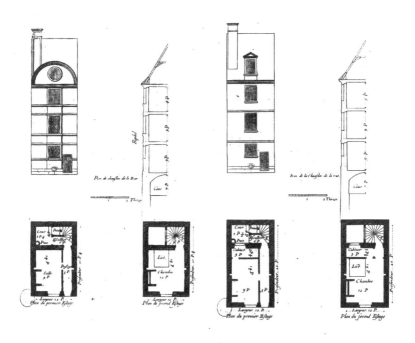

4.3 Pierre Le Muet, plate from *Manière de bien bastir pour toutes sortes de personnes*, 1623.

squares built in the seventeenth and eighteenth centuries—from Place des Victoires to Place Vendôme—augmented the spread of the formulaic character of the *architecture d'accompagnement* as a new template of urban architecture that found its culmination in the endless façades of Haussmann's boulevards. Yet, as Giudici notes, the proliferation of this formulaic residential architecture was not just motivated by civic decorum, but was also—and especially—seen as the suitable envelope of commercial housing initiatives.[9] Increasingly ruled by financial speculation, housing for the middle and upper classes in large metropolises like seventeenth- and eighteenth-century Paris was not defined solely by its use value, but also by its exchange value as a property asset. This prompted wealthy owners to build houses that were easily subdivided into rentable units for transient tenants. Consequently, a vast market for standardized housing models emerged as a way to ease the building of speculative projects. *Architecture d'accompagnement* was thus the byproduct of the transformation of housing into a commodity. It is not surprising that this approach to producing residential architecture became influential in eighteenth- and nineteenth-century England, where financial speculation dominated every aspect of life, especially the production of houses. As in Paris, in London the architectural model for housing speculation took form with the building of a royal square, Covent Garden, designed by architect Inigo Jones in 1630 and financially backed by the duke of Bedford. Although accompanied by a plain church of Palladian inspiration, like its French predecessors Covent Garden essentially consisted of the mere aggregation of standardized townhouses.

The architecture of Covent Garden represents a hybrid of the Palladian classicism that dominated English aristocratic architecture until the late nineteenth century and the monotonous character of bourgeois architecture of the same time.[10] Inigo Jones attempted to give form and proportion to an architecture whose repetitive, almost industrial nature largely downplayed the decorum of classicist proportions. The success of projects like Covent Garden encouraged landowners to initiate speculative residential developments, fueling the proliferation of formal abstraction that ultimately produced the terraced housing type. The decision to build this typology was informed by mere financial parameters:

fig. 4.4

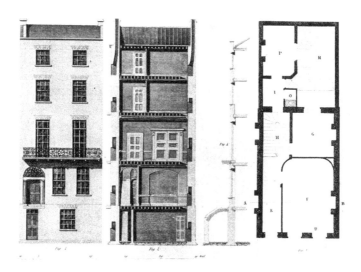

4.4 Second-rate terraced house, plate from Peter Nicholson,
New and Improved Practical Builder, 1823.

terraces were not built for specific clients but for the market. The production process was similarly shaped by economic constraints, starting with the landowner appointing a surveyor to design the street layout and subdivide the buildable area into parcels. Partitioned areas were then rented to builders who, once the bare house carcasses were complete, would sell them to individual owners.[11] The latter would own the house but not the land, which they leased from the landowner. With the expiration of the lease, property rights to both land and house returned to the landowner, who would revise the leasing agreements and increase the rental fee. As a business scheme, the whole arrangement was designed to allow the landowner to extract a profit from the estate. Because a lease would expire in 70 or 80 years,[12] profit was not immediate, but this was not a problem for a landowner with accumulated wealth. In dire need of immediate return were the builders, whose speculative business cycle was dependent on selling houses and was thus far shorter than the prolonged profit structure of aristocratic estates. In order to generate short-term profit, builders developed a commercial way of designing and building, in which every aspect of construction—use of materials, selection of building type, and hiring of subcontractors for carpentry and finishings—was economized. This austerity of means was reflected in the architecture of the terraced house, which was built fast and was not meant to last long, since the building would inevitably be returned to the landowner once the lease expired. These houses were built as commodities—fundamentally different from traditional houses that were strictly built for their use. While the latter were built to endure for long periods, commodified houses were built as disposable objects, and obsolescence was embedded in their very design and construction. Unlike previous kinds of houses, the terraced houses, with their thin walls and repetitive details, suggest a sense of uncertainty. Their commodity status is precisely embodied in this uncertainty. With the terraced house, housing is no longer a durable object determined by use value; rather, as an object to be consumed and marketed, it is determined by its exchange value.

Not by coincidence, when Marx described the difference between the commodity's use value and exchange value, he referred to a ruthless London builder of terraced houses: Nicholas Barbon.[13] *Use value* is the effective utility of an object; *exchange value* is its economic value, the price of an object on the market independent of its material properties. Barbon celebrated his building activity not as "art" but as a successful form of business, given the large number of subsidiary trades involved. From this vantage, a house is not a building but an apparatus based on myriad economic transactions: buying, leasing, standardizing, renting, and selling. What matters is the creation of value; as Barbon (quoted by Marx) wrote, when value is the purpose of a process, "one hundred pounds worth of lead or iron is of as great value as one hundred pounds of silver and gold."[14]

The result is a powerful form of abstraction. A window or a door is no longer just the outcome of handicraft but also, and especially, the result of parameters imposed by the market. The extensively standardized terraced house embodied the abstraction of commodity exchange by reducing the house to a plain kit of parts consisting of walls, windows, doors, stairs, fireplaces, closets, decorations, and other elements. For the first time in history, domestic space was devoid of symbols reflecting its content. The terraced house has a front and back, yet the plan and section show a neutral disposition: front and back parlor, front and back bedroom are interchangeable. This spatial logic transcended social class and included a variety of domestic arrangements. The extent of the abstraction of the terraced house is fully revealed in the detail of the wooden window frame, which is set back to minimize exposed woodwork, reduce fire hazard, and reveal the unornamented brick wall. In the terraced house architecture was reduced to an object, and this exposed objecthood was the product of abstract economical facts.

The sheer commercial nature of this type of architecture—and its potential lack of permanence—is why architects were reluctant to participate in its design. In fact, design was conducted by the builders themselves, who were also able to coordinate a vast array of craftsmen and produce highly rationalized housing for the sake of profit. Everyday experience and accessible "pattern books"—such as *The Modern Builder's Assistant* compiled by architects Robert Morris and William and John Halfpenny in 1757—were the main sources of their design knowledge.

It is important to understand what is meant by "builders." Initially, they were master masons who subcontracted work to artisans for carpentry and finishings. In time, builders became "undertakers" of projects, entrepreneurs who made a profit by planning the entire building process.[15] As discussed in chapter 1, it was in the context of planning that the word "project" became part of architectural culture. Within the commerce of building practice, project became the "plot" carefully devised by the "undertaker" to make a profit. Based on its lucrative nature, the building "project" was not only a widely practiced trade in Georgian and Victorian England but was also the very symbol of entrepreneurship.[16] The realization of architecture through speculative projects drastically changed the nature of the building process. Until the late eighteenth century, with the exception of military undertakings, assessment of a building's value was done during construction or after completion of the building. Alternatively, to prevent costs from escalating and possible legal disputes between clients and builders, all parties involved in a speculative project would determine detailed specifications before beginning the work. As Stefan Muthesius noted, in nineteenth-century England building became an economic activity in which success was dependent on predetermining every minute detail by contract.[17] This meant that every transaction between builder, contractor, craftsmen, landowner, and client was mediated by financial and juridical terms. The architectural project was hence substantiated in the contract, within which every architectural feature was optimized to generate profits for the builder. With his extremely lucrative large-scale construction business, nineteenth-century London-based builder Thomas Cubitt demonstrated that extraction of surplus value was only possible through rigorous standardization of plans, elevations, and construction details—meaning that the possibility of profit was contingent on devising a *project*. In contrast to the Renaissance, the project here does not address the authority of the architect but rather the economic power of the builder, who in many cases worked as the investor, designer, and contractor, de facto controlling the entire cycle of building production. As John Wilton-Ely has argued,[18] builders like Cubitt could negotiate competitive tendering on a lump sum basis because, as in a factory, they employed the necessary labor force on a permanent basis. This allowed builders to replace, almost instantly, the expensive piecemeal work of master craftsmen. Paramount in every sector of building activity, this project-oriented attitude was especially important in the construction of factories, where the demand for quick and cheap work could not afford traditional and expensive craftsmanship.

A Place for Production and Control

Unlike the terraced house, the factory is not a building typology but a mode of production, a diagram of functional relationships in space. According to Andrew Ure, one of the first apologists of industrial manufacturing, the factory is the combined operation of many working people under the system of productive machines continuously impelled by a central power.[19] The power addressed by Ure was the engine that moved the machines, which was propelled first by water power and later by steam engines. Yet the true power of factories was the capital that investors put into these large-scale "undertakings," which made every aspect of the project, from beginning to end, strictly defined in financial terms. What escaped the realm of economic rationality was the sheer brutality of the system—the fact that the factory was one of the most exploitative apparatuses ever conceived. The limited scope of this study cannot fully document the extent to which, from the onset of the factory system, tending machines was an exceedingly alienating form of labor for workers, both physically and mentally.[20] People had no choice but to accept wage work in factories given that since the fifteenth century the English peasantry had been dispossessed of its land and sources of self-subsistence and subjected to the "bloody code" that severely punished unemployment.[21] As Marx noted, this aggressive process of "primitive accumulation" of capital ensured early capitalists an abundant supply of labor for the factory system. The diffusion of cheap commodities was another important factor in the rise of the factory. Once dispossessed of their livelihood and made wage-dependent, workers were compelled to buy everything they needed and to become consumers of basic goods like textiles. The greatest influence on the mechanization of production and the rise of early factories in England—such as those built by entrepreneur and engineer Richard Arkwright—was the introduction of cotton, which made textiles more affordable to a larger customer base. Machines for carding and spinning cotton soon replaced silk-throwing machines that spurred the construction of the first factories.[22]

Before the factory system, peasants and artisans controlled—at least partially—their means of production. This was reversed in the factory. The worker entered the factory as an individual, and any tool or form of cooperation between workers was mediated by the machines. As Marx noted, it was not the workers who used the machines in the factory but the other way around: the machines guided and choreographed the workers, assigning tempos to their tasks.[23] To a certain extent the machine *abstracted* the gestures of the workers, making them conform to a pattern of activities that were predictable and measurable in time and space. The uniformity of the factory escalated with the replacement of water-powered mills by the steam engine, whose steady source of energy gave an unnatural regularity to the rhythm of the machine. Despite the apparent automatic rhythm of the work, the factory was more than a place of production; it was a place of control.

For the entrepreneur, the extraction of surplus value did not depend exclusively on technological advancement. It also, and especially, required the docility and constant discipline of the factory workers. From the beginning, it was apparent that control of the workers was only possible when their position was in full view of a manager and their movements and actions were as limited as possible. Not by chance, an early advocate of workers' discipline was the naval engineer Samuel Bentham, whose brother Jeremy invented the modern detention system known as the *panopticon*. This surveillance device, which enabled the observation of a multitude of inmates by positioning one supervisor at the center of a circular structure, was first conceived by Samuel Bentham as a system for controlling workers in a woodworking plant designed in 1791 for the Prince Potemkin in Critchoff (Krichev), Russia.[24] As a general inspector of the British Royal Navy in the years immediately preceding the Napoleonic wars (1803–1815), Samuel Bentham was responsible for the reorganization of the dockyards and their manufacturing capacity. Notably, he persuaded the Royal Navy to produce their own pulley blocks instead of buying them from external contractors. To increase both the production and precision of these important ship components, he proposed to manufacture them using labor-saving machines propelled by steam engines.[25] He thus reorganized the labor structure to completely tie workers to machines and to avoid acts of insubordination. He further abolished any form of apprenticeship—which was customary among carpenters—and hired only waged workers. Jobs were also reclassified according to the nature of the task itself and therefore did not distinguish between the professions of carpenters and joiners. All the workers at the factory were called "woodmillers."[26] With the help of engineer Marc Isambard Brunel, Bentham conceived a manufacturing system where workers were strictly assigned to a task that required little movement. They therefore worked faster and were easily controlled by a supervisor. Customarily, before Bentham's reorganization of their production in the factory, pulley blocks had been fabricated by specialized craftsmen whose handicraft combined design and manual skills. Bentham and Brunel's system, based on a linear chain of automated machines, intentionally destroyed the workers' unity of head and hand and transformed their skilled work into generic laboring activities.

With the same intentions, Samuel Bunce, an architect and member of the staff in Bentham's office, designed the Portsmouth Block Mills, the factory that produced pulley blocks for the Royal Navy, built in 1800. The factory was designed as a sequence of well-lit halls, each programmed with a specific task. Machines and workers were placed in a clockwise linear configuration, an arrangement that expedited the transfer of blocks from machine to machine. For this reason, the building was reduced to a rectangular enclosure carefully dimensioned to calibrate the optimal distance between machines and the water reservoir located below the factory. Designed to ensure efficiency, the layout subscribed to the diagram of production engineered by Bentham and Brunel. This strictly functionalist approach reduced architecture to its most generic properties—namely, the load-bearing structure. Yet ornamental features survived in small but significant details, such as the Tuscan order of thin posts in the one-story skylighted hall at the center of the complex. With their tall base, the columns made the hall resemble a church or basilica. Even though early factories were built mostly by engineers whose main concern was efficiency rather than representation, these professionals and their clients were reluctant to surrender to the brutal logic of

fig. 4.5

4.5 Portsmouth Block Mills, view of the interior. © Bob Comlay.

the factory form. Minimum embellishments such as pediments, cupolas, and arches are visible in factory buildings built in the eighteenth and nineteenth centuries. A remarkable example of a factory that mixes the typical industrial plan and preindustrial architecture is the Old Casting Hall of the British Cast Plate Glass Manufactory at Ravenhead, built in 1773. The building's interior fig. 4.6 is divided into three long narrow spaces defined by large pillars made of bricks. The roof over the taller central section is supported by pointed brick arches, and a scaled-down version of the same motives covers the side aisles. The space was clearly designed to make the factory floor flexible and to look like a restrained version of a Gothic church. Observing the anachronistic tropes used to mask the unprecedented nature and consequences of industrial production, Marx wrote that "precisely in such periods of revolutionary crisis [people] anxiously conjure up the spirits of the past to their service and borrow from them names, battle cries and costumes in order to present the new scene of world history in this time-honoured disguise and this borrowed language."[27] In early factories, the architectural language of institutions like public halls and churches was borrowed in an attempt to legitimize the factory as infrastructure for the public good. With the massive proliferation of factory buildings in cities, following the introduction of steam engines, engineers and their clients were no longer motivated to add ornamental details. At this moment, the factory was truly without architecture—a rectangular block with minimum load-bearing structure and uniform fenestration—as evident in the cotton factories of Union Street in Manchester sketched by Schinkel.

Typical Plan and "Rational Architecture"

In the late eighteenth century the machine system clearly demanded a specific spatial arrangement that was incompatible with any previous architectural typology except one: that of storage. Forms of storage had existed for millennia and were mainly used to store grain. In medieval Europe, the granary, or *Kornhaus*—as it was called in German—was often built as a large hall. This kind of building spawned a specific architectural form that offered large, unobstructed, flexible space. With the rise of mercantilism and the explosion of colonial trade in the sixteenth century the granary evolved into a storehouse for commodities in general. At this time the term "factory" described the establishment of merchants and factors in a foreign country. The factor was a trader who specialized in buying and selling goods on commission, and the factory was the premises of such business, which required large storage facilities.[28] The factory was thus not born as a place for mass-manufacturing goods, as is commonly assumed, but as logistic infrastructure to support long-distance trade, and thus storage spaces were crucial.

In terms of scale and capacity, the most impressive storage facilities were built at the Isle of Dogs in the early nineteenth century by Robert Milligan, a powerful and ruthless factor. The facilities were conceived as a militarized compound of storehouses built along docks to ease loading and unloading of merchandise. Among these warehouses, No. 10, built on the East Quay and designed by the engineer Thomas Morris in 1809, is an extreme example of abstraction in the design and construction of this typology. Nothing more than a stack of unpartitioned floors, the building is supported by a load-bearing structure reduced to a grid of cast-iron posts carrying beams and girders made of timber.[29] This warehouse represents an early case of the typical plan—an undivided floor plan supported by a regular grid of the smallest possible load-bearing columns. Precisely because of its economy and flexibility, the typical plan became the structural model for early factories.[30]

The typical plan was ultimately a matter of structure rather than typology. The dimensional shape of the floor plan, the height of each floor, and the span between columns strictly adhered to the spatial organization of machines. Yet it was also expected to be flexible to accommodate unforeseen changes. The architecture of the factory was accordingly the outcome of design parameters, not formal moves. The governing parameters were few and basic: maximum distance between vertical posts to make the factory floor spacious and flexible; maximum fenestration to increase ventilation and reduce the need for artificial lighting; maximum floor plate depth to ease spatial organization and supervision. Above all, the tendency to design factories as one-room spaces was

4.6 Old Casting Hall of the British Cast Plate Glass Manufactory at Ravenhead, built in 1773.
From John Gloag, *Industrial Art Explained* (London: Allen and Unwin, 1934), plate II.

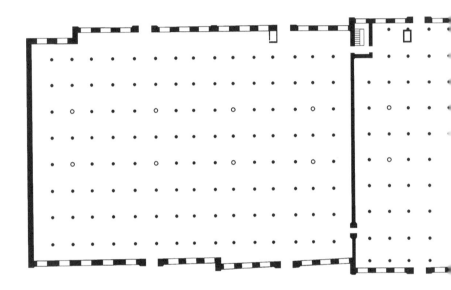

4.7 Warehouse No. 10, built on the East Quay, Isle of Dogs, London, and designed by the engineer Thomas Morris in 1809, plan. © Georgios Eftaxiopoulos.

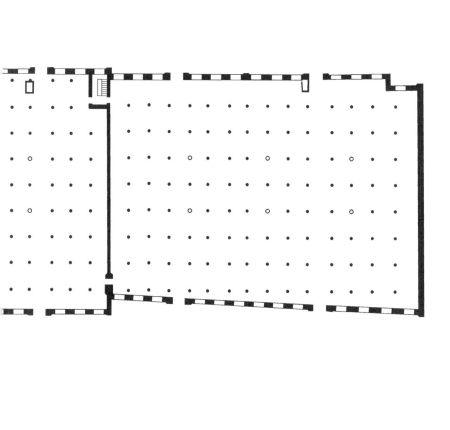

motivated by the owner's desire to optimize surveillance, making the production space a panopticon. Over time, the height of the building became an exceedingly important design consideration. Steelworks and heavy industry in the nineteenth century made multistory buildings unviable. The architecture of the factory was therefore further reduced to a network of one-story shed buildings grouped together in a planned compound. This approach was first tested in the Soho Foundry in Birmingham built by James Watt and Matthew Boulton in 1796.

Reduced to the barest form possible—a grid of vertical supports and a façade with homogeneous fenestration—the factory's abstraction is a visible index of the general abstraction that rules both capital and the industrial system. Within capitalism, the socially necessary labor time is a datum of management that is primarily, although not exclusively, an abstraction of the amount of labor time performed by a worker of average skills and productivity working with tools of average output capacity.[31] This metric of time is also concrete insofar as it regulates the exchange value of commodities in trade and sets every parameter for the organization of the labor force and the production of commodities. The architecture of the factory, informed exclusively by productive parameters, is the most direct physical embodiment of capital's capacity to abstract everything into quantifiable data: the ground zero of what we can call "rational architecture."

The term "rational" is often used in architectural discourse and typically refers to a design attitude inspired by a strict economy of means. As discussed in chapter 2, rational architecture emerged in France between the seventeenth and eighteenth centuries when architects—pressured by engineers—shifted their focus from issues of beauty and proportion to construction understood as a material and pragmatic problem. This rationalization, which was cemented in the teachings of the postrevolutionary École Polytechnique, occurred slightly before the rise of the factory as the dominant mode of production in society. Prior to the nineteenth century, "rationalization" was limited to an economy of construction that aimed to streamline time and expense. With the emergence of the factory, the logic of rationalization expanded from construction to the management of workers. In the history of industry, the term "rationalization" addresses, in fact, the deliberate and careful planning of things and people for the sake of profit.[32]

In the second half of the nineteenth century, the rationalization of both the building process and management of workers became more intense and systematic in the United States than in England. This shift was instigated by the different conditions of the labor force in the two countries. After three centuries of the violent dispossession of workers' means of production through Parliamentary enclosures and the enforcement of restricted wage levels, labor power in England was abundant and thus cheap. In the United States, securing labor power was far more difficult because, until the early twentieth century, people were more likely to pursue economic fortune in the western "frontier" than remain on the East Coast and become workers in factories.[33] In contrast to British workers, American workers were expensive, prompting American factory owners to more regularly invest in technological innovation. Investments in technology were made to minimize labor costs. Not just a matter of entrepreneurial initiative, the organization of the factory by capitalists and engineers was an "applied science"—the scientific organization of production to reduce costs and increase profits.

Scientific research applied to industry became known as "technology," a term introduced by physician and Harvard professor Jacob Bigelow in 1829.[34] As argued by historian David F. Noble, the development of technology in the United States cannot be disentangled from the rise of capitalism and its incarnation in the manufacturing industry. The imperatives of utility and profit made science, particularly in America, a form of capital accumulation by applying discoveries in the field of physics and chemistry to the production of commodities.[35] In the development of factory architecture, scientific research played a decisive role in advancing the handling of materials. Indeed, in the space of the factory the movement of materials in conjunction with workers was the most delicate aspect in the optimization of production costs. Exemplary of the challenges of moving resources was the meatpacking industry. The elaborate process of transforming live animals into sausages required an extremely efficient system of overhead conveyors, endless chains, and moving benches to eliminate the wasteful manual handling of carcasses through the packing house. Confronting issues of logistics, early theorists of the factory system—such as F. W. Wilder in his influential treatise *The Modern Packing House* (1905)—were the first to argue that plant design and layout were central to the manufacturing process.[36] For Wilder, a successful plant accommodated a high degree of work flow in a frictionless choreography. Achieving this design task challenged engineers to fuse building, management, and business into a singular professional expertise. No longer focused exclusively on materials, engineering as the management of workers was first systematized in Frederick Taylor's *The Principles of Scientific Management* (1911), in which the Philadelphia engineer proposed a rationalization of laboring activities by subordinating them to careful time-space planning.[37]

Rationalized plant design could not rigidly adhere to one single work flow diagram, because incessant competition and technological innovation compelled factory owners to constantly update both machines and the organization of the labor force. Production that required both strict planning and the accommodation of change was a paradoxical condition that created the need for a space where—in the words of engineer Charles Day— "the building did not exist at all."[38] The desired realization of the factory as an empty shell with minimal vertical structures provoked engineers to use reinforced concrete. Fireproof and capable of eliminating machine-induced vibrations, reinforced concrete most notably allowed unprecedentedly long spans between columns. First introduced in the construction of infrastructure in France in the second half of the nineteenth century, reinforced concrete gained widespread popularity in the United States through its use in buildings like warehouses and factories. Early applications of reinforced concrete were expensive. When cast as a monolithic structure, it required expensive formwork made with complicated carpentry that could only be fabricated by specialized workers. Price-restrictive obstacles were overcome by casting the load-bearing structure in parts and using recyclable formwork. Compared to other building techniques, this method required low-skilled labor and gave the engineer full control over the workers' process.

The use of reinforced concrete, therefore, presented an opportunity to rethink not just architecture but also the labor of construction. Experimentation with the labor of producing reinforced concrete was evident in Ernest L. Ransome's design for the Pacific Coast Borax factory built in 1903 by the United Shoe Machinery Corporation in Bayonne, New Jersey. While an earlier phase of this factory, built in 1897, used reinforced concrete in imitation of masonry, the 1903 phase was instead designed by Ransome, to use Reyner Banham's words, as "a regular grid of plain rectangular horizontals and verticals, framing almost total glazing."[39] Banham celebrated the formal purity of the structure and yet, as historian Michael Osman has emphasized, the method in which columns, girders, and beams were molded as precast units, placed by derricks, and united by a light slab poured in place was driven by Ransome's goal of reducing costs and the desire to deskill manual labor by reducing it to extremely simplified operations.[40] Similar to Taylor's principles, which required the complete subordination of the workers to centralized management, Ransome's design implied the total subordination of construction workers to a plan that quantified materials and labor time. As Osman also argues, "The influence of management, first to organize the material into a standardized construction system and then to fully transform it into a set of data, made concrete fit for expanding systems of mass production."[41] The result was what Osman has called "managerial aesthetics," a pseudo-architectural language made of graphs, diagrams, and endless tabulations of any discernible data all compiled in construction drawings.[42] For Osman, the best literature on managerial aesthetics was *A Treatise on Concrete, Plain and Reinforced* (1907) and *Concrete Costs* (1912), two books on the technology of concrete authored by Taylor in collaboration with engineer Sanford Thompson.

In the first book the authors provide guidelines for handling concrete based on data collected in the study of contractors; in the second book, following the approach outlined in *The Principles of Scientific Management*, Taylor and Thompson list, among other things, tabulations of labor time obtained from direct observation of workers. In this approach to design and construction—as Osman argues—labor and material coexist in a single plane of value.[43] Built structure is infused with the key principles of Taylorism: the deconstruction of work into measurable temporal units. The result was an elementary architecture reducible to a kit of parts, optimized to save costs and control every aspect of the production process. Rationality, a concept celebrated by countless twentieth-century architects and theorists, was in fact, as evident in Ransome's architecture, the outcome of the most refined form of capitalist accumulation applied to the building site.

From Columns to Envelopes

No architect would have a greater impact on the history of industrial architecture than Albert Kahn, who brought the rational design and construction of factories to its extreme conclusion. Apprenticing in architectural firms at a young age, Kahn established his practice in Detroit in 1896 and immediately became involved in the design of factories. During Kahn's lifetime, Albert Kahn Associates (AKA) built approximately 2,000 projects, of which the majority were factories.[44] AKA designed factories for many companies, but, given the firm's location in Detroit, the epicenter of the automobile industry, Ford Motor Company was the office's most important client. AKA realized this monumental amount of work because Kahn, from the outset, conceived the office as a form of architectural "mass production." In the late 1930s the office was 600 people strong. Moreover, Kahn understood that the design of large-scale engineering projects, like factories, required a vast amount of specialized knowledge. For him, architecture—understood as "form-giving"—was a minimal part of realizing industrial-scale buildings. It is well known that Kahn characterized his approach to architecture as "90% business and 10% art."[45] What he called "business" was a vast conglomeration of expertise that needed to be rigorously combined and contained in a systematic hierarchy of many managers and workers, very much reflecting the conditions of a factory. Within AKA, collaboration between different professionals adhered to a rigidly defined division of labor that deconstructed the design process in stages: from layout of space to structural calculations to cost estimations, each task was assigned to a specialized team. Kahn essentially employed the same production process—the assembly line—that Ford had adopted in his factories since 1909. Inspired by the meatpacking industry, the assembly line entailed mechanically moving a partially finished element through a series of workstations until the final whole was produced.[46] At each workstation, quasi-skilled and deskilled workers added parts to the moving assembly. Workers' jobs thus consisted of specific and highly repetitive tasks. The goal of this process was threefold: to increase production, cut costs, and above all prevent worker insubordination. Because of the exacting nature of this process, the factory was designed in strict accordance with the assembly line diagrams. Moritz Kahn, Albert's brother and an AKA associate, explained the collaboration between architect and client in frank terms: "An architect who specializes in the design of industrial buildings is not expected to be an expert in process layout. The works managers are best capable of preparing their own process diagrams. Being in possession of such a diagram, architects should confine their effort to building around that layout a factory which is best suited to the scheme of operation."[47] In other words, the task of Kahn's office was to devise the appropriate physical enclosure for the assembly process and minimize the obstructing presence of vertical supports. Like Ransome, Kahn reduced architectural form to the solution of two design problems: the perimeter and the vertical structure. With these two elements minimized, the space of the factory could offer both minimal friction to the spatial unfolding of the assembly line and a degree of flexibility in case the production process had to be modified or updated.

Kahn's earliest factories, such as the Packard Plant No. 10 in Detroit built in 1905 and the Geo. N. Pierce Plant in Buffalo built in 1906, were not produced for Ford, and yet their design demonstrates the spatial organization that endures through all of AKA's work. The Packard plant saw the first use of reinforced concrete in an automobile factory. With the design of this plant Kahn perfected the structural grid, creating a relentless modularity that defined the whole architecture of the factory. Yet it was in the Pierce plant—a one-story structure in which production progressed horizontally rather than vertically—that Kahn unveiled the logic of space that would characterize his career. Interestingly, in the Pierce plant the structural grids of the interconnected buildings followed different modules, each optimized for the specifics of a different production requirement—including manufacturing, assembly, and body finishing. In later designs, this module variation was discarded, as AKA realized that optimizing

fig. 4.8
fig. 4.9

4.8 Albert Kahn, Geo. N. Pierce Plant, Buffalo, built in 1906, view of the interior of the manufacturing building, photo by Joseph Klima. From Grant Hildebrand, *The Architecture of Albert Kahn* (Cambridge, MA: MIT Press, 1974). © Bentley Historical Library.

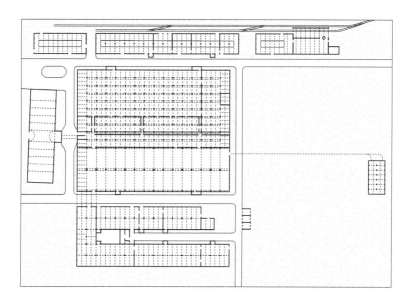

4.9 Albert Kahn, Geo. N. Pierce Plant, Buffalo, plan. © Dogma.

production depended on the utmost possible eradication of vertical elements. The entire oeuvre of AKA can be summarized as a gradual yet relentless process of spatial abstraction where vertical structure is reduced until it ultimately becomes absorbed in the building envelope.

This process of structural rarefaction started with the first factory designed for Ford at Highland Park in 1909, a four-story building which included the entire Model T assembly line under one roof. This factory epitomized the daylight factory model, a flexible, well-lit interior in which the *floor*—the artificial reconstruction of the ground—became the primary form of architecture. Spacious interiors were maximized by longer structural spans and the considerable reduction of supports. This spatial logic responded to Ford's managerial vision, in which everything, in order to be improved in terms of efficiency and productivity, was constantly under trial of optimization. As Ford put it, "We measure on every job the exact amount of room that a man needs; he must not be cramped—that would be a waste. But if he and his machine occupy more space than is required, that is also a waste."[48] But one must not fall prey to Ford's relentless ideology of efficiency. Behind this maniacal vision of efficiency lies the fundamental process of capitalist extraction of surplus value from labor power. According to Marx, labor power is not a "thing" but the generic human faculty to produce anything.[49] This faculty does not coincide with what has been already achieved but rather is the *potential* to produce. To capture and mobilize labor power, architecture must approximate its generic character as an infinite range of yet unrealized potentialities.[50] Precisely for this reason, labor power is most effectively embodied in the free plan of the daylight factory. However, the first Highland Park Plant was a multistory building and therefore resisted the relentlessly smooth process pursued by Ford. In light of this inefficiency, after perfecting the multistory concrete structure with the six-story building known as the "New Shop," Ford and AKA adopted the simplest building form possible: a single-story steel structure. From then on, this skeletal structure was the dominant model at Ford's sprawling factories built in River Rouge in the 1920s and 1930s. AKA first tested this model not for Ford but for Packard in what is arguably one of the most impressive factories ever built:

fig. 4.10

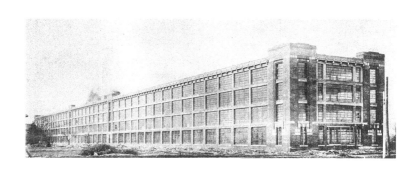

4.10 Albert Kahn, Highland Park Plant, view from southwest, 1909 (Henry Ford Museum).
© Bentley Historical Library.

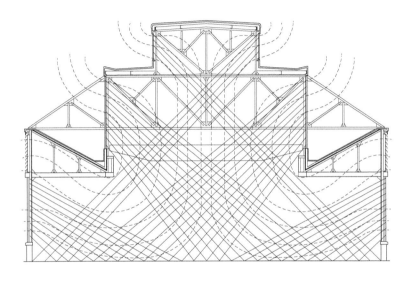

4.11 Albert Kahn, Packard Forge Shop, 1911, section. © Dogma,
adapted from Albert Kahn Associates.

the 1911 Forge Shop. The defining feature of this building is the roof structure, whose trusses span a 72-foot void and support 70-foot-long crane beams. Consequently, the plan of the building fig. 4.11 is an empty hall devoid of any vertical obstruction other than the thin enclosing wall. Both inside and outside, the architecture of the Forge Shop consists of the persistent repetition of the structural module, which recurs 23 times. The Forge Shop is thus the foremost manifestation of the typical plan in which emptiness, not structure, becomes the ultimate form of the factory. It is informative to compare Kahn's design to Peter Behrens's AEG Turbine Factory in Berlin, another clear-span structure built just two years before the Forge Shop. While Behrens's structure, with its rusticated corners and monumental rounded pediment, is a clear nod to classical architecture, AKA's structure is devoid of any reference that is not structure itself. Moreover, while the Highland Park Plant had corners marked by small decorative towers, meant to break the repetitive character of the structural grid, in the Forge Shop the uniform structural system was left open-ended, implying that the structure could expand ad infinitum. The logic of a shed that could endlessly expand became the hallmark of the factories envisioned by Kahn and Ford, starting with the Eagle Plant for assembling antisubmarine patrol boats. Built in 1917, this factory was devised by AKA as a simple sequence of five immense aisles, each 51 feet wide and 1,700 feet long. While previous Ford factories were tailored to a precise production diagram, the Eagle Plant was conceived as a space with a program that would inevitably change, since the production of antisubmarine boats would all but stop with the end of World War I.

Abstraction as "Uncertain Space"

The Eagle Plant inaugurated a spatial logic of architecture meant to be indifferent to content. Structural scale was magnified so as to host any kind of productive program. The vacuous space of the shed contrasted with the traditional notion of Fordist design as a rigidly choreographed mode of production in which form follows function. Instead, with the Eagle Plant, Ford and AKA embraced uncertainty as a spatial principle in the design of factories. Rather than buildings made of concrete, for both Ford and

AKA the ultimate factory was a simple clear-span shed built with steel. These buildings were easy to dismantle, so once the factory's function became obsolete it was deconstructed and its material was recycled for use in other new buildings. Like the terraced house a century before, factories had a rather short lifespan, largely due to the rapid pace of innovation and change in the organization of the production process. The potential obsolescence of facilities became even more likely in wartime, when industrial mobilization put enormous pressure on the establishment and organization of large industrial facilities whose use after war was uncertain. Kahn's office referred to these war factories as "five years plants," because, as Albert's brother and AKA associate Louis Kahn explained, "at the time they were built, five years was the maximum productive life expected of them."[51] Historians Adam Lauder and Lee Rodney labeled this contingent condition "uncertain space."[52] An impressive example of a five-year plant embodying the logic of "uncertain space" was the Willow Run manufacturing complex located between Ypsilanti and Belleville, Michigan. Conceived for the production of World War II bombers, Willow Run was designed and built in nineteen months. Opened in phases beginning in 1941, when completed in 1942 the plant was the largest industrial building ever constructed. In designing this unprecedented building at an unprecedented speed, AKA's customary factory-like design approach was tested by a high degree of uncertainty, as the production layout was not yet defined when design started. With this work, uncertainty, alongside flexibility, became a fundamental parameter of AKA's factories. Lauder and Rodney assert that Willow Run, with its gigantic scale and speed of both construction and obsolescence, embodied capitalism's experimentation with planned obsolescence and creative destruction.[53] The eventual precarity that many industrial cities like Detroit experienced once they were no longer the epicenters of heavy industrialization was already built into the logic of industrial production, where relentless development outlives everything caught in its momentum. Willow Run was the latest and clearest manifestation of a foundational principle of the architecture of the factory: the rapid obsolescence of its technology. It is now evident that this obsolescence was the outcome of the accelerated evolution of the factory, but it is a mistake to understand this process as merely driven by innovation. The factory's constant change and obsolescence were also the consequence of the workers' struggle against their condition as factory workers. As mentioned earlier, a decisive aspect in the development of the factory in the United States was worker reluctance to be employed in a factory setting. With the great waves of European immigrants needing work, capitalists finally acquired a labor force in large quantities and at a cheap price. But this labor force was far from amenable: rebellions and strikes were widespread beginning in the late nineteenth century in the United States, and their scale and impact were far greater than in Europe. Additionally, as noted by Mario Tronti, workers' struggles in the United States were less ideological than those in Europe because they were exclusively focused on wage issues.[54] Such struggles dictated precise parameters to factory owners, who responded not just with repression but by refining the production process to achieve the impossible: increase wages and profits at the same time. This was the intent of the Five-Dollar Day promoted by Ford in 1914.

The fast-paced cycle between struggle and change is precisely what marked the evolution of AKA's factories from multistory to one-story, from concrete to steel structure.[55] The ambition of this advancement was the design of spaces that could accommodate change in all its possible manifestations, from expansion in scale to the introduction of new machinery to the alteration of the spatial distribution of workers' stations. Ford did not evade his workers' discontent, but rather appropriated its momentum in order to advance his radical reform of working conditions, building welfare facilities like schools and housing, progressively extending the paternalistic logic of the factory from the workplace to society.[56] Reflecting on the history of labor struggles in the United States in the early twentieth century, Tronti argued: "Working-class struggles are an irreplaceable instrument of capital's own self-consciousness: without them, it does not recognise its own adversary and thus does not know itself."[57] From the class struggle, American capitalism learned that conflict and uncertainty were not collateral effects, but a structural condition of capital itself.

Toward the Big Box

As AKA's factories moved away from the multistory concrete structure toward a structure of emptiness, they gave form to what today
is called the "Big Box." Perhaps the most radical incarnation of
this archetype is AKA's design for the Glenn Martin Assembly
Building near Baltimore, built in 1937. The Assembly Building
housed the production of the PB2M Mars, the largest flying boat
to serve in World War II. Arguably, this factory is architecture at
the pinnacle of abstraction. On the exterior, the building is a box
clad with a uniform sequence of horizontal bands of glass and
topped by trusses that allowed for a column-free interior with a
structural span of 300 feet. Services, including toilets, lockers, and
supervision offices, were located in a two-story annex positioned
along one side of the box. The result was an enormous expanse of
empty space sandwiched between a uniform floor and the relentless grid of trusses, making it the epitome of modern abstract
space as continuous and uniform. In its pronounced emptiness
and uncertainty (the building was not expected to last long), the
Glenn Martin Assembly Building anticipated the spatial conditions of late capitalism in which everything was subjected to the
volatile logic of permanent flexibility. To celebrate the structure,
AKA commissioned a photograph that famously captures the
gigantism and monumentality of the building, but this image is
illusory: the building ceased operations soon after completion,
in 1945. In 2006, the plant was sold to private developers to be
transformed into a mixed-use complex.[58]

While teaching at IIT in the 1940s, Ludwig Mies van der
Rohe was interested in the "clear-span" steel structure. AKA's
designs popularized the "clear-span" model in the United States,
and Mies wanted to appropriate this structural principle as a
"timely" architectural form applicable to any kind of public
building. Mies's formal approach was profoundly impacted by
the writings of architectural historian and theorist Karl Bötticher,
for whom the essence of architectural style was the way in which
specific building techniques—from Greek post-and-lintel systems to Gothic pointed arches—solved the problem of enclosing
space.[59] Informed by this historical perspective, Mies understood

clear-span structures, which concentrate structure on the perimeter of the building to free the enclosed space from obstruction, to be the ultimate historical conclusion of industrial building techniques in which the use first of iron and later of steel played a crucial role.[60]

In 1942, Mies wanted to test the clear-span solution and asked one of his students to find a photograph of a large clear-span industrial building and insert a concert hall in it. When the student found a photograph of the interior of the Glenn Martin Assembly Building, Mies suggested that a theater be conceived as a composition of minimal partitions hung from the factory's trusses. The result—one of the most famous collages in architectural history (which exists in several versions)—features cut-and-pasted pieces of paper rendered as abstract planes of color. The collage seems to suggest a unity of intent between the abstraction of fine art, evoked in the composition of flat surfaces, and the abstraction of modern building engineering represented by AKA's factory. The concert hall inserted into the Glenn Martin Assembly Building can be interpreted in two ways. First, as a sublimation of industrial-capitalist production into a codified form of Architecture. After all, as Detlef Mertins suggested,[61] Mies's design method consisted in the refinement and expression of structural and spatial types that were first generated in the industrial vernacular, elevating *Bauen* to *Baukunst*. Mies domesticated the rarefied abstraction of Kahn's architecture by using clearly defined proportions and precious materials like travertine and marble. After the 1940s, building-as-shed became the dominant motive of Mies's designs—as evident in the Farnsworth House in Plano, Illinois, built 1945–1951, Crown Hall at the IIT campus in Chicago, built 1953–1954, and the unbuilt National Theater in Mannheim, designed 1952–1953. Second, it is possible to interpret the concert hall collage as a subtle commentary on the fate of architectural form in the age of buildings *without* architecture. Confronted with the ultimate abstraction of industrial architecture—an abstraction that is not only physical but also economic and managerial—architecture is relevant only at its most generic, reduced to mutable partitions installed and dismantled as needed. In this way, Mies's concert hall embodies the same flexibility and uncertainty manifested in AKA's disposable

fig. 4.12

4.12 Ludwig Mies van der Rohe, Concert Hall, 1942. Collage over photograph,
29½ by 62 inches. The Mies van der Rohe Archive. © The Museum of Modern Art/
Licensed by SCALA / Art Resource, NY.

industrial architecture, in which spatial management becomes the very liturgy of capitalist space.

An extremely appropriate and yet involuntary commentary on the purpose of such space lies in the presence of a statue of an Egyptian scribe pasted on the concert hall collage after Mies gave it to the sculptor Mary Callery. For the earlier (and exhibited) version of the collage, Mies had suggested that the student include a sculpture by Aristide Maillol. When Callery received the collage, she replaced the photograph of Maillol's sculptural figure with the scribe.[62] The scribe represents the essence of bureaucratic power, the translation of things and people into the abstraction of writing and computing. This is also the language of the industrial megamachine. Here the abstracting power of the scribe can be seen as the summa of what is at stake when Schinkel called the early industrial architecture of Manchester "building without architecture." In the absence of "architecture," building becomes the physical translation of an abstract space where nothing remains permanent except the endless management of construction and destruction in pursuit of surplus value.

5   Formalism, Rationalism, Constructivism

"Form" and "space" are familiar words in architectural parlance. Not only are they used constantly (and often interchangeably) when we talk about architecture and the city, but form and space are foundational to many theoretical and critical discourses about modern and contemporary architecture.[1] Our extreme, and somehow casual, familiarity with them conceals the reality that "form" and "space" are novel words that were seldom used before the nineteenth century. In earlier times art and architecture lacked an idea of either "form" or "space." Today these terms are used to address the aesthetic experience of a building (or of its reproduction in a drawing or photograph), but before the nineteenth century it was impossible to disentangle experience from symbolic or social values. Appreciation of form and space, as they exist today, is a product of "aesthetics," a branch of philosophy that emerged in the eighteenth century and focuses on the way humans perceive things. The word "form" comes from the Latin *forma* which means figure, or contour of an object. *Formae* was also the name of the cadastral tablets on which Roman state officials recorded property titles. In Rome, form was defined as the contour line that delimited physical things or land—and until the nineteenth century this was the sole meaning of the word "form." The word "space" has a more recent origin; it derives from *spatium*, which since the thirteenth century was used to address both a specific place and the distance between things. Within aesthetics, "form" and "space" do not address figures, objects, or distances. Rather, the terms designate the relationship between things, especially between subject and object. This *aesthetic* understanding was advanced in eighteenth-century German culture; the first philosopher to introduce aesthetics as a proper discipline was Alexander Baumgarten in his seminal essay *Philosophical Meditations on Some Requirements of the Poem* (1735). Baumgarten argued that, in poetic form, sensual perception of words and sounds is more important than the ideas represented by these words. Aesthetics thus originated in defense of sensual perception against the cognitive thrust of rational thinking. Indeed, from Plato to Descartes, sensual experience of physical things was assailed as too subjective and therefore impossible to convey in a systematic and methodical theory. Aesthetics was born as the attempt to systematize sensual cognition, even if sensory experience was not (always) explicable in rational terms. Baumgarten's aesthetics was advanced not against rational metaphysics, but in order to broaden the metaphysical horizon by including sensible experience in its purview. This integration was necessary because Baumgarten considered sensible experience the main criterion for judging art. Yet the major written contribution to aesthetics—Immanuel Kant's *Critique of Judgment* (1791)—does not deal with art, but rather with the general modes of human cognition. For Kant, form is the process of comprehension through which humans mediate intuition. As discussed by Rodolphe Gasché, for Kant form is the method of perceiving things through space and time, which for him are a priori categories, indeed criteria of intuition.[2]

Therefore, for Kant, form is not the image of things but the process through which we *understand* things. Undoubtedly, Kant's *Critique of Judgment* is a major breaking point in the history of aesthetics because it does not merely defend sensual experience, but defines the very transcendental conditions of spatial experience— space and time. In Kant's treatise, form is the process of synthesis without which no cognitive process or sensible experience could exist. Kant's *Critique* was conceived as applicable to any aspect of knowledge, and yet it became particularly instrumental in the consolidation of artistic formalism. This was largely due to the simplification of Kantian aesthetics by Johann Friedrich Herbart, for whom aesthetics became not *a* but *the* theory of the arts.

According to Herbart, aesthetics concerns the relationship between sensible facts. Tones, lines, colors, and ideas are all examples of his notion of "facts." The main goal of art is to render these sensible facts *autonomous* from anything else. For Herbart, form in the Kantian sense of *comprehension* is assumed as an autonomous realm of thought. Herbart is thereby responsible for the first use of Kantian aesthetics as the basis of the autonomy of art. Artistic work can therefore be theorized as the manipulation of formal relationships devoid of any meaning outside their pleasing effect. Aesthetic judgment is consequently based on human perception, the conception of sequences like the notes in a musical composition, colors in painting, or spaces in architecture. Importantly, Herbart claims that the proper state of mind for aesthetic "formal" experience is absolute indifference, which is equidistant from both depression and excitement. This position not only radicalizes the

Kantian idea of "disinterest" as ground for aesthetic judgment, but, as will become evident below, unwittingly makes explicit the political intent underlying artistic practice.

Aesthetics cannot be disentangled from the rise of the arts—especially painting, sculpture, and architecture—as liberal professions, clearly distinguished from the work of craftsmen. As previously outlined, the emancipation of art from the artisanal took many forms, from the designation of drawing as a cognitive task to the disenfranchisement of the professional guild. As a theory of art, aesthetics further fortified artistic practice as a liberal discipline precisely when artisanal craftmanship was destabilized by the ideology of precision enforced by scientific thought and industrial labor. By disconnecting artistic form from social and economic implications, aesthetics permits artists to evade the debasement of productive activity—including art—by commodification. The autonomy of art was appealing not only to artists but also to critics, theorists, and patrons. In a social condition geared entirely toward the instrumental reason of profit, the autonomy of artistic values offered the illusion of a genuine "disinterested" cultural experience. This consolatory, yet enabling, function is precisely why aesthetic formalism became a dominant ideology of artistic production beginning in the nineteenth century.

In his essay "The Age of Neutralizations and Depoliticizations," Carl Schmitt argued that "aesthetics" was not only the intermediate passage between *ancien régime* metaphysics and bourgeois moralism, but also the main collateral effect of a way of life dominated by economy and industry.[3] The more industrial production became ubiquitous, reifying any aspect of human production, the more art was understood as "fine art," that is to say, art disconnected—at least ideologically—from the realities of its social status. Within these conditions, the concept of *form* manifested as the main object of aesthetic experience.

What Formalism Is

The theory of autonomous form was advanced by the collector and theorist Konrad Fiedler and the sculptor Adolf von Hildebrand, who concurrently theorized form as perception defined by an active ordering process rather than the passive reception of things. Fiedler's work emancipated form not only from content but also from language itself. He argued that form was the pure act of seeing, the human capacity to sharpen optical vision as the primary form of knowledge.[4] This argument was reinforced by Hildebrand in his seminal book *The Problem of Form in Painting and Sculpture* (1893), which promoted the influential thesis that the primary purpose of the work of art is to augment our optical faculty, independent of any historical or stylistic criteria. Both Fiedler and Hildebrand asserted an understanding of form that lacked any historical contingency. The influence and dominance of this approach was especially amplified by the work of Heinrich Wölfflin, whose books *Renaissance and Baroque* (1888) and *Principles of Art History* (1915) are considered foundational to formalist theory in the twentieth century even beyond the visual arts. In contrast to Fiedler's and Hildebrand's ahistorical theory, Wölfflin applied formalism to the history of art. Essential to this approach was the articulation of art as a dialectic of formal concepts including linear and painterly, plane and recession, and closed and open form. Consequently, the history of art was read not as a narrative based on the biographies of artists, but as a succession of formal approaches. Even if Wölfflin offered a historical reading of art, his objective was to establish a universal grammar of plastic form which would hypostatize "visuality" as the main experience of art. In doing this, he abstracted form from its social or symbolic context as a datum *in itself*. However, in regard to architecture the challenge of isolating form in its pure plasticity forced him to search for a scientific basis to his theory, which he found in modern psychology as theorized by Wilhelm Wundt, Oswald Külpe, and Theodor Lipps.[5] With the aid of psychology, Wölfflin not only gave scientific legitimacy to his art historical categories but made seeing a mode of spatial organization beyond mere spectatorship. In his seminal book *Prolegomena to a Psychology of Architecture* (1886), Wölfflin argued that form could not be reduced to "quantifiable" metrics like construction or proportional systems, but depended on the viewers' mood, or their *lived experience*, which could only be rationalized in psychological terms.

This psychological understanding of architectural form shaped the most successful and influential theory of formalism in architecture—August Schmarsow's theory of *Raumgestaltung* (space forming), which emerged in books published in the late nineteenth and early twentieth century. As noted by historian Mitchell W. Schwarzer, Schmarsow was the first to formulate a comprehensive theory of architecture as a formal creation.[6] The main tenet of this theory was that architectural space is experienced through bodily movement, rather than from a stationary point of view as in the case of painting. In emphasizing the body, Schmarsow argued that spatial images built up over time. He thus defined *Raumgestaltung* as the active process of ordering spatial images through coherent spatial intuitions. For Schmarsow spatial intuitions, which are bodily encounters, went from simple and unconscious impulses to sophisticated constructions, and yet his history is described in purely psychological rather than social or technological terms. As Schwarzer argues, in the application of this methodology to different historical periods, Schmarsow refrained from either speculative or materialist explanations, always basing his conclusions on psychological perception.[7]

At stake in Wölfflin's and Schmarsow's formalism is first and foremost the centrality of perception as a physiological and thus *innate* human feature. Second, their theories address the process of abstraction through which sensations derived from the experience of physical and material situations are ordered into discernable principles. Although Wölfflin and Schmarsow focused on premodern examples of architecture, their formal approach transcended historicity and was applicable to any building. Particularly in Schmarsow's theory, the essentializing and ahistorical approach was motivated by dissatisfaction with late nineteenth-century stylistic eclecticism. Its essentialist approach to form is specifically why formalism appealed to artists and architects in the early twentieth century. Undoubtedly, the rise of abstraction in art and architecture was nurtured in the tradition of nineteenth-century German aesthetics. However, this very same tradition infused artistic abstraction with the politics of bourgeois aestheticism, resulting in the divorce of the experience of form from its social and political context.

Formalism Goes to Russia

Ironically, formalism, the preeminent bourgeois "project" in nineteenth-century arts, radically manifested in Russia—

in Moscow and Petrograd,[8] to be precise—at the eve of and in the decade following the 1917 Bolshevik revolution. There are many links between nineteenth-century German aesthetic debates and cultural movements in Soviet Russia, but for this study one is of particular importance. In late nineteenth-century Russia, it was customary for middle- to upper-class families to send their children to study in Germany. For Jewish families this was the only way to overcome tsarist Russia's restrictions on their access to higher education.[9] Many Russian artists and intellectuals coming of age in the early twentieth century attended German fine arts academies and universities and received formalist training rooted in the theories of Fiedler, Hildebrand, Wölfflin, and Schmarsow. Beyond the visual arts, formalism became a paradigm for culture in general and especially for the study of poetry and literature, which were simultaneously dominated by symbolism.

An early manifestation of formalism in Russia was in literature with the activities of the Moscow Linguistic Circle and the OPOYAZ (Society for the Study of Poetic Language), founded in Moscow and Petrograd in 1915 and 1916, respectively. These groups aimed to advance the study of literature in scientific terms by foregrounding the formal properties of poetic and literary language, such as syntax and the sound of words.[10] In this ambition, the formalists were reacting against symbolist literature and poetry. Less focused on the formal qualities of texts, symbolism primarily concerned words' capacity to evoke meaning. In contrast, the formalists were interested in the opacity of language, its aversion to mere representation and its capacity to defamiliarize reality, especially within the language used in literary work. The formalist groups understood poetic and literary language as the possibility of downplaying the referential use of words in order to emphasize their phonetic and syntactical consistency. Another end pursued by the formalists, and clearly enunciated in Viktor Shklovsky's essay "Art as Device," was the power of poetic language to slow down the perception of things, so that readers don't merely recognize them by their name but *see* them in their appearance.[11] For example, Shklovsky observed how Tolstoy's lengthy and detailed descriptions rendered things as if they were seen for the first time, before those things even acquired a customary definition.[12] For Shklovsky, the function of poetic and literary language was to estrange familiar things, so that they could be saved from the automatism of reality.

In his reconstruction of the vicissitudes of Russian formalism, Boris Eichenbaum recounts Wölfflin's outsized influence on the movement and how his emphasis on the formal description of the work of art suppressed both the biography of the artist and the historical circumstances of the artwork's production.[13] Eichenbaum therefore argued that formal reading addressed the artwork's structural properties rather than its content. In terms of poetic language, the application of Wölfflinian formalism was especially fruitful because it foregrounded language's syntactical functioning rather than its meaning. For poets, formal reading abstracted language from its communicative function and made it available for unforeseen uses. Demonstrative of this condition was the poetry of the Russian futurists such as David and Vladimir Burliuk and Velimir Khlebnikov. In Khlebnikov's "Zaum" experiments words did not spell any coherent content, but were organized in terms of their rhythmic and phonetic properties. By composing nonreferential poems, such poets both criticized language as a coherent institution and liberated it from its traditional representative function.

Outside of poetry, an initial approximation of the formalists' and futurists' attempt to free language from its denotative function was Kazimir Malevich's cubofuturist paintings, in which he presented random juxtapositions of figures, objects, words, and planes of color.[14] Through these experiments, Malevich countered the representative role of painting by depicting incoherent assemblages of abstract signs. This approach found its extreme resolution in his programmatic *Black Square* made in 1915, which reduced painting to its material zero-degree of color pigment on canvas.[15] According to Malevich, *Black Square* was not abstract but a realist painting, because in the expulsion of the "representational" role of art, the true material aspects of painting—color pigments on canvas—were revealed. This extreme abstraction of painting—which Malevich defined as "suprematist"—was not only the beginning of nonreferential abstraction, as commonly assumed by art historians, but also the logical conclusion of aesthetic formalism as it had emerged in Germany since the nineteenth century.

Like the formalists and the futurists, Malevich believed that, once freed from the restraints of representation, language—in his case pictorial language—was open to still unknown uses. Here lies the "revolutionary" aspect of these artistic experiments, although, in these cases, revolution was located within the form of the work of art itself. In Russia, revolutionary forces were also imminent within society at large. Russian formalism, futurism, and suprematism developed parallel to but independently of the political upheaval that led to the October Revolution. Since the time of Peter the Great, Russia's elite had been extremely receptive to Western artistic and political movements, embracing even the most extreme as an antidote to Russia's economic backwardness.[16] Although these political and artistic movements share a common root, the political avant-garde focused on class politics, while the artistic avant-garde focused on a renewal of art without any class perspective. Many of the protagonists of artistic movements—like the literary critic Osip Brik and the poet Vladimir Mayakovsky—were ardent supporters of the political revolution and played official roles in its aftermath, but their early poetic experiments were not inspired by politics. Rather, their work was stimulated by the life of the metropolis, which many of them had experienced not just in Moscow and St. Petersburg but also in Paris and Berlin. The new urban landscape composed of industrial buildings, anonymous housing blocks, and traffic of people and goods prompted the formalists and futurists to trust the nonreferentiality of language as the only legitimate medium for artistic invention. They reasoned that, in a world completely infiltrated by industrial life, the symbolic role of language was no longer viable. The manifestation of language as an opaque and alienated "object" was necessary to sustain it within the alienation of modern life. Compelled by this reasoning, the formalists maintained an especially ambiguous role in regard to the October Revolution: they welcomed its momentum as a trigger for cultural renewal, but they were determined to safeguard the independence and autonomy of their formal research from any political manipulation. Movements that followed the October Revolution, like constructivism and production art, criticized artistic autonomy as rooted in bourgeois thinking; however, their method of work retained the formal approach inherited from the pioneering work of the formalists. As one might expect, it was in architecture that tension between formal concerns and political pressure reached its most intense and contradictory stage.

Form Is Rational

In postrevolutionary Russia, the institution that most embodied the tensions between formalism and the class politics of the newly established Russian Soviet Republic was VKhUTEMAS (Higher Artistic and Technical Studios). Founded in 1920, the school hosted programs in architecture, painting, graphic and textile design, metalwork, and ceramics. Scholars often draw comparisons between VKhUTEMAS and the Bauhaus, which was founded in Weimar the year before.[17] Both schools attempted to merge art and industrial design, yet while admission to the Bauhaus was restricted by a selection process, at VKhUTEMAS it was unrestricted and free of charge. This was a crucial difference. From the outset, VKhUTEMAS's pedagogical activities were deeply conditioned by the large number of students admitted, and the demands of mass education left its mark on the way knowledge was organized and transmitted. No longer relying on beaux-arts "virtuosity" typical of selective academies, teachers were forced to develop a more accessible form of artistic training. In confronting this challenge, VKhUTEMAS architect Nikolai Ladovsky and his collaborators Vladimir Krinsky and Nikolai Dokuchaev introduced a foundation course as a prerequisite to all the specialized programs. Known as the "space" course it consisted of step-by-step design exercises on space and form. As noted by Luka Skansi, the methodological premises of the course were deeply influenced by the theories of Wölfflin and Schmarsow, whose writings were made popular in Soviet Russia by the important theorist and art historian Alexander Georgievich Gabrichevsky in two seminal essays, "Architecture" and "Space and Volume in Architecture," both published in 1923.[18] Gabrichevsky argued that architecture is an art that primarily concerns not the simple accommodation of utilitarian functions, but the dialectic between space and volume.[19] By *space* Gabrichevsky implied the dynamic experience of observing the entirety of a building, and with *volume* he addressed the tectonic qualities of architecture. The interplay of space and

fig. 5.1

volume was thus understood as the very essence of architectural form, and it is precisely such an interpretation of architecture that the space course at VKhUTEMAS introduced to its many students. In her monumental study of VKhUTEMAS, Anna Bokov provides a detailed analysis of Ladovsky's space course;[20] here it suffices to mention that the course was organized as a sequence of exercises that focused on the basic properties of architecture: surface, frontal space, volumetric form, spatial form, mass and weight, deep space. This sequence was organized in terms of increasing complexity in relation to the viewer's experience of architecture, from the static perception of frontal space to the dynamic experience of volumetric and interior space. Each exercise was carried out by the students without site or program, enabling the creation of forms without any functional or technical limitations. This resulted in the prolific production of models in cardboard and clay. Most impressive for their formal elaboration were those made of clay, where prismatic forms were modeled in order to produce volumetric complexity.

Significantly, these exercises avoided the use of plans and sections as the generators of architecture. Architecture was immediately identified with its volumetric appearance, excluding anything not incumbent to a building's formal organization.

Ladovsky's exercises are notably similar to Malevich's *Arkhitektony*, which were models of programless architectural compositions. Produced in 1923 following his drawings of *Planity* (planets), *Arkhitektony* were an attempt to translate Malevich's suprematist compositions into architecture. Unlike the VKhUTEMAS volumetric exercises, Malevich's models are rather restrained in complexity and composed according to a clearly discernable ordering system in which a basic prismatic volume was flanked by smaller symmetrically arranged volumes.

fig. 5.2

Malevich's architecture appears to be an attempt to overcome the limitations of painting and realize formalism in three dimensions. In translating painting into architecture, he preserved the literalness of his formal elements, which in painting were planes of color and in architecture were volumes of matter. Through the whiteness of plaster, any sense of materiality was downplayed to enhance the pure volumetric appearance of architecture. The models produced by Ladovsky's students were more

5.1 Exercise on the articulation of volumetric form, from the space course at VKhUTEMAS, Moscow, 1928–1929. From Anna Bokov, *Avant-Garde as Method: VKhUTEMAS and the Pedagogy of Space, 1920–1930* (Zurich: Park Books, 2021).

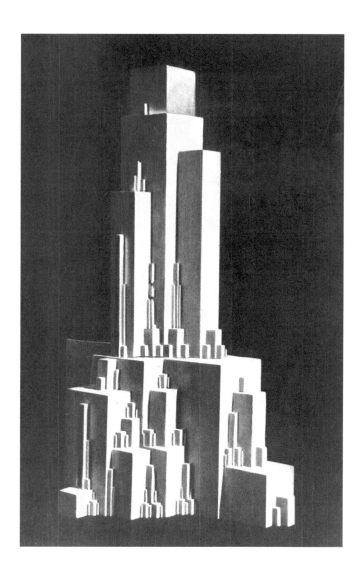

5.2 Kazimir Malevich, *Arkhitekton, Gotha 2*, 1921. From *Nova generatsiia* 3, no. 2 (1928).

rudimentary and left their materiality exposed, but the goal of the academic exercise coincided with Malevich's pursuits: the liberation of architecture from any constraint that was not pure formal composition. Clearly the inspiration for this volumetric idea of architecture was Wölfflin's and Schmarsow's interpretation of architecture as the composition of space and volume. However, in both historians' analyses, the abstraction of architecture as volumetric composition remained implicit, since the focus of their reading was Renaissance and baroque architecture. With both Ladovsky's space course and Malevich's *Arkhitektony* the abstraction of pure plasticity became the explicit goal of architecture. This goal is evident in Ladovsky's use of precedents in the space course. To familiarize students with historical work, Ladovsky and his collaborators pinned reproductions of architecture, sculpture, and paintings to display boards. The purpose of the boards was not to educate students in the history of architecture, but to allow them to extrapolate formal themes *from* history for use in any kind of architecture. This methodology exposes an unexpected kinship between Ladovsky's pedagogical approach rooted in architectural abstraction and what he opposed, namely the more traditional teachings of architects such as Ivan Zholtovsky, Ivan Fomin, and Alexei Shchusev. Though it is inaccurate to identify their influence on the Soviet architectural scene with the rise of Stalinist architecture, Zholtovsky, Fomin, and Shchusev were professionally and pedagogically active immediately after the Bolshevik revolution, and their work was supported by the state, which trusted their professional skills far more than those of their more progressive colleagues.[21] Furthermore, while their architecture is often assumed to have been "classicist," this was far from the case. Projects like Zholtovsky's design for an All-Russian Handicraft Exhibition in 1923 and Fomin's competition design for a Workers' Palace in Petrograd in 1919 demonstrate a high degree of formal invention in which classicist tropes such as arches, columns, and pediments are estranged from their traditional use and identity. In this architecture a combinatory approach emerges that Ladovsky himself further developed in his own projects and pushed to its extreme consequences in the space course. Crucially, the difference between Ladovsky's teachings and those of the supposedly more "conservative" architects was the role of virtuosity in the design of architecture. Zholtovsky and Fomin belonged to a tradition of architectural training that emphasized mastering the design of complex features—like moldings and capitals—and elaborating compositions in plan and elevation. The space course was instead devised to overcome virtuosity and allow anyone to gain an understanding of form and space without requiring exceptional skills in drawing and model-making.[22] Indeed, despite their formal inventiveness, the models produced at VKhUTEMAS are rough and look effortless. The radicality of the space course method was thus its accessibility to students, who at VKhUTEMAS were in large part of modest background and lacked any previous artistic training. In the history of formalism, Ladovsky's space course represented the supposed democratization of form-making, a way to make formal composition as easy as possible, accessible to virtually anyone. Yet fundamental to the accessibility of the space course was an idea of art and architecture that was born within the quintessential bourgeois aesthetic mentality of severing the production of art from more humble forms of craftsmanship.

Ladovsky's approach to form was not simply pedagogical, but reflected an understanding of architectural design as labor.[23] For Ladovsky, to make and experience form was not only a pleasing activity but also an expenditure of psychic energy. The desire to economize this energy led him to rationalize the production and encounter of form through a psychological and perceptual approach to architecture. Economy of form-making was the grounds for qualifying his approach to architecture as "rational"—a theoretical label that was also assumed by the architects gathered in the ASNOVA (Association of New Architects) group, founded in 1923 and of which Ladovsky was the undisputed leader. Seemingly at odds with design wholly defined by formal intuition, rationality, for Ladovsky, did not pertain to structural or functional requirements, but rather involved the possibility of assigning a comprehensive combinatory system of forms. Only rigorous scientific analysis of the production of architectural form would provide the architect with the necessary data to guide design methods. In the psychology of labor theorized by the American scientist Hugo Münsterberg, Ladovsky found an operative tool to assess form-making in scientific terms.[24] A follower of Frederick Winslow Taylor's scientific management, Münsterberg reinterpreted Taylorism within the field of psychology in an effort to rationalize not just movement but also perception and cognition. Following Münsterberg's psychological Taylorism, at VKhUTEMAS Ladovsky founded a psychotechnical laboratory that evaluated architectural effects, where the production and experience of form by teachers and students was defined in statistical terms and compiled into spreadsheets. Needless to say, this ambitious and somewhat absurd program of the Taylorization of formal production did not arrive at any substantial "scientific" result, but for some time it did legitimize the creative work of both the VKhUTEMAS space course and ASNOVA's professional output, best represented by Konstantin Melnikov's sophisticated architectural compositions.

Their endeavor to translate formal intuition into "rational architecture" led to harsh criticism of both Ladovsky and ASNOVA. Because of the alleged autonomy of formalism, already evacuated of any technical, economic, or functional constraint, Ladovsky's and ASNOVA's mechanical formal approach was seen as the justification of architecture "by means of architecture." This critique of architectural formalism became the theoretical foundation of the "constructivist" approach to architecture.

Construction versus Composition

The term "constructivism" is often used as an all-encompassing label for early Soviet art and architecture. This term is also often used interchangeably with another one—"avant-garde"—by which Western liberal culture flattens the most cutting-edge art produced in Russia in the early twentieth century into a progressive narrative. Even when defined narrowly, constructivism remains an elusive term, due to its double origin—first in the visual arts and then in architecture. Perhaps the most precise way to understand constructivism is to focus on the object of its critique: the formalist approach as it emerged in the early period of the Soviet Republic, first in painting and sculpture and then in architecture.

Constructivism was born when artists Karl Ioganson, Konstantin Medunetsky, Aleksandr Rodchenko, Georgii and Vladimir Stenberg, Varvara Stepanova, and Aleksei Gan formed the First

Working Group of Constructivists at INKhUK (Institute of Artistic Culture) established by Narkompros (People's Commissariat of Enlightenment), the Bolshevik administrative organ for cultural and educational matters.[25] The Institute was founded to promote research on art in scientific terms, and its director was Wassily Kandinsky. In strict opposition to the subjective and romantic understanding of art supported by Kandinsky, the First Working Group of Constructivists formulated its theoretical premises. At the core of constructivism was the difference between *construction* and *composition*.[26] For the constructivists, composition was the traditional process of art-making, which presupposed a play with form completely divorced from social and material conditions.[27] Composition was ultimately based on artists' subjective choice in arranging things together, according to their own taste. Against an individualistic mode of making art, the constructivists advocated "construction" as a more objective methodology that eradicated the influence of subjective choice.

In order to move from composition to construction, the constructivists proposed art that was useful in everyday life. For this reason, the group was drawn to architecture and design in general. Ironically, it was Ladovsky—whose formalist approach would eventually be attacked by constructivist architects—who provided the founders of constructivism with the terms to define their method. During a discussion at INKhUK, Ladovsky suggested that composition entails the hierarchy and coordination of volumes, while construction is a combination of shaped material elements according to a given plan where "there are no superfluous materials or elements."[28] In adopting this definition of construction the constructivists asserted the need for their art to be *planned*—like architecture itself. Not an architecture composed of spaces and volumes, the constructivists' idea of construction coincided with what Rodchenko called "laid-bare construction," in which the technical structure of things and buildings was related to their material fabrication. This definition implied the absorption of the traditional role of the artist into industrial design. Aleksei Gan clearly expressed this position in his 1921 manifesto "Constructivism," declaring that constructivism was the "art of production."[29] Art theorist Boris Arvatov further radicalized this position when he attacked artists who were still working as traditional "artists" in spite of the alleged "revolutionary" content of their work, such as Tatlin and Malevich. For Arvatov, artists could only exit their bourgeois mode of artistic production and become workers themselves by embracing not art, but production *tout court*. Arvatov's position was too extreme to accept—even for those critical of traditional form-making—but it elucidates the constructivists' desire to fine-tune the production of art with the reality of industrial work. This aspiration was best reflected in Rodchenko's teachings at VKhUTEMAS, where he was in charge of both the graphic construction course and the metalworking department. Against the intuitive formalism of Ladovsky's space course, Rodchenko's graphic construction course promoted a rigorous approach to form-making based on deductive exercises. Students were asked to arrange basic forms like circles, triangles, and rectangles in the most logical manner, taking into account the format of the support structure and the geometric relationship between figures. Rodchenko's exercises were meant to instigate planning and design *prior to making*, which students would later apply to a multitude of industrial objects like advertisements, textiles, or architecture. The architectural aspiration of constructivist art and its emphasis on planning clearly made it appealing to the architects who later adopted the movement's concepts in the mid 1920s.

More Program, Less Form

Constructivism's transition from art to architecture was in many ways instigated by two well-known and extremely influential designs for theatrical stages: Aleksandr Vesnin's stage design for Aleksandr Tairov's *The Man Who Was Thursday* in 1924, and Lyubov Popova's stage design for Vsevolod Meyerhold's *The Magnanimous Cuckold* in 1922.[30] These designs emphasized bare construction; theatrical backdrops were built not as traditional solid surfaces but as open scaffolds. The use of scaffolding conveyed an idea of architecture where structure is visible and becomes more important than volumetric form. With Vesnin's and Popova's stage sets, architecture was rendered, to return to Rodchenko's terms, as laid-bare construction.

This principle is also at work in projects by the Vesnin brothers, such as their competition design for the Palace of Labor in 1922 and for the Arkos Building in 1924, both in Moscow. In these projects the internal load-bearing concrete frame is visible in the façades and the volumetric appearance of the buildings directly reflects the interior program. Unlike the rationalists' approach, which starts with the building's sculptural perception, in the Vesnin brothers' approach architecture is the result of structure and program. This led to a far simpler and matter-of-fact architectural language. Abstraction was no longer the outcome of excessive volumetric effects but of an economy of construction means.

Constructivism in architecture and its critique of rationalist formalism fully emerged with the formation of OSA (the Organization of Contemporary Architects) in 1925 and the publication of its journal *SA* (*Sovremennaya arkhitektura*, Modern architecture) which, from 1926 to 1930, documented the projects and research carried out by the architects associated with the organization. Among the group was Moisei Ginzburg, whose writings and designs became a crucial contribution to the work of OSA.

Despite his constructivist allegiances, Ginzburg's work exhibits the influence of formalism: his first publication, *Rhythm in Architecture* (1923), was devoted to the study of architectural form in a Wölfflinian fashion. In this book, Ginzburg argued that rhythm underlies the totality of human experience.[31] Ginzburg distinguished between two kinds of rhythm: *active*, like music or dance, and *static*, which consisted of sequences of elements temporally perceived.[32] For Ginzburg architecture was static rhythm where walls, columns, and ornamental features marked intervals of space. Following Wölfflin, Ginzburg asserted that the viewer did not passively receive images, but was an active interpreter whose perception organized space.[33] Reducing architecture to a rhythm of vertical and horizontal elements potentially eased the user's experience of space. Following this logic, while complex and convoluted architectural compositions provoked perceptual distress in the user, simpler and organized compositions relieved perception. Ginzburg illustrated his approach with a series of stenographic diagrams that made it possible to reduce any architecture, whether modern or ancient, to rhythmic cadences. In *Rhythm in Architecture*, which represents Ginzburg's "formalist" phase, there already exists an implicit critique of Ladovsky's

fig. 5.3

formalism as it emerged in the space course at VKhUTEMAS. Form for Ladovsky was the composition of volumes, while for Ginzburg form stemmed from the sequence of simple elements. Ginzburg's approach emphasized the partitioning of space into clearly defined intervals and declined the sculptural drama of architecture found in the buildings designed by ASNOVA members. Ginzburg's approach emphasized what architecture framed, particularly program, rather than architecture itself.

Ginzburg and the OSA architects opted for simpler architectural structures made of elementary forms, where composition was dictated by technical and programmatic constraints. This approach to architecture became especially important to OSA's work in relation to housing, which became an urgent issue at the end of the Russian Civil War and with the inception of the NEP (New Economic Policy). The NEP was created to introduce a state-controlled market economy in support of a moderate form of capitalism, en route to the gradual transition toward socialism. Intended by Lenin to last for decades (in reality it only lasted a few years), the NEP was understood by the OSA architects as a period of transition in which socialism would be built not only through large-scale policy, but also by making quotidian life more attuned with collective forms of living.[34] Aiming to foster this transition, OSA architects undertook the analysis of housing as documented in the pages of *SA* and culminating in their contribution to the research carried out by STROIKOM (the State Building Committee) and GOSPLAN (State Planning Committee) during the first five-year plan. This work was published in Ginzburg's book *Dwelling*, which provides an overview of both his and OSA's housing investigations through 1932.

Dwelling opens with an analysis of the history of domestic space from ancient to modern times, focusing on the relationship between forms of life and housing types.[35] The book highlights a fundamental aspect of Ginzburg's and OSA's work, namely their choice to focus on typological design rather than formal composition. Ginzburg conceived architecture as the aggregation of housing cells, where the design of cells responded to OSA's rigorous critique of the traditional bourgeois family apartment. Formal organization was the outcome of social organization, that is, the organization of the house as a collectivized infrastructure. The

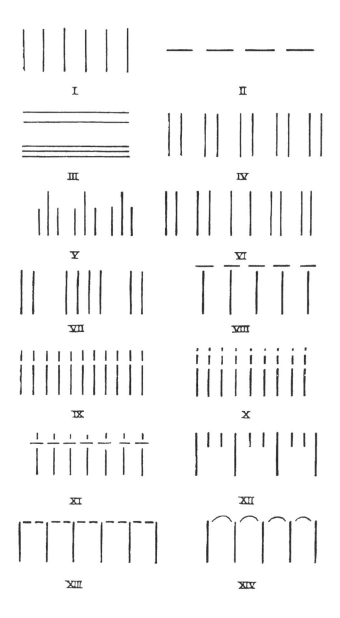

5.3 Moisei Ginzburg, stenographic diagrams. From Moisei Ginzburg, *Rhythm in Architecture* (London: Artifice Press, 2017, originally published in 1923).

political direction of this work stemmed from the social reforms of marriage and family introduced by the early Soviet Republic in the aftermath of the revolution. In light of these reforms, architects attempted to completely reorganize domestic space toward a more communal form of living. From this premise the Dom-Kommuna (communal house) type emerged as a new kind of collective housing, where domestic facilities such as the kitchen were shared. The Dom-Kommuna was not invented by members of OSA, but they perfected this model of habitation through the design of large-scale housing prototypes—of which Mikhail Barshch's and Vyacheslav Vladimirov's collective housing for single dwellers, designed in 1928, is perhaps the best and most extreme example.

However, Ginzburg understood the potential stress of concentrating many dwellers in large-scale structures. Under the influence of sociologist Mikhail Okhitovich's "disurbanist" theory, Ginzburg proposed smaller independent units to be dispersed across vast landscapes equipped with communal services and served by motorways and railways. Disurbanism projected the gradual replacement of the city as the center of political and economic accumulation, aiming toward an even distribution of people and infrastructure across the vast Russian territory. Defining the project were two fundamental tenets of communism: elimination of land property and the gradual dissolution of the family. Ginzburg's and Okhitovich's disurbanist vision took form in three projects: Green City, a competition entry for a settlement near Moscow in 1929; Kombinat, a competition entry for the building of the industrial city of Magnitogorsk in 1929; and the master plan for a settlement strip developed for the department of socialist housing of GOSPLAN in 1930. This last project proposed a strip of land served by an infrastructural backbone fringed with vegetation. A road that links places of industrial and economic importance is flanked by a park with communal settlements. Beyond the park are dwellings of various kinds that range from one-room houses to hostels, housing blocks, and communes. The housing typologies were organized to provide a multitude of individual and collective living arrangements. Similarly, Ginzburg's Narkomfin housing block in Moscow, proposed in 1928, contained the aggregation—within a single slab—of a variety of housing unit types, from cells to apartments. The GOSPLAN settlement

fig. 5.4
fig. 5.5

fig. 5.6

186

was also made of a diverse range of housing types meant to achieve a gradient of associations, from private to communal. In aggregating a multiplicity of housing types and designing them as light and thus movable timber frames, Ginzburg intended to offer the inhabitants the choice to live alone or together.

At the large scale, the GOSPLAN settlement was represented by a diagram indicating the frequency of collective facilities placed along the road. This diagram reveals the noncompositional logic of Ginzburg's proposal: the urban settlement is conceived not as clearly delineated form, but as the linear distribution of punctuating entities. The diagram reinterprets the concept of rhythm explored by Ginzburg in *Rhythm in Architecture*, but instead of addressing the form of architecture the project dealt directly with the social organization of space.

Ginzburg's proposal operated from the scale of the territory down to the scale of the construction details of the prefabricated housing units. In the GOSPLAN settlement model, formal expression was overcome by prioritizing spatial organization and technical implementation. The overarching focus on typology confirms that for constructivist architects the primary objective of architecture was not only construction but also—and especially—the organization of social relationships. Within this trajectory of research, architecture was abstracted to its minimum—the line of the road or the freestanding housing unit. This concept of architecture, driven by programmatic concerns and realized through an extremely simplified vocabulary, was best developed in the work of arguably the most talented architect of the OSA group: Ivan Leonidov.

Architecture Is a Big Empty Circle

Between 1926 and 1931 Leonidov produced a body of projects whose formal and programmatic coherence is nothing less than a theory of architecture. Within this theory, the social organization of his architecture is achieved with a minimum of form. His approach is both an outcome and a critique of rationalism and constructivism. In order to understand how Leonidov formulated this theory, it is useful to review three of the most representative projects of his early body of work: the Workers' Club of a New

5.4   Moisei Ginzburg et al., GOSPLAN RFSFR, Department of Socialist Housing,
plan for a settlement strip in an arbitrary place. From *Sovremennaia Arkhitektura*, no. 6 (1930).

5.5 Moisei Ginzburg et al., GOSPLAN RFSFR, Department of Socialist Housing, general plan for distribution of social facilities within the ribbon. From *Sovremennaia Arkhitektura*, no. 6 (1930).

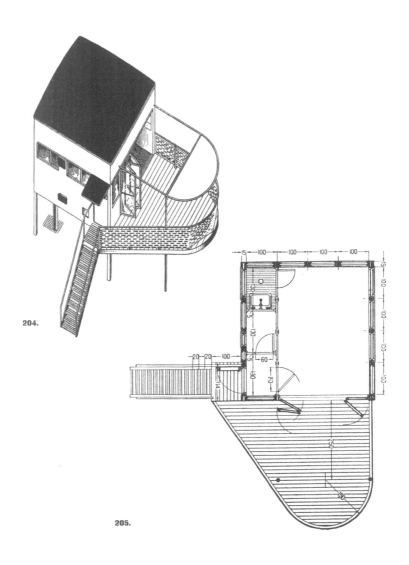

204.

205.

5.6 Moisei Ginzburg, GOSPLAN RSFSR, one-room unit, plan and axonometry.
From Moisei Ginzburg, *Dwelling: Five Years Work on the Problem of Habitation* (Moscow:
Fontanka, 2017, originally published in 1934).

Social Type from 1928, the House of Industry designed between 1929 and 1930, and the proposal for a socialist settlement at Magnitogorsk proposed in 1930.

The workers' club was a research project presented at the First Congress of Constructivist Architects, which took place in Moscow in 1929. The proposal—published in *SA* in three variations based on the same program—was Leonidov's response to the Moscow workers' unions, which, in their 1928 plenum, put forward a program to build a large number of workers' clubs in the Soviet capital and its outskirts.[36] The *rabochiye kluby* (workers' clubs) were introduced by Soviet authorities in the immediate aftermath of the 1917 October Revolution and were organized under the supervision of unions and other social groups. The clubs were the descendants of the "People's Houses" established both in Europe and prerevolutionary Russia by philanthropic institutions, unions, and political parties. Soviet authorities encouraged the proliferation of clubs as "schools in which to learn urban culture," with a primary focus on educating those who had just migrated to large cities. As spaces of recreation and education, they offered a variety of programs such as cinemas, theaters, cafés, dance halls, and other amenities. The early Soviet workers' clubs did not have a defined typology. Between 1917 and 1925, they were built in old public palaces, deconsecrated churches, and storage spaces. The spatial organization of these improvised structures was one of the first tasks assigned to architects after the revolution. However, after 1925, clubs were built in close proximity to large workplaces, and their purpose was mainly to offer a large auditorium, complemented by a sizeable foyer and other multifunctional spaces. The most significant manifestations of this type of workers' club were the Zuev Workers' Club, designed by Ilya Golosov, and the Rusakov Workers' Club, designed by Konstantin Melnikov, built in 1929 and 1928 respectively. It was precisely in reaction to this paradigm of workers' club that Leonidov conceived his proposal.[37] His workers' club consisted of parabolic domes, identical cubical volumes, and a low, wide-span plinth made of concrete. In this striking proposal the club is no longer a building where every activity takes place indoors. Leonidov proposed the workers' club as a park where buildings were reduced to a minimum footprint and open space was maximized.

fig. 5.7

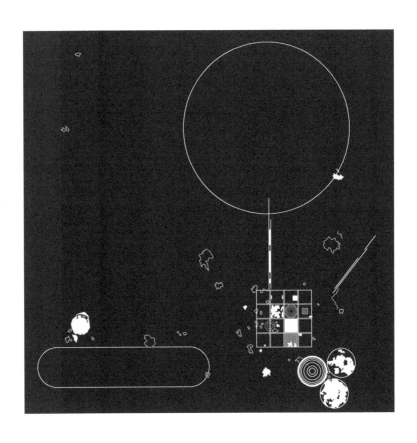

5.7 Ivan Leonidov, Workers' Club of a New Social Type, 1928, plan.
© Dogma, adapted from Ivan Leonidov.

He further not only challenged the club's building type but also reimagined its program, rejecting the inclusion of the theater and auditorium that were considered the most important spaces of the traditional club. In doing so he argued that these functions encouraged passive spectatorship and therefore were not compatible with the desire to make the clubs active and participatory spaces.[38] Instead, he proposed to include activities and programs like gardening, a scientific planetarium, facilities for athletics and gymnastics, a kindergarten, and a space equipped for broadcasting and listening to radio programs. The large plinth was intended as a multifunctional space in which demonstrations, motorcycle races, open-air cinema, and hot-air balloons could all coincide. This unconventional program resulted in an unprecedented formulation of the workers' club, which unsettled Leonidov's colleagues at OSA not only because of its rejection of traditional programs like the theater but also—and especially—for the lack of a clear relationship between the proposed forms. Other OSA members could not comprehend the arrangement of circles and squares and the activities that were supposed to take place in them.[39] During the first OSA congress, when Leonidov was questioned about the functionality of his design in regard to the proposed program, he answered that multiple activities could take place in the same structure. This was not a response of careless relativism, but rather was informed by Leonidov's close consideration of the volatile nature of programs that could be improvised at any moment without rigid predetermination. This is why he rejected the auditorium: a stage fronted by rows of seats was too deterministic, as it presupposed a specific spatial relationship between the attending audience and the performance on stage. Instead, all the activities proposed by Leonidov, such as gardening or playing, did not presuppose specific spatial arrangements but rather generic architectural conditions, such as indoor or outdoor space. Additionally, as noted by Richard Anderson, Leonidov imagined the activities at the club to be increasingly engaged with new media, such as listening to or broadcasting radio programs, with which it was difficult to associate a building type.[40] Leonidov's only concession to a recognizable architectural form was the planetarium, which was located in one of the parabolic domes. Besides this structure every other element of the club was conceived by Leonidov as "nontypological," designed without adhering to a specific activity.

Leonidov's nontypological approach to architecture is fully evident in the most iconoclastic feature of the project: the circular platform, a recurring theme in his work. The platform's simplicity was clearly inspired by Malevich's suprematist pictorial language, especially by the drawings contained in the painter's influential book *From Cubism and Futurism to Suprematism New Painterly Realism* (1916). On one page of the book, Malevich plainly displayed a black circle drawn on a white page.[41] Certainly, Leonidov was deeply impressed by Malevich's presentation of this "fatherless figure" as a radical formal gesture, and attempted to translate its irreverent force into the simplest architectural expression possible: an "empty" circle, within which anything could take place. It is this blunt architectural language that differentiates the work of Leonidov and makes it unique even amidst the research of his colleagues at OSA—who were appalled by the formal abstraction of the Club of a New Social Type. A mere formalist understanding of Leonidov's work cannot do justice to his approach, which exceeded the design of form by rigorously contemplating and challenging the conventions of the workers' club program. Accordingly, at the constructivist conference he presented the project not in terms of formal invention but as the ambition to reform the club program. His main concern was overcoming the limitations of the workers' club as a building, not the creation of novel forms. The diagrammatic quality of his projects emphasized the capacity of architecture to subdivide and thus organize space, creating complementary spatial situations— such as open and enclosed, indoors and outdoors, soft and hard, high and low, big and small, transparent and opaque—which can be deployed when needed. For Leonidov, reducing—or, better, abstracting—architectural form to its zero-degree as spatial partition made it possible to emphasize architecture's organizational potential, without resorting to a deterministic functionalism. This approach is even more evident in his proposal for the House of Industry, made in 1929, which he presented as an entry to the competition organized by the VSNKh RSFSR (Supreme Economic Soviet of the Russian Republic) for its nine-story headquarters next to Red Square. Leonidov's approach to the project—as he

fig. 5.8

fig. 5.9

5.8 Kazimir Malevich, *Suprematist Element: Circle*, 1923. Pencil on paper, 18½ by 14⅜ inches.
© The Museum of Modern Art/Licensed by SCALA / Art Resource, NY.

wrote—departed from accepted ideas of work and management. The project noticeably anticipates neoliberal capitalist strategies that include leisure activities in the workplace to increase productivity. In the design of the office building, Leonidov (from a socialist perspective) proposed delineating a zone on each floor for activities such as physical exercise, rest, reading, eating, and bathing, while services like staircases, elevators, and bathrooms were concentrated in a core protruding from the volume of the building. Cleared of functional requirements, the rest of the floor space was kept open and marked with a grid, painted on the floor, that allotted each worker five square meters of space to be used according to their individual needs and wants. In Leonidov's vision, the close proximity between the grid of workstations and the strip of leisure activities permitted workers to have frequent half-hour or ten-minute breaks. The floor plan presented a sequence of three spatial situations: the grid of workstations, the strip of leisure activities, and the mechanical services. No corridors, no rooms: the interior of the House of Industry is reduced to the ultimate abstraction of an open floor where the location of different activities is simply traced directly on the floor. This abstraction is further accentuated in the treatment of the tower's envelope as a continuous glass façade, the first of its kind in the history of architecture, which would later become pervasive with the introduction of the curtain wall.

The uniform façade and axonometric representation of the House of Industry resembled El Lissitzky's *Prouns*, the well-known compositions made of prisms that he first created in 1920. The *Prouns* translated Malevich's suprematist compositions into three-dimensional renderings of geometric forms (and in turn inspired Malevich to work on the *Arkhitektony*), which Lissitzky employed both in his paintings and in installations such as the *Proun Room* in 1923. By depicting *Prouns* through different axonometric views, or hanging them in different positions, Lissitzky attempted to create a space devoid of any preestablished direction such as up, down, left, or right. Freed from orientation, the *Prouns* demonstrated the infinite potential of simple forms to become the building blocks of an alternative social landscape.[42] Lissitzky collaborated with suprematists, rationalists (ASNOVA), and constructivists (OSA) alike, and to a certain extent his *Prouns* can be considered a "metalanguage" that both synthesized and transcended the different contributions of these movements. Yet Lissitzky's *Prouns* are neither too ethereal, like Malevich's *Arkhitektony*, nor too mechanical, like Rodchenko's "construction"; neither too complicated, like Ladovsky's space course models, nor too functionally deterministic, like OSA's buildings. Leonidov's reinterpretation of Lissitzky's *Prouns* was thus a way to distance himself from both the complex formalism of ASNOVA and the cause-and-effect constructivism of OSA, aiming at redefining architecture as a generic container for human activities. The boldest gesture of Leonidov's proposal for the House of Industry was the allocation of all the required functions into one monolith-like volume. This operation allowed him to restrain form, almost completely, into one simple block. Like the workers' club, the House of Industry's complex program is met with the simplest formal vocabulary. A similar approach is evident in what can be considered the apex of Leonidov's architectural work: his proposal for the socialist settlement at the industrial *Kombinat* of Magnitogorsk, which was presented at the competition organized by GOSPLAN in 1930. This is the same competition for which Ginzburg and Okhitovich proposed their iteration of the Green City settlement model. Leonidov's proposal was also influenced by Okhitovich's disurbanist theories; and similar to Ginzburg's entry, he proposed to develop the new settlement in a linear fashion. But in contrast to Ginzburg's, Leonidov's scheme was regimented by a checkerboard pattern stretched for 25 kilometers in a straight line. The gridlike subdivision of the strip separated built and unbuilt areas and prevented disorderly accumulation of buildings by imposing a settlement logic that was easy to use and left abundant space for future buildings. Although Leonidov proposed two types—high-rise towers and two-story pavilions—both consist of the same housing module. This module is conceived as a nine-square grid that organizes sixteen single-person rooms around a double-height cruciform communal space where each arm is devoted to specific programs such as a winter garden or gym. The nine-square grid was a reiteration at a smaller scale of the checkerboard pattern of the settlement, thus making the grid its all-encompassing logic. Leonidov imposed a uniform organization defined by the geometric sameness of the square, making the organization of the city immediately legible

fig. 5.10

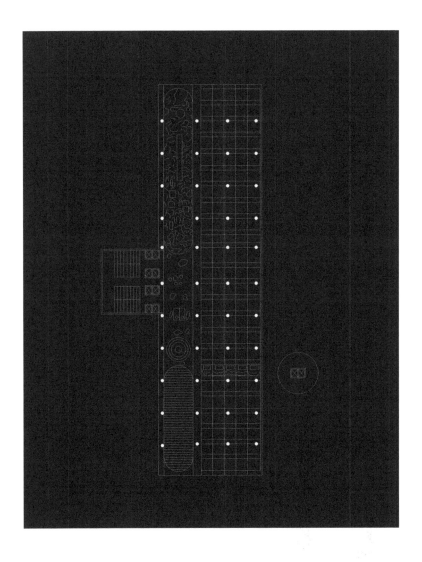

5.9 Ivan Leonidov, House of Industry, designed between 1929 and 1930, plan and axonometry.
© Dogma, adapted from Ivan Leonidov.

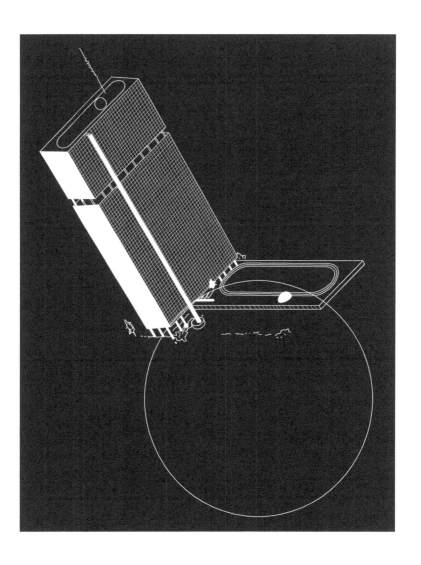

and abolishing any hierarchical relationship between the different spaces. The even distribution across the settlement, from giving each inhabitant the same room regardless of gender or age, to the regimented placement of services and facilities such as kindergartens, stadiums, or museums within or along the linear strip, was established by Leonidov to approximate a classless urban space freed of hierarchies and servitude. In Leonidov's architecture, the refusal of complex architectural compositions was thus grounded not in outright simplicity but on the reality of a socialist habitat where privilege and class were to be eliminated. Leonidov's architecture pushed the formalist tradition to the extreme and exceeded it: formal expression and construction were eclipsed by the organization of life.

A Necessary Irony of History

For the organization of life, formalism, rationalism, and constructivism were scrutinized by Soviet authorities under Joseph Stalin's rule. The standard "Western" narrative claims that in the early 1930s, with the abolition of all artist and architect groups and the creation of unifying state-led associations, there was a return to order under the direct control of the state. Centralized authority forced architects and artists to reject abstraction and move to more traditional forms of expression. This story is of course measured against the incomparable artistic innovations of the 1920s and constructed to emphasize the conservative character of Stalin's authoritarian rule. The reality of this political scenario is captured in the "character assassination" of Leonidov by the architects associated with VOPRA (Association of Proletarian Architects) who accused the young architect of indulgence in formalism and disregard for programmatic and technical aspects of architecture.[43] Based on such episodes, historians have assumed that the Soviet artistic "avant-garde" was eradicated by the state because the art and architecture movements were considered "petit bourgeois" and "formalist," two terms that in the polemics and accusations of the time were often interchangeable. Despite its general acceptance, some scholars—most notably the cultural theorist Boris Groys—have argued that this standard story is not entirely correct.[44] According to Groys, the constructivists' dream of art and

200

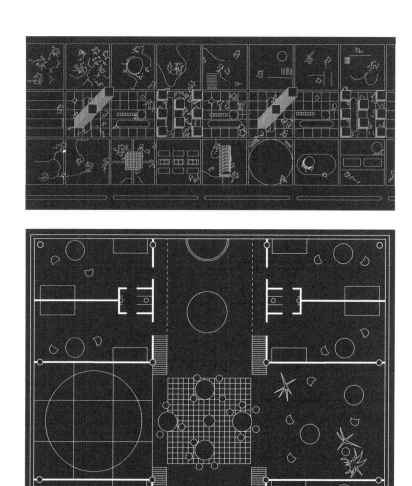

5.10   Ivan Leonidov, competition entry, socialist settlement for the chemical-metallurgic *Kombinat* at Magnitogorsk, 1930. © Dogma, adapted from Ivan Leonidov.

architecture as the organization of life through aesthetic means was fully accomplished under Stalinist rule. Socialist realism, the aesthetic doctrine that became hegemonic in Soviet Russia in the 1930s, shared the constructivist goal of using art beyond cultural bourgeois institutions (the museum, the academy) to influence people in their everyday life. Ironically, socialist realism's critique of constructivism as a deviation from the socialist cause—because it was too indulgent in formalism and thus incapable of appealing to the masses—was not dissimilar from the constructivist's critique of rationalism's obsession with form.

It was not art-related policies that dealt the major blow to the rationalists' and constructivists' aspiration to offer "the armature of everyday life" to the working class. This goal was undermined by the changing politics of the late 1920s when, with Stalin's rise to power, centralized planning replaced the tactical and gradual strategy of the NEP.[45] With the inauguration of the first five-year plan in 1928, Stalin made *real* the constructivist idea of "construction" as an organizing totality. In this new context artists were no longer independent agents offering or teaching their knowledge to the masses: in the name of the dictatorship of the proletarians, they were asked to subordinate their work to the directives of the Party. It is important to consider this situation beyond accepted notions of Stalin's authoritarian rule. At stake was not simply the suppression of artists under the Party's rule, but something more significant and perfectly aligned with the socialist principles of Soviet power: the critique of the bourgeois artist's intellectual disposition as it emerged in the nineteenth century.

Under Stalin, workers and peasants took positions of power in the Soviet Union. This phenomenon of social mobility, carefully researched by Sheila Fitzpatrick, was not only the consequence of the 1917 revolution, but was orchestrated by Stalin himself as a way to realize Marx's idea of the dictatorship of the proletarians (and reinforce his leadership).[46] While Lenin entrusted intellectuals to "make the revolution" on behalf of the working class, with the inception of a centralized economy Stalin empowered the working class (or a selection of it) and subordinated intellectuals to this new class composition.[47] This specific context should be considered to fully understand Soviet state criticism of the artistic and architectural movements of the 1920s. What was questioned was precisely their bourgeois conception of art as an autonomous sphere of intellectual activity, distinguished from any other form of labor; their conception of form and space as depleted of any ideological or symbolic connotation was a direct consequence of this legacy, and one of the main critical points for Stalinist critics. This mentality, which survived even within constructivism, was strongly rooted in the Russian intellectual class that considered their mandate as not subordinate to the state and thus felt authorized to propose their own solutions. Notwithstanding the nomenklatura's often crass accusations against abstract and constructivist art, what was being critiqued was precisely the recalcitrant attitude of the "avant-garde" toward the class politics of the Soviet state.

The crisis of "avant-garde" movements in the age of Stalinist centralized planning was discussed by a group of architectural historians and intellectuals led by Manfredo Tafuri in the late 1960s and early 1970s at the Istituto di Storia dell'Architettura of the school of architecture in Venice, Italy.[48] This discussion was a response to both the intensification of students' and workers' struggles in Italy at that time and the concurrent renewed interest in the art and architecture of early Soviet Russia. This interest, which started in the early 1960s with the rediscovery of Russian formalism and pioneering studies on Russian architecture like those by Vittorio De Feo and Vieri Quilici, resonated with the protesting students and their search for alternative ways to practice art and architecture. It was precisely by critiquing the alleged "progressivism" of the avant-garde, and especially the idea that there could be a perfect coincidence between political revolution and artistic revolution, that Tafuri and his colleagues scrutinized the fate of formalism and constructivism after the 1920s. For them, this fate had to be interpreted beyond Stalinism and in light of the problematic nature of "artistic" work within actualized socialism.

In his contribution to this discussion, Tafuri stressed the centrality of formalism in all the 1920s art and architecture movements in Soviet Russia.[49] He also noted their troubled relationship with the class politics of the revolution, precisely because of the alleged political neutrality of formalism. This relationship becomes even more problematic when artists and architects *themselves* decided to support the revolution by moving from a theoretical stance to a propositional—"projective"—approach. For Tafuri, the core of the formalist project—which, according to him, informed both rationalism and constructivism—was the insistence on the estrangement of quotidian language which artists and architects pursued as a way to achieve a socialist reconstruction of the world. This pursuit, however radical and leftist, remained grounded in the traditional role of artists who—as confident manipulators of their disciplinary tools—*voluntarily* offered their knowledge to the Party and the working class. This position implied that the artist or the architect was a sovereign agent, and it was precisely this intellectual "agency" that, according to Tafuri, was at odds with the class politics of the revolution, within which there was no "special role" for artists or intellectuals other than the one of workers among workers.

In 1930, Lazar Kaganovich, a member of the Politburo and close associate of Stalin, declared that the "communist city" existed immediately when the Bolsheviks took power in 1917.[50] This statement was intended to criticize the disurbanist experiments of constructivist architects, reminding them that the first five-year plan prioritized heavy industry and thus aimed to consolidate the city as the primary focus of urbanization; Kaganovich's statement was also a reminder to artists and architects that there was no need to invent a new socialist world, because the latter was already immanent in the existing socialist life of the Soviet Union. Inferred in this statement is that art and architecture were not expected to teach people new things, but to provide appealing and legible forms to the masses to amplify their commitment to socialism. In the Stalinist Soviet political context, art and architecture played a fundamental role, and to a certain extent even the legacy of constructivism and suprematism survived (are not the Moscow skyscrapers built after the Second World War a reinterpretation of Malevich's *Arkhitektony*?). Discarded was the legacy of formalism, which, as has become evident, extracted its radicality from nineteenth-century bourgeois aesthetic detachment. After all, that formalism found in Soviet Russia its ultimate and most radical expression was—in Tafuri's words—a "necessary irony of history."

6 Experience and Poverty: Abstraction and Architecture from Dom-ino to Data Centers

In 1933 Walter Benjamin wrote an essay titled "Experience and Poverty," in which he declared: "a new poverty has descended on mankind."[1] For Benjamin, this new poverty was not a lack of material things but the outcome of the disintegration of experience, understood as the kernel of wisdom that for millennia had guided people's lives. Benjamin noted that experience was encapsulated in proverbs and stories transmitted from one generation to another and constituting a shared ethos among communities.[2] The rise of industrial production, which found its most brutal manifestation in the mechanized warfare of World War I, destroyed the possibility of building meaningful, durable, and transmissible experiences. Reflecting on the silence of the people who returned from the war, Benjamin observed that for the first time soldiers confronted with a "force field of destructive torrents and explosions" could not recompose the vicissitudes of warfare into a transmissible "story."[3] With industrialization and its intense forms of existential uprooting, any form of genuine experience was destroyed and replaced with more abstract and indifferent "information"—like the news delivered by industrialized media such as newspapers and radio. For Benjamin, the flipside of experiential poverty was the "oppressive wealth of ideas that has spread among people" such as astrology, chiromancy, gnosis, and spiritualism. This wealth of ideas compensated for existential uprooting with a thin layer of "tradition," and it was precisely against these compensations that, in a dramatic twist, Benjamin invoked the new poverty not just as a given condition but also as a *possibility*, which the German critic addressed as the subjectivity of the "barbarian." As is well known, "barbarian" was the derogatory term the Greeks used for foreigners. The origin of the word is onomatopoetic: *bar-bar* is said to be, to the Greeks' ears, the stammering sound of foreign languages. Benjamin appropriated this negative definition and transformed it into a "positive concept": the barbarian as the only genuine way of being within the predicament of the modern industrial world. For modern barbarians, "poverty of experience" is an invitation to start from an existential tabula rasa "to make a little go a long way; to begin with little and build up further, looking neither left nor right."

Benjamin gave examples of barbarians such as Descartes, who launched his own philosophical program based on a single certitude—"I think, therefore I am"—or Paul Klee, whose artistic approach to painting was, in Benjamin's view, modeled on the engineer rather than the bohemian and romantic artist. For Benjamin, the most radical form of modern barbarism was embodied by those artists who work as mathematicians and "build the world from stereometric forms, like the cubist." From this vantage Benjamin evokes the image of modern architecture as a positive expression of the poverty of experience. He makes direct reference to "modern" architects including Adolf Loos and Le Corbusier. According to Benjamin, it is possible to interpret the bare form of modern architecture as an attack on the bourgeois interior, in which the abundance of furniture and decoration was meant to reinforce the homeowner's sense of possession.[4] Notwithstanding Benjamin's rather loose interpretation of these architectural sources— certainly Loos's interiors were far from bare—in his evocation of twentieth-century architecture as bare structures that prevent dwellers from leaving any trace he identifies, if not a tradition, at least a historical thread concealed by popular and reassuring definitions such as the "modern movement" and "functionalism." Benjamin's interest in architecture was informed by the writings of Sigfried Giedion, especially Giedion's book *Building in France*, in which the Swiss critic and historian introduced the German public to the most advanced forms of building engineering at that time. Moreover, Benjamin was acquainted with the debate on modern architecture due to his collaboration with the journal *G: Material zur elementaren Gestaltung* founded by painter and filmmaker Hans Richter and filled with contributions by artists and architects whom Benjamin would well have identified as radical barbarians, such as El Lissitzky, Raoul Hausmann, Ludwig Mies van der Rohe, and Ludwig Hilberseimer. The journal and its contributors actively searched the most rarefied forms of industrial production for the seeds of a new aesthetic vision which today would likely be defined as "accelerationist."[5] Juxtaposing photographs of modern architecture with industrial buildings, or reproductions of Piet Mondrian's paintings with commercial advertisements, the editors of *G* hoped to accelerate the merging of art and architecture with the ethos of mass production. Yet, as Detlef Mertins argued, the approach pursued by the editors of G exudes a certain idealism which aimed to preserve artists' and architects' professional integrity in relation to a world dominated by industrial reification.[6]

Contrary to this tendency, Benjamin's invocation of poverty of experience was meant to smash any remnant of artistic (or architectural) integrity and expose the production of art and architecture to the most industrially reified conditions possible. Rather than the idealism that characterized—with the exception of Dada—the stance of early twentieth-century avant-gardes, Benjamin refers to an attitude that combines disenchantment with commitment to the present condition.

Given that poverty of experience is a condition that far exceeds what is generally recognized as modernity and was accelerated by the massive technosocial development of the recent decades, Benjamin's quandary can help situate the last century of architectural production beyond the usual labels of modernity, postmodernity, avant-garde, neo-avant-garde, digital or postdigital, and so on. Across multiple means of production—material or immaterial, Fordist or post-Fordist, mechanical or digital—poverty of experience still persists, unfolding in even more radical terms than before and producing ever more illusory compensations in the form of "traditions" and "cultures." Against cheap acts of compensation, certain architectural ideas or projects—purposely or in spite of themselves—revealed in striking terms the truth of the poverty of experience, that is, the impossibility of properly inhabiting or building "meaningful" spaces. By stripping architecture bare to the abstract form of a container lacking any symbolic trope, the architectural ideas revisited in what follows evoked the life of the barbarian as someone who lived and continues to live through the *longue durée* of our industrial civilization.

Tabula Rasa Architecture: Starting from Scratch

The most obvious yet powerful representation of poverty of experience in architecture is Le Corbusier's famous perspective of the house system known as Maison Dom-ino. Initiated in 1914, the Dom-ino was conceived during a period of intense frustration

fig. 6.1

and depression for Le Corbusier.[7] The system's name likely refers to both *domus* (house) and *innovation*. It can also be interpreted literally as *domino*, one of many tiles, twice as long as they are wide, assembled according to specific rules in the game that bears the same name. The housing system consisted of a multistory structural skeleton made of horizontal slabs and vertical piers. Everything else, including the façades and internal partitions, was to be filled in by the inhabitants.

Le Corbusier's perspective is deceptive on several accounts: it shows with realistic matter-of-factness an unrealistic structure; moreover, the building would never be seen empty as it is represented, since the skeleton would inevitably be hidden by the façade and internal partitions. Despite its abstract representation, the Dom-ino project was motivated by Le Corbusier's wish to generate a picturesque grouping of houses based on four plan types. As is visible in his drawings, where he projected the future inhabitation of the Dom-ino, elevations and plans were filled with rather traditional façades and floor plan subdivisions.[8] Even the piers were not yet the iconic and sculptural *pilotis* that would become characteristic of many of his later buildings: the piers did not have a round section and, set back from the edge of the slab, they would disappear once the façade was added. The most important conceptual aspect of the project, when it was developed between 1914 and 1916, was not the skeleton itself but the separation between load-bearing structure and façade. Accordingly, the internal partitions and façade could be changed without affecting the structure. The possibility of separating structure and walls was revealed to Le Corbusier by Emil Mörsch's *Die Eisenbetonbau*, the book that introduced him to techniques of reinforced concrete. In 1909 *Die Eisenbetonbau* was translated into French by Max Du Bois, the engineer who reluctantly helped Le Corbusier in devising the Dom-ino structure.[9] In the book, Mörsch suggested that, by separating structure from vertical walls, a building could be built with reinforced concrete and still look conventional. This result is exactly what Le Corbusier anticipated in the Dom-ino project. While he would later present this project from a radical position, in his initial conception he did not intend to leave the structure visible, making the iconic Dom-ino perspective highly deceptive. Only retrospectively, after eight or nine years, did he

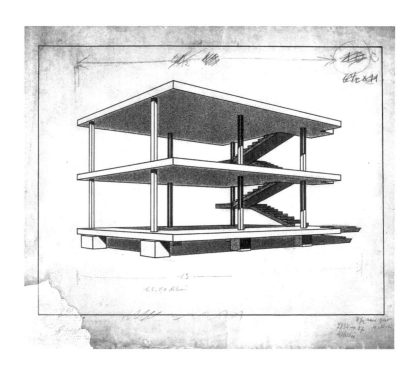

6.1 Le Corbusier, Maison Dom-ino, 1914. Crayon on paper, unsigned, undated. © FLC/ARS, 2022.

finally understand the dramatic implications of his model. By separating the load-bearing structure from the enclosing skin, the Dom-ino model implied the total relativization of both façade and internal partitions: any distribution of infill was possible. Moreover, pulling the columns back from the edge of the horizontal slab eradicated the post-and-lintel structural motive, a dominant feature in the structures that inspired Le Corbusier, including Ottoman timber-frame houses and Auguste Perret's concrete structures.[10] With its radical abstraction, the Dom-ino prefigures the possibility of unlimited flexibility, of constant change and adaptation, and thus the impossibility of "experience" in dwelling.[11] For millennia, dwelling was supported by the enduring continuity of habits and rituals: the way we enter a house, the way we eat at or sit around a table. With time, the architecture of the house was formalized around these gestures. With its radical blankness, the image of the Dom-ino's empty structural frame suggests a situation in which no habit or ritual is supported by a defined spatial organization: anything can take place, any use is possible, any form of life can start *from scratch*.

Le Corbusier proposed the Dom-ino system as row houses, apartments, and even single-family houses. In one variation, he even incorporated workspaces.[12] Yet this unprecedented flexibility became explicit only when, after reflecting on his realized projects, Le Corbusier presented his proposal in the pages of the first volume of the *Oeuvre complète* in 1929.[13] It is here that the iconic perspective is appreciated as the formal datum for many of his projects—especially his famous villas—most of which were based on the separation between load-bearing structure and façade. Nonetheless, in his subsequent work Le Corbusier appears to exorcise the generic bareness of the concrete frame. In his houses, such as Villa La Roche (built 1923 to 1925), Villa Savoye (built 1928 to 1931), or Villa Stein (built 1926 to 1928), the enclosing walls acquire a sculptural, almost monumental presence that completely masks the generic logic of the load-bearing system. Beginning with Villa La Roche, Le Corbusier transformed the structural pier into the elegantly sculptural *pilotis*. If Dom-ino marks the starting point of his understanding of the structural tectonic of concrete, in this later work he seems to retreat from the radical implications of his 1914 model. Perhaps he understood and feared Dom-ino's unlimited potential to make architecture generic and to completely undo architecture as a sculptural practice, as the *jeu savant*. Further, he likely recognized an even more disturbing implication of his model: the total elimination of the architect as author of singular, unique buildings. While working on the project, he fantasized about establishing a company that would produce the concrete formwork and any accompanying standardized fixtures such as windows and door frames.[14] The Dom-ino was not a proposal for a building but for a building system based on the mass production of its parts. This was not an original idea: Le Corbusier adopted it from the production of factories like the "daylight" factories designed by Albert Kahn for Packard and Ford in the early 1900s. As discussed earlier, in these factories architecture was literally reduced to its load-bearing skeleton, which consisted of long-span fireproof structures and a minimum of vertical support. This structural arrangement allowed flexible, well-lit interiors in which the *floor*—the artificial reconstruction of the ground—became the primary form of architecture. Potentially extendable ad infinitum, the industrial floor creates an even spatial condition in which workers, machines, and goods occupy the same horizontal datum.

To a certain extent, the uniform logic of the smooth and continuous factory floor can be interpreted as a physical translation of the principle of the money economy—the equivalence of all things determined by the abstraction of exchange value. On the abstract floor of the factory it was possible to reduce workers and machines to measurable parameters to improve productivity. Further, in accordance with the drive for profit and the need to constantly upgrade manufacturing technology, the bareness of the factory floor and structure permitted flexibility and constant transformation. Le Corbusier's Dom-ino project should be understood as the intuitive application of the factory's structural rationale at the scale of domestic dwelling. The tectonic form of Dom-ino is even more abstract than Kahn's factories. Dom-ino removed the supporting beams from beneath the horizontal slabs, which are conceived as perfectly smooth objects. Like a factory, the Dom-ino model is not derived from a building type, but from the logic of building elements. Dom-ino is the reduction of architecture to a few standardized generic elements—slabs, piers, stairs—that repeat to define a modular frame. Du Bois, the engineer working with Le Corbusier, understandably expressed skepticism about the prospect of building Dom-ino. The novelty of the model was grounded in Le Corbusier's plan to mass-produce the house by uniting large industry, responsible for the concrete and formwork, and the small-scale low-skilled labor that would complete the structure. This system forecast the proliferation of concrete structures such as the Turkish *gecekondu* or the Greek *polykatoikia*, which today represent one of the most ubiquitous building techniques around the world.

However, it was precisely the proliferation of a generic model that Le Corbusier attempted to avoid in his subsequent work. Despite efforts to collaborate with the building industry and exploit its modus operandi, Le Corbusier would not concede the role of the architect, and he especially wanted to preserve the sculptural effect of form. Tim Benton noted that Le Corbusier negatively reacted to Henri-Marcel Magne's praise of reinforced concrete as a means for designers to devise architecture as a scientific fact.[15] In the margin of a text where Magne expressed this position,[16] Le Corbusier scribbled: "the architectural problem is a sculptural matter." This conviction prevented him from fully realizing the premise of the Dom-ino model. The famous Dom-ino perspective embodied the dilemma of architects confronted by the abstraction of architectural form made possible by industrialized concrete. The perspective displays two seemingly opposite conditions of architecture: in Adolf Max Vogt's words, "the perfectly pure" and the "raw real."[17] While the perfectly pure is the structure's formal abstraction, the raw real is its construction system, whose logic was meant to dissolve architecture into a pure engineering process. Dom-ino marked the beginning of Le Corbusier's architectural grammar, which would be crystallized in his famous five points—among which the most important was the *plan libre* defined by the decoupling of structure and partition. More fundamentally, Dom-ino was the threshold between architecture freed from any symbolic association—but still endowed with its plastic presence—and architecture reduced to the logic of its technical building process.[18] Although Benjamin endorsed Le Corbusier's architecture as the embodiment of the destruction of experience, Le Corbusier's buildings eventually recuperated "experience" by pursuing architecture as plastic gesture which became the very leitmotiv of his oeuvre.

A Metropolis of Barbarians

While Le Corbusier withdrew from the radical implications of the framework of industrial concrete, Ludwig Hilberseimer pushed the logic of this building system to its utmost conclusion. In 1925, Kurt Schwitters published Hilberseimer's book *Grosstadtbauten*, a small pamphlet that condensed the themes more thoroughly developed in the book *Grosstadtarchitektur*, published in 1927. Unlike the more famous book, which was an overview of the day's most advanced architecture, the small pamphlet focused only on Hilberseimer's projects, prefaced by a concise and lucid exposition of his thesis on architecture and its relationship with the modern metropolis. In the second chapter, Hilberseimer presented the important thesis (which would appear in the first chapter of *Grosstadtarchitektur*) that there was a grand divide between the traditional city and the metropolis, since the latter is the product of capitalistic accumulation.[19] While this was an obvious observation in the field of political economy, it was a novel and unprecedented statement in architecture and urbanism, because, with few notable exceptions, most of the literature on city-making situated the metropolis as a mere enlargement of the historical city. Contrary to this assumption, Hilberseimer claimed that the difference between the historical and the "new" city was not simply quantitative but also—and especially—qualitative. For Hilberseimer, capitalistic accumulation was more than a concentration of people and goods. It was a distinct mode of production founded on the division of labor and driven by profit. A member of the German Social Democratic Party, he was influenced by the revisionist theses put forward by Eduard Bernstein for whom capitalism—once tamed by state legislation—could become a means to achieve socialism. For Bernstein, it was the moment of circulation and distribution—and not production—that had to be reformed in order to evenly allocate the profits of capitalistic accumulation.[20] From this perspective, economic and spatial planning were seen as critical to a more "rational" reorganization of capitalism. It is in this context that Hilberseimer grounded his approach, with the ultimate goal of designing buildings not as singular events but as "gears" within a comprehensive plan for the city.

In *Grosstadtbauten* he presented a series of his own designs as exemplary projects, including rowhouses, a single-family house, a block made of rental housing, a mixed-used building that combined housing and workspaces, an office building, and a boardinghouse. He also proposed two urban schemes, one for fig. 6.2 a satellite city and one—the famous Vertical City developed in 1924—which represented the culmination of his project for the city. Each project responded to a belief that the three vital elements emerging in the capitalist city were housing, offices, and the factory. While he did not present any projects for the factory apart from his proposal for a mixed-use high-rise/factory building, its architectural and structural system dominated many of the designs presented in *Grosstadtbauten*. This influence is evident in one of the most striking projects presented in the book: Hilberseimer's theoretical project for the 1922 Chicago Tribune headquarters. His project consisted of two rectangular towers fig. 6.3 placed on a block. The structure is visible on the façade and the even fenestration renders the composition of volumes as one monolithic entity. Yet the most revealing feature of the project is the plan, which consists of a large unobstructed space punctuated only by load-bearing columns and elevators. Hilberseimer is here appropriating and further radicalizing the typical plan of American skyscrapers, but unlike many extant examples of early twentieth-century high-rises, his building façade is not clad with motives other than the simple projection of the internal structure. In doing so, Hilberseimer refers to the "literal" logic of Albert Kahn's factories like the Old Shop at Ford's Highland Park Plant, where the internal structural bay is directly projected onto the façade. Appropriation of the factory's architecture for buildings conceived for white-collar work reflects an emerging social tendency in Germany during the Weimar Republic: the rise and proletarization of the white-collar worker known as the *Kopfarbeiter*, the brainworker—a clear forerunner of the contemporary knowledge worker.[21] This subjectivity became prevalent in large cities like Berlin, where unprecedented numbers of press, administrative, and service jobs were available. The *Kopfarbeiter*'s condition was the focus of unions close to the German Social Democratic party, who saw the rise of this type of worker as part of a larger process of proletarization of the middle class.[22]

Within this societal trend Hilberseimer applied the architecture of the factory to office space. The typical plan of the factory—with its minimum of vertical elements—served to foster constant adjustment of the assembly line, thus its use in the landscape of the office could accommodate the volatile spatial demands of more immaterial forms of work. Anticipating the *Bürolandschaft*—the open office plan of the 1940s—Hilberseimer envisioned a plan for the Chicago Tribune building hospitable to radically flexible labor conditions, where everything but the building's structure was movable or adaptable. The typical plan of his Chicago Tribune building is thus rendered "empty": yet this emptiness was far from empty. Architecture could only provide a minimum definition to the multitude of activities that would ultimately fill the plan. Hilberseimer's reductive method of abstracting architecture to structure and envelope was not a search for pure form but rather a desire to reckon with the ever-changing nature of the metropolis. This attitude cannot be separated from his active role as an art and architecture critic, a commitment which guided the conceptual background for his work as a designer. In particular, his interest in and praise of the abstract cinema of Hans Richter and Viking Eggeling—which reduced the filmic experience to an elemental language devoid of any naturalistic or mimetic connotations—clearly resonated with his own design trajectory.[23] Hilberseimer noted how Richter and Eggeling intensified the experience of polarity by counterposing simple geometric forms, thereby establishing a process in which individuals could arrive at a unity of experience out of a multiplicity of sensations. This remark is notable because it suggests that in Hilberseimer's work, unity is not proposed an a priori form but as a counterweight to the differentiated experience of the metropolis. Form can only attempt to contain and organize, not express, the dissonant programs and activities of the city.

Here emerges the fundamental difference between Hilberseimer's (and Mies's) approach to form and the approach of abstract artrists such as Theo van Doesburg and El Lissitzky in their architectural work. In projects like the Maison Particulière

fig. 6.4

6.2 Ludwig Hilberseimer, proposal for a boardinghouse, 1924.
© Ryerson and Burnham Art and Architecture Archives.

6.3 Ludwig Hilberseimer, proposal for the Chicago Tribune headquarters, Chicago, 1922, perspective. © Ryerson and Burnham Art and Architecture Archives.

by Van Doesburg and Van Eesteren, the neoplastic free play of vertical and horizontal datums is applied to a private house without consideration of program of structure. In contrast, Hilberseimer's elementarism operated as a container of given conditions. As stated in *Grosstadtbauten*, rather than approach architecture as a sculptural pursuit, he routinely started from the most abstract and yet concrete datum of architecture: the plan. For Hilberseimer the plan was a concrete abstraction because it not only formalized the conditions of land use (i.e., the parcelization of the land) but also elaborated the use of the building. The relationship between land use and the programmatic condition of the singular building was, indeed, the very object of Hilberseimer's design. A preoccupation with both factors is evident in his proposal for a satellite town, where he reinterprets Ebenezer Howard's garden city model. In this project, Hilberseimer reintroduces collective ownership of the land, a critical premise of Howard's theory that was lost when garden cities were realized as suburbs. For Hilberseimer this communal model of land tenure allowed the settlement to be rationally planned as a uniform distribution of blocks consisting of housing organized in bars. This organization not only increased sun exposure and ventilation, but also improved the layout of the housing unit. Hilberseimer conceived of housing as a linear composition of apartments where the only fixed elements were entries, vertical circulation, and wet walls for bathrooms and kitchens: everything else was considered movable. A highly flexible apartment was thus realized, where different rooms could merge to become larger spaces. Additionally, much of the furniture was designed following fabrication techniques employed in American hotels and the cabins of transatlantic liners. The bedrooms, conceived as *Schlafkabine*, also evoked a ship's cabin in that they were only large enough to accommodate sleeping. In Hilberseimer's satellite city the fig. 6.5 coherent organization of the whole urban system subsumed the individuality of buildings in the logic of planning, defined by the imperative of rational land use and the standardization of both design and construction.

This attitude toward the planning of the city and its archi- fig. 6.6 tecture was further developed in what would become his most well-known project: Vertical City, proposed in 1924. This proposal

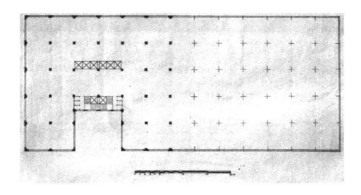

6.4 Ludwig Hilberseimer, proposal for the Chicago Tribune headquarters, Chicago, 1922, plan. © Ryerson and Burnham Art and Architecture Archives.

offered a critique of both the high-rise and the satellite city projects. Hilberseimer recognized that the typologies of his past projects, despite having some advantages, were products of speculation: while the narrow footprint of the high-rise maximized land value, the satellite city sought the cheapest land available. In Vertical City, Hilberseimer reorganized the metropolis by compacting its residential and working areas into an extremely dense settlement surrounded by green areas. The settlement was made by the repetition of a single block composed of three layers: workshops and offices on the bottom, retail and restaurants in the middle, and housing on the top. While the lower level conformed to the rectangular gridiron like a traditional perimeter block, the upper level—the housing—was made of north-south-oriented slabs. Vertical City was distinguished by the overlapping of functions, made possible by zoning laws that developed in the early twentieth century. Hilberseimer advanced this solution to resolve what he considered the most pressing problem of the large metropolis: commuter traffic between center and periphery. In *Grosstadtarchitektur* he presented Vertical City as a critique of Le Corbusier's theoretical model for a City of Three Million Inhabitants proposed in 1922.[24] Hilberseimer argued that the separation of housing and workspaces in Le Corbusier's model would drastically reduce the city's capacity to handle traffic. Beyond the pragmatic issue of traffic, the differences between the two city models were both subtler and more substantial. Le Corbusier's City of Three Million Inhabitants was a composition of different building typologies—Cartesian skyscrapers, the *redents* blocks of flats, and the *immeubles-villas*, stacked villas ordered in a classical concentric manner. Hilberseimer's Vertical City, on the contrary, was a repetition of the same typology that sectionally combined the total program of the metropolis. Further, Le Corbusier's housing typologies demonstrated rather traditional household arrangements and addressed the family as the main subject, while Hilberseimer offered flexible apartments that resembled the units of a residential hotel. A relevant aspect of the German middle class in the 1920s was its mobility, which expressly impacted large cities like Berlin, the metropolitan scale clearly referenced in Vertical City. Hilberseimer's proposal both accommodated and accelerated this condition of mobility, pushing its underlying "indifference"

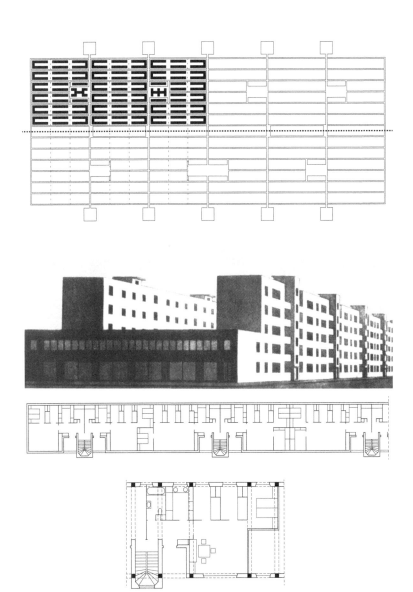

6.5 Ludwig Hilberseimer, proposal for a satellite town, 1922, plans and perspective view.
Plans © Dogma, adapted from Ludwig Hilberseimer; perspective view
© Ryerson and Burnham Art and Architecture Archives.

6.6 Ludwig Hilberseimer, proposal for Vertical City, 1914, north-south perspective.
© Ryerson and Burnham Art and Architecture Archives.

to place to its limit. In his celebrated essay on the metropolis, Georg Simmel claimed that "indifference" was the main attribute of human association in the city.[25] Supported by an even distribution of transport networks such as roads, trams, and trains, Vertical City is the embodiment of a postindustrial metropolis constituted by both constant flux and indifference, where the main productive activity is no longer large-scale manufacturing but services and tertiary work. Hilberseimer reduced architecture to a bare minimum—to its structure—as an attempt to frame the scale and complexity of the metropolis and order it according to sheer rational criteria. In amplifying the extreme bluntness of rational structure, Hilberseimer embraced the essence of the barbarian's metropolis and rejected "the traditional, solemn, noble image of man, festooned with all sacrificial offerings of the past."[26] The starkness of Hilberseimer's work evokes a "posthumanism"[27] opposed to the grand visions of the modern metropolis. Urban reform is proposed with a realist attitude that accepts the poverty of experience of modernity and eradicates nostalgia for previous urban and architectural attachments.

Abstracting the Interior

More than any other scholar, Benjamin focused on the bourgeois domestic interior as the paradigmatic form of capitalist society. While Marx described the evolution of private property as a political and economic historical process written "in letters of blood and fire," Benjamin saw private property evolving more subtly, but no less harmfully, in the ideology of bourgeois *decorum*. After experience was emptied and abstracted by life in the industrial metropolis, cultivating the nineteenth-century interior became the *purpose* for dwelling. As noted in his famous essay "The Paris of the Second Empire in Baudelaire," since the days of the citizen-king Louis-Philippe, the bourgeoisie desperately sought to compensate for the inconsequential nature of private life in the big city by indulging in the interior design of the private apartment.[28] For the bourgeois inhabitant, domestic space became the illusion of individual personality against the anonymity of the city. Against this style of dwelling, Benjamin imagined a "traceless" way of living so as to liberate the city dweller from the trap of domesticity, not only economically and politically but also, and above all, anthropologically. In one of his most subtle and radical *Denkbilder*, or thought images, written in 1931 (just before "Experience and Poverty," as his own life became increasingly precarious), Benjamin invoked the possibility of a "destructive character." This character "knows only one watchword: make room. And only one activity: clearing away. His need for fresh air and open space is stronger than any hatred."[29]

Benjamin's invocation to "make room" and "clear away" is embodied in the domestic interior of Hannes Meyer's *Co-op Interieur*, a photograph of a room staged by Meyer as part of a series of projects, artworks, exhibitions, and theater plays that he conceived between 1923 and 1926 as educational propaganda for the cooperative movement. The room was minimally furnished by Meyer himself using found products like a bed, a foldaway chair, a foldaway table, and a shelf holding jars. On the table was a gramophone whose exuberant form introduced a sense of enjoyment in what was otherwise a deliberately stark interior. In 1925 the German critic Adolf Behne used a cropped version of the photograph to accompany an article he wrote for the monthly magazine *UHU*, commenting that Meyer's room was "extreme" and not to everyone's taste.[30] Yet, for Meyer, *Co-op Interieur* was not a matter of taste but economy. He produced *Co-op Interieur* during a crucial period of his life, when he was gradually moving away from his involvement in the Swiss cooperative movement—for which he had designed Siedlung Freidorf in Basel from 1919 to 1921—and toward a more explicit Marxist position. The plain theatricality of *Co-op Interieur* was an extension of the scenography he designed for his *Theater Co-op* at the first International Cooperative Exhibition in Ghent in 1926. With *Theater Co-op*, Meyer staged a series of short vignettes displaying the domestic advantages of cooperation as against middle-class individualism. As in Bertolt Brecht's theater, Meyer wanted the audience not to stare romantically at the idyll of cooperativism but to assess this way of life and take a position. His article "The New World,"[31] for which *Co-op Interieur* was the main illustration, can be seen as Meyer's rejection of making art and architecture as an idealization of the world. In this article, which reads as an accelerationist manifesto, Meyer described the experience of modernity as driven by incessant

fig. 6.7

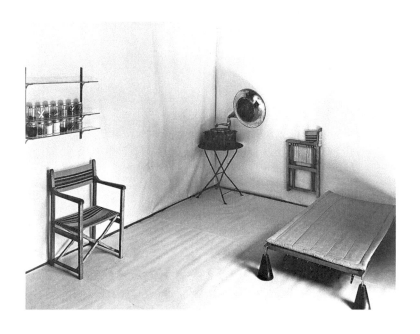

6.7 Hannes Meyer, *Co-op Interieur*, 1924. © Galerie Berinson.

technological development and increasing uniformity of human habits. Meyer also, and importantly, observed the intense form of socialization already evident in capitalism. As he wrote, "The standardization of mental fare is illustrated by the crowds going to see Harold Lloyd, Douglas Fairbanks and Jackie Coogan. . . . Trade unions, co-operatives, LTD., Inc, cartel, trust, and the League of Nations are the forms in which today's social conglomerations find expression; the radio and the rotary press are their media of communication. Co-operation rules the world. The community rules the individual."[32]

For Meyer, cooperation—social exchange—emerged from modes of production dependent on standardization of objects and human life. A fundamental aspect of this emerging subjectivity was the increased uprootedness and nomadism of metropolitan living, as workers roamed from place to place, from city to city, from nation to nation. Meyer himself was living such a life, constantly traveling through different European countries such as Belgium, France, and Germany, often living in hotel rooms.[33] *Co-op Interieur* thus reflects an uprooted way of life, and as such it remains a hauntingly enigmatic image. It is not clear whether Meyer's *mise-en-scène* is the promise of a better life or the merciless description of an increasingly atomized and precarious existence. Even if dominated by capital, Meyer argued in his article, standardization and uniformity of life were evidence that "cooperation rules the world." Outside these explicit claims, Meyer's *Co-op Interieur* can also be understood as a critique of domestic space. Rather than illustrate his manifesto with the design of a new city, Meyer addressed the most intimate yet most common space of the modern metropolis: the private room. While architects like Le Corbusier or Hilberseimer always presented their interiors within specific housing typologies that suggest established forms of life and kinship networks, Meyer proposed the *Co-op Interieur* as a universal space for a generic worker. Moreover, the name of the room made it clear that this unit was part of a cooperative where, presumably, other domestic functions such as cleaning, childcare, and cooking were no longer assigned to the family but instead were professionalized and undertaken by a communal organization. Here lies the most important and radical aspect of *Co-op Interieur*: its rejection of domestic conventions such as gendered furniture or specific forms of interior decoration. By keeping the room as abstract and generic as possible Meyer challenged the very idea of the interior that, according to Benjamin, forced the inhabitant "to adopt the greatest number of habits—habits that do more justice to the interior he is living in than to himself."[34]

In *Co-op Interieur*, the attributes that contributed to the individualization of the modern laboring subject—male, female, adult, child, wife, husband, parents and siblings, master and servants—were gone. Meyer's room stood against the *Existenz-minimum* promoted by the CIAM architects, who attempted to reduce the typical family apartment to a minimum dimension and set of functions. As the fragile enclosure of the *Co-op Interieur* conveyed, the single dweller exhibits a mentality that is always open to new forms of collective association that may well exceed the juridical framework into which human association is inscribed by law. Its genericness and anonymity promised its inhabitant the possibility of a life liberated from the anguish and the burden of the enduring obligation of ownership. *Co-op Interieur* can be imagined dialectically, as both the rendering of an increasingly precarious domestic life and as a space for anyone—a universal basic right. Against a life encased by false and shallow images of dwelling, Meyer embraced abstraction as liberation from domestic life and its enduring tropes of possession and privacy.

From the second half of the nineteenth century, under the pressure of workers' uprisings, capitalists and governments were increasingly concerned with "housing" workers. In Victorian England, philanthropists and social reformers proposed housing models to confine the working class to ordered households. At the core of these models, such as those illustrated in the influential pamphlet *The Dwellings of the Labouring Classes* written by the American architect Henry Roberts in 1851, was the introduction of workers to petit bourgeois values. This spatial pedagogy was achieved by proposing housing layouts that individuated the nuclear family by subdividing the house into rooms with specialized functions. A central objective of this model was to privatize the household by providing a bathroom and a scullery in every unit, so that families had no need to share space or to collectivize their work outside their home. Furthermore, the ultimate purpose was to domesticate the working-class family and secure the reproduction of workers' labor power. A primary target of this process of domestication was women, whose role in the home provided unwaged reproductive labor. As argued by Maria Mies, the transformation of women into housewives dependent on the income of their husbands became the model for the sexual division of labor under capitalism.[35] While social reformers in the United States, England, and Germany expected reproductive labor to be provided as a labor of love, women's movements such as Bund Deutscher Frauenvereine pushed for the recognition of reproduction as a proper working activity, and for a consequent reorganization of the dwelling.[36] For both the bourgeois and the socialist wings of the German women's movement, it was increasingly clear that the house was a workplace in its own right, and this conception of it as a site of labor conflicted with the romantic image of the home as cozy abode.

The need to rationalize housekeeping alongside the general architecture of the house became even more explicit when, in countries like Germany, women started to enter the job market and had less time for domestic tasks. In facing this reality, debates about housekeeping referenced books like Christine Frederick's *Household Engineering: Scientific Management in the Home*, published in 1915 and translated into German in 1922. Frederick argued for a rationalization of the home in order to drastically reduce women's laboring efforts, and yet, as has been noted, her understaning of women's role was conservative at best: she represented women as efficient housewives and, above all, as expert consumers of domestic products.[37] Frederick came from a long tradition of middle-class feminism that started with Catharine Beecher's influential *The American Woman's Home* (1869), which introduced the discipline of home economics as the parallel to what Beecher perceived as a male-dominated political economy. The goal of home economics was not liberation from domestic chores, as later advocated by many feminists, but the rationalization of women's role as housewives.[38] For this reason, Beecher proposed to transform the typical single-family cottage into a machine for living *ante litteram*, featuring built-in drawers and movable partitions and where the kitchen was the main infrastructure of the house. Imagined as the cook's galley of a steamship with walls made of open shelves, this kitchen was defined by Beecher as a "workshop," making explicit the productive nature of this space. Frederick further developed home economics by referencing Frederick Winslow Taylor's management studies for the workplace, aiming to shorten the time necessary to perform specific tasks. Like Beecher, Frederick focused her domestic reform on the kitchen, where she proposed a compact grouping of equipment in order to minimize movements across the room and to ease cleaning and maintenance.

It was precisely this process of mechanization and rationalization of kitchen work that inspired the most famous model of the rational kitchen: Margarete Schütte-Lihotzky's Frankfurt kitchen, designed in 1926 for the workers' houses built under the Neue Frankfurt program directed by Ernst May. Schütte-Lihotzky was not new to the task of designing kitchens; prior to her involvement with Neue Frankfurt, she had worked on two kitchen models as part of the Social Democratic Party's efforts to support the settlers' movement in Vienna. In 1923, Schütte-Lihotzky contributed to the "Small Garden, Settlement and Housing" exhibition, which featured the achievements of the Viennese settler movement, by designing three settlement homes, titled *core houses*—"Type 4," "Type 7," and "Type 52." These types were all conceived as modular structures that expanded as the number of household members increased, and featured standardized furniture that was at odds with the self-building and ad hoc ethos of the Viennese settlers. Schütte-Lihotzky designed two versions of the kitchen: the live-in kitchen and the cooking niche. In both models she attempted to compact all of the kitchen equipment into one block, not only to facilitate cooking and cleaning operations, but also so that the kitchen could be purchased as a single prefabricated block. While the design of the live-in kitchen retained the image of the traditional kitchen, the elements of the cooking niche, including the floor, were poured in a block of concrete. Despite its rational organization, the live-in kitchen model retained, through its vernacular image, its symbolism as the "hearth" of the house, while the cooking niche rendered the kitchen as merely utilitarian infrastructure, whose materiality and shape denied the dweller's expectation of the quintessential domestic core. As noted above, Schütte-Lihotzky's approach to kitchen design, especially evident in the cooking niche, clashed with the settlers' self-building habits. The Viennese settler movement arose amidst

fig. 6.8

the economic scarcity which followed the end of the First World War. Members of the movement were directly involved in the production of their own abodes, which allowed them to reclaim the very act of *dwelling*. Schütte-Lihotzky's prefabricated kitchen presumed the industrial manufacture of home components and thus the radical depersonalization of the house interior. Besides being expensive, her kitchen models, especially the cooking niche, stripped domestic labor of its sentimental and symbolic value, making them unpopular among the settlers.[39]

While both Viennese kitchens were conceived as part of the living room, the most notable feature of the subsequent Frankfurt model was its arrangement as a room of its own. The kitchen consisted of a small space in which all furniture and appliances—stove, cooling counter, haybox, fold-out ironing board, dish drainer, cupboard, sink, and plate frame—were located along the walls, making the walls an infrastructure that women could operate while sitting on a rotating stool, like an industrial machine operator. Schütte-Lihotzky designed the disposition of the appliances by measuring movements with a stopwatch, a quantifying technique similar to those used in factories to increase the productivity of workers.[40] To make it affordable, the whole kitchen was prefabricated and could be reassembled. This reproducible approach followed the Neue Frankfurt program, devised by May in order to produce a large number of houses in a relatively short time. Schütte-Lihotzky designed the kitchen as a confined cabin where one spent as little time as possible. Besides rationalizing the kitchen, she wanted to eliminate the sentimentality that had historically naturalized domestic labor as the duty of the housewife and her "labor of love." By industrializing and prefabricating the kitchen, Schütte-Lihotzky made explicit the productive nature of domestic labor as "reproduction"; and yet, by proposing a kitchen that could be embedded in each private household, the Austrian architect also confirmed the housewife as an isolated worker, prisoner of the domestic compound. The segregation of the kitchen from the living room further isolated women from the rest of the household. For this reason the design was met with resistance by working-class women.

The Frankfurt kitchen demonstrates the ability of industrialization and mechanization to abstract even the most resilient

6.8 Margarete Schütte-Lihotzky, Frankfurt kitchen, 1926. In *Die Deutsche Wohnung der Gegenwart* (Königstein im Taunus: Langewiesche, 1930). © The Museum of Modern Art/ Licensed by SCALA / Art Resource, NY.

remnant of traditional dwelling—the kitchen. Ultimately, this process of abstraction, where the movement of the housewife was calibrated by geometry and time, reinforced the traditional scene of bourgeois households, where modernization coincided with the naturalization of the nuclear family whose reproduction was dependent on the unpaid labor of women.

The City as Factory

Ludwig Hilberseimer's Vertical City, Hannes Meyer's *Co-op Interieur*, and Margarete Schütte-Lihotzky's kitchens revealed that the logic of mass production was no longer confined to the factory but had in fact penetrated every aspect of human life, thus mobilizing the entire spectrum of social relationships. Their merciless depiction of all-encompassing industrial existence prompted many postwar architects to adopt a more humanist approach to architecture. In the aftermath of World War II, architects, including those affiliated with the revisionist group Team X, continued the reformist premises of modern architecture within the social and economic reality of the European welfare state but attempted to recuperate "dwelling experience," something they believed had been lost in the ethos of interwar modernism. This altruistic intention is evident in projects like Alison and Peter Smithson's competition entry for the Golden Lane social housing estate designed from 1959 to 1962 or Aldo van Eyck's Municipal Orphanage in Amsterdam designed and built between 1955 and 1960. Both projects exemplify how these architects attempted to counter the abstraction of modernist architecture by introducing a nuanced formal approach that aimed to express the dweller's embodied use of space. In both projects, features such as galleries, domes, and playgrounds were not just functional spaces but forms meant to spatially augment the user's experience. As Alison Smithson wrote, "My act of form-giving has to invite the occupiers to add their intangible quality of use."[41]

Against this humanist reinvention of architecture stood the Italian group of architects known as Archizoom, whose body of work consisted mostly of theoretical projects. Archizoom did not retreat from the industrial logic of society but attempted to make this logic visible as the dominant reality of welfare state capitalism. Officially founded in Florence in 1966, Archizoom's conceptual premises were defined in 1963 when some of its founding members worked together in a design studio at the school of architecture in Florence and produced a project titled Città Estrusa (the Extruded City). The studio brief tasked students to design new premises for the school of architecture at Sesto Fiorentino, between Florence and Prato, in the so-called *piana* or plains, a place that, at that time, was saturated by small-scale textile factories. Archizoom's response to both brief and context was to imagine the new school of architecture as a "knowledge factory," thus equating the university to the burgeoning industrial character of its context.[42] Inspired by Le Corbusier's linear housing structure for Algiers—the Plan Obus proposed in the early 1930s—Archizoom imagined the school of architecture as a linear structure that connected the most important functions of the *piana*—school, housing, and factories—as one coherent urban system. Archizoom rejected the idea of the university as an autonomous institution, divided into departments and contained within its campus. Instead, they conceived the new project as an overarching productive system that organized work and leisure, education and housing. The goal of this project was to "extrude" the productive logic of the city itself. As future Archizoom member Gilberto Corretti wrote about Città Estrusa, "The concept of the project is banal, and it comes from the idea of the city understood as the transmission belt that unites into one system the territory between Florence and Prato. . . . Città Estrusa is the extrusion of all the urban entities of the contemporary productive apparatus."[43]

A year before Città Estrusa, the Italian philosopher and communist militant Mario Tronti published, in the second issue of *Quaderni Rossi*, a long essay titled "The Factory and Society," in which he argued that, with the advancement of capital, all social relationships had come under the domination of the productive logic of the factory. In this essay—which became seminal for the movement known as Operaismo and was an important text for Archizoom members—Tronti argued that the more capitalism advances, the more it needs to incorporate and control all aspects of labor power, both inside and outside the workplace.[44] Not just production but also distribution, exchange, and consumption become moments of a process that transforms all of society into an extended factory. For Tronti, this was not necessarily bad for workers, because the extensive domination of the factory over society implied not just capital's domination but also—and especially—the *possibility* of the working class's power. Tronti saw the development of capital as the result of workers' struggle: the more workers challenged capital, the more capital had to develop and incorporate all of society within its workings. Therefore, capitalist development was the measure of working-class power. Through political organization, capital's apparent power could be reconstituted as workers' power. Tronti maintained that capital at its highest form of development offered workers the possibility of taking power over the factory and therefore over society itself. This thesis was advanced at the apex of welfare state politics in Italy, which, in the span of a decade—between the 1950s and 1960s—turned the country into an economy largely based on industry. This condition gave rise to a new "alienated" working-class subjectivity, no longer driven by the traditional values of socialism but by the ethos of an increasingly consumerist attitude that the Operaists aimed to harness for revolution. The Operaists called this new subjectivity the *mass worker*, represented by the workers of the assembly line, completely indifferent to their job and seeking "to earn more and work less." Tronti and the Operaists declared this subject "a rough pagan race,"[45] because its ethos was the outcome of a social condition in which the old "humanist" aspirations of both liberalism and socialism were collapsing under the pressure of intense industrial development. In a sense, the Operaists' rough pagan race was a new embodiment of Benjamin's barbarian.

It was Tronti's thesis that inspired the Florentine students to conceive of the city as a large-scale assembly line. Instead of designing a city for an alternative political or economic system, the future members of Archizoom chose to depict the existing reality of the capitalist city with unrelenting realism. Città Estrusa can thus be considered an anticipation of Archizoom's most important theoretical project: No-Stop City, conceived from 1970 to 1972. Initially titled City as Assembly Line of Social Facts and published with this title for the first time in the magazine *Casabella* in 1970,[46] No-Stop City consists of a series of drawings that depict a vast hypostyle space occasionally populated by freestanding walls, topographical elements, and furniture. For Archizoom, No-Stop City was not meant to be a proposal, nor a utopian vision of a future and better society, but the radicalization *ad absurdum* of the existing capitalist city. A scenario where capital reached its final stage of complete social colonization was imagined as an urban system devoid of any limit and form, thus capable of becoming ubiquitous. In terms of architecture this condition was expressed as the overlapping of the three main *topoi* of the capitalist city: the factory, the parking lot, and the supermarket. For this reason, Archizoom reduced the city to an endless interior built like a factory, artificially lit and mechanically ventilated. The group first tested this design strategy in 1968 in a competition proposal for the reuse of the Fortezza da Basso, the sixteenth-century Florentine fortress designed by Antonio da Sangallo the Younger for duke Alessandro de' Medici. The competition brief asked participants to adapt the fortress for use by the national craftsmen's association as an exhibition space. For their project, Archizoom filled the entire pentagonal enclosure of the fortress with an industrial shed, designed with a "typical plan" that clearly referred to the architecture of the factory. Archizoom presented this project as an attempt to create an architecture of vast empti-ness capable of accommodating any program. The building itself was reduced to prefabricated steel elements to achieve an utmost generic and indifferent kind of architecture.

In 1970, this approach was translated into a series of dia-grams that Archizoom members drew with a typewriter in an effort to mimic the style of a computer drawing. One of these drawings, *Diagramma abitativo omogeneo* (*Homogeneous Housing Diagram*), was posited as a "hypothesis for a nonfigurative archi-tectural language." The drawing, a repetitive grid of periods punctuated by Xs (each of which represents a load-bearing ele-ment), insinuated an understanding of the city as a continuous, inhabitable expanse, with no divisions between interior and exterior spaces. In this vision of the city, there are no more rooms, houses, blocks, streets, piazzas, parks, or monuments. This is an urban landscape broken down to its most rudimentary parts: a column every 5 meters, a bathroom every 10 meters, a lift every 50 meters. This conceptual "nonfigurative" city was later trans-lated into a series of 20 drawings called the *Nondiscontinuous and*

fig. 6.9
fig. 6.10

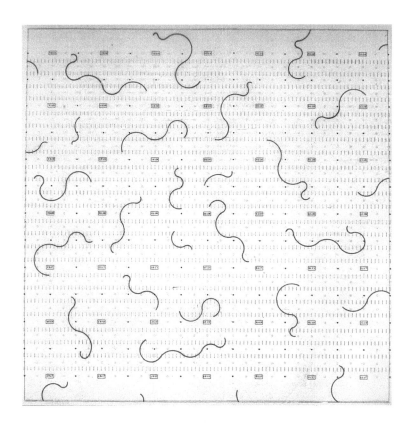

6.9 Archizoom Associati, No-Stop City, 1970–1972, plan. © Andrea Branzi.

ARCHIZOOM ASSOCIATI
DIAGRAMMA ABITATIVO
OMOGENEO

IPOTESI DI LINGUAGGIO
ARCHITETTONICO NON FIGURATIVO

struttura montante.

maglia dimensionale.

6.10 Archizoom Associati, *Homogeneous Housing Diagram*, 1970. © Andrea Branzi.

Homogeneous City and constituted the bulk of the first published presentation of the project in *Casabella*. In these drawings, which can be understood as variations of the concepts notated in the typewriter diagrams, Archizoom appropriated the structural logic of Mies van der Rohe's 1929 Barcelona Pavilion, made of a grid of columns and freestanding walls, and expanded it as a continuous field. Another iteration of No-Stop City was conceived by Archizoom in response to a competition held for the building of the new University of Florence campus located in the same plains for which Città Estrusa was designed. Archizoom proposed to cover the plains with a homogeneous grid made of transportation lines that granted access to a series of large multistory containers. One of the competition panels compared the section of No-Stop City with other canonical urban models such as Haussmann's Paris, Le Corbusier's Unité d'Habitation, and Peter Cook's Plug-in City, demonstrating how Archizoom's model was no longer a city made of buildings but a continuous, homogeneous habitat, a "city without architecture."[47] In this respect, No-Stop City was an elaboration of Hilberseimer's Vertical City, where the endlessly repeatable stacking of housing, offices, and recreational activities within the same block posited an idea of the city as a totalizing productive apparatus. Archizoom knew Hilberseimer's project because it was discussed by Manfredo Tafuri in his seminal essay "Per una critica dell'ideologia architettonica" published in the Operaist journal *Contropiano*.[48] For Tafuri, Hilberseimer completely accepted capitalism's integration of urban life in its cycle of production. Analyzing Hilberseimer's project for the city, Tafuri wrote:

> Once the true unity of the production cycle has been identified in the city, the only task the architect can have is to organize the cycle. Taking this proposition to its extreme conclusion, Hilberseimer insists on the role of elaborating "organizational models" as the only one that can fully reflect the need for Taylorizing building production, as the new task of the technician, who is now completely integrated into this process. For Hilberseimer, the object was not in crisis because it had already disappeared from his spectrum of considerations.[49]

Archizoom's No-Stop City was thus the allegory of an urban condition defined not by architecture but by the organization of technical components within a continuous plan. Yet, unlike Hilberseimer's Vertical City, No-Stop City indicated not the advent of a supremely rational civilization, but the counterpart of capitalist development: the unlimited growth of working-class power as a "wild reality" within and against the unlimited expansion of capitalist development. Following the Operaists' belief that capitalist development is driven by workers' struggle, Archizoom wrote that No-Stop City reflects the working class as a force that "represents both a leap forward and the obscure intent of a foreign body within a rational mechanism."[50] For Archizoom, the relentless homogeneity of No-Stop City aimed not at maximum rationality but at making "the brain of the system mad," so that workers—through both their total integration within the system and their refusal of work—could interrupt the continuity of the productive process.

The ultimate iteration of No-Stop City was No-Work City, which Archizoom developed in the form of neutral interiors sparsely populated by misplaced furniture that suggested multiple forms of inhabitation. The rooms of No-Work City are a radical critique of the home as the ultimate place of work, the locus of the reproduction of the labor force itself. Archizoom was aware that industrial design contributed enormously to the naturalization of domestic labor by transforming the home into a microfactory, or, in Le Corbusier's words, a "machine for living." Designs such as Schütte-Lihotzky's Frankfurt kitchen eased reproductive labor and preserved the presence of the kitchen (and its labor) within the home. The neutral rooms of No-Work City further developed the abstraction and hedonism of Meyer's *Co-op Interieur*, arriving at interiors barren of quality or form where poverty of experience consisted in unlearning the urban and domestic habits that made dwellers productive. In one interior, a bust of Marx was juxtaposed with rows of beds, representing workers' emancipation and characterizing sleep as the ultimate refusal of work.

Toward Computational Abstraction

Although produced through analog means, the drawings for No-Stop City—especially the typewriter diagrams—were meant to imitate computer graphics, suppressing both virtuosity and the authorial aura of the architect's hand drawing to approximate the statistical aesthetic of the city-as-factory. The typewriter diagrams for No-Stop City are similar to maps produced more or less at the same time by the Landscape Architecture Research Office (LARO) fig. 6.11 based in the landscape architecture program at Harvard University. LARO was among the first design groups to experiment with computer graphics and sophisticated means of digital mapping.[51] Their maps synthesized coherent graphic systems of information on surveyed territories by inscribing empirical evidence in a grid cell pattern. In these maps, geographic and social issues were rendered through continuous fields where pattern variations replaced delineated marks. Crucial in both Archizoom's plans and LARO'S maps is the rendering of the urban field not through cadastral lines, as in modern cartography, but through patterns. This apparently minor graphic detail signaled a paradigm shift in urban representation. With massive quantities of data to be managed and translated into a coherent representational system, patterns became more instrumental than line drawings. While cadastral lines delineated each topographical feature according to its specific singularity, patterns imposed a statistical homogeneity on reality, implying that any geographical or social issue could be translated into the abstraction of numerical or alphabetic symbols.

As Catherine F. McMahon has argued, the emergence of mapping techniques, such as those elaborated by LARO, was a reaction to the many conflicts that erupted in the 1960s, as states and corporations were eager to equip themselves with predictive machines to survey and tame these conflicts.[52] It is not by chance that the golden age of early computer research, both in the United States and in Europe, was contemporaneous with intense workers' struggles and the civil rights movements. In this context of permanent instability, the objectivity of computing and its potential ubiquity were harnessed as an effective form of governance and, unsurprisingly, most of the research in the field was heavily funded by the state. Laboratories at major academic powerhouses including Harvard, MIT, and Stanford all received federal funding.[53]

Computational governance in the form of cybernetics—computer science applied to a vast range of fields from production to politics[54]—established a common ground for the seemingly opposed political policies of the welfare state and neoliberalism.[55] Whether they augmented or downplayed the role of the state with respect to market forces, both economic policies were informed by the possibility of reducing social complexity to measurable datasets.[56] Computation evolved as the ultimate "concrete abstraction" of late capitalism, in which all of life is reduced to data that informs the organization and governance of everything that exists, as exemplified by GIS cartography. Archizoom's No-Stop City presented urbanization as a continuous field of built equipment such as columns, elevators, and air-conditioning machines, while mapping systems such as GIS made urbanization a continuous field of fungible data to be extracted as commodities. Computing must then be understood not only as a technique that allowed institutions of power to manage large quantities of information and parameters, but also as an apparatus that facilitated the translation of everything into economic value.

Computation primarily entered the field of architecture through the adoption of CAD-CAM technologies, which originated in the aerospace industry and specifically in the manufacture of the Boeing 727 aircraft.[57] In the mid 1950s, Boeing's aerospace division equipped its factory with computers so experienced machinists, known as parts programmers, could translate engineering drawings into a series of simplified steps required to produce a part. As argued by historian Norman Sanders, it was these early CAM technologies that led to the development of CAD, and not the other way around as is commonly assumed.[58] Computer-aided design developed to allow engineers to fully control computer-aided manufacturing, bypassing the agency of machinists who were the first to operate computers in factories. CAM and CAD are both instances of the division between manual and intellectual labor, because these technologies removed control from the hands of the worker in the factory and expedited the passage from ideation to execution. CAD-CAM technologies certainly solidified design's control over manufacturing, but they also significantly enabled budget control over the design process. From the 1970s to the 1980s CAD-CAM technologies entered architectural design via corporate offices to increase production and better organize the division of labor among a multitude of

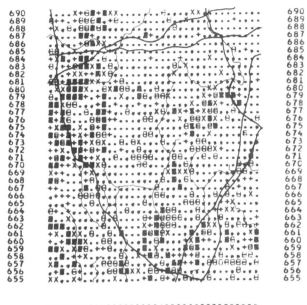

III.8.8 Ian L. McHarg

COMPOSITE:
CONSERVATION-RECREATION-URBANIZATION SUITABILITY

```
. 0 = Low Recreation/Low Conservation/Low Urban
, 2 = Low Recreation/High Conservation/Low Urban
+ 3 = Low Recreation/Low Conservation/High Urban
X 4 = Low Recreation/High Conservation/High Urban
O 5 = High Recreation/Low Conservation/Low Urban
θ 6 = High Recreation/High Conservation/Low Urban
⊖ 7 = High Recreation/Low Conservation/High Urban
■ 9 = High Recreation/High Conservation/High Urban
```

6.11 LARO (Landscape Architecture Research Office), Ian L. McHarg, composite land use analysis for conservation, recreation, and urbanization, 1969, original map by Ian L. McHarg. From Carl Steinitz, Timothy Murray, David Sinton, and Douglas Way, "A Comparative Study of Resources Analysis Methods," Landscape Architecture Research Office, Harvard University, 1969. Reproduced from Arindam Dutta, ed., *A Second Modernism: MIT, Architecture, and the "Techno-Social" Moment* (Cambridge, MA: MIT Press, 2013).

workers. Only after computing appeared in large-scale offices did it become a theoretical banner for avant-garde architects who, in the 1990s, attempted to translate computing's abstraction into an expressive language.[59] The work of this avant-garde became rapidly obsolete, as it relied on technologies that were soon surpassed. It was inevitable that "digital architecture" of the 1990s should have become anachronistic, not because computing lost relevance (far from that), but because these architects aimed to apply computation in the service of geometric virtuosity, which is precisely what advanced computation surpassed. In computation, geometric projection is replaced by an algebraic set of procedures.

Perhaps more than any other architect, Philippe Morel embraced the eclipse of geometric abstraction and worked with computation as a totalizing apparatus that annexed everything, including architecture. According to Morel, architecture in the future will be generated by computational procedures based in machinic "superintelligence" that have a scale and impact far beyond the capacity of human perception.[60] At the core of what Morel defines as "superintelligence" is *calculation*, which has an unrestrained power to abstract the world. For Morel, this computational intelligence, which is rooted in the very history of mathematical thought, is already forming an "artificial general intelligence" that integrates all existing knowledge into a universal system, stripping cognition of any anthropocentric or humanist pretension.[61] Morel maintains that this condition is not a sudden novelty, or "digital turn," but part of a five-century history of algebraic calculation that pushed quantification far beyond the limits of arithmetic and geometrical thinking.[62] Here lies Morel's most significant observation: no longer based on geometry, computation's more abstract algebraic logic represents the generalization of mathematical thought in any aspect of reality. Pivotal to this line of thinking is Alan Turing's seminal essay "On Computable Numbers, with an Application to the Entscheidungsproblem," which opened the possibility of a universal computing machine.[63] The calculating power of this machine cannot be reduced to any geometric thinking, thus making it impossible for architecture as a "visual" medium to represent reality with geometry. For Morel, architects should embrace the logic of the universal computing machine and give up the pretense of representational form. In a sense, Morel's project further develops Archizoom's No-Stop City by envisioning a reality where the world exists entirely under the spell of unrestrained computational possibilities. To support his thesis, Morel created a series of experimental prototypes that hint at the use of computation as a method of design. One of these prototypes is Universal House, which Morel's practice EZCT produced in 2009. Although this name suggests a relation fig. 6.12 to "classicist" theory, Universal House is neither "universal" in the essentialist or humanist sense nor a house understood as a traditional "domestic space." EZCT's Universal House represents the attempt to devise a generic integrated building system made of self-interlocking discrete blocks that can be arranged in any direction. The result is a gridlike architecture that can expand in any direction and can give form to any space or program. For Morel, only this fully abstracted architectural language lacking anthropocentric or representational features can embody the logic of a building organized by computational procedures. The gridded and pixel-like form of this prototype represents architecture reduced to an infinitesimal construction unit, capable of becoming any kind of inhabitable structure.

Universal House crucially rejects any form of composition outside its pattern-like order. Once this order is initiated, the architecture evolves in ways that are impossible to conceive in advance according to a *project*. According to Morel, human thought cannot compete with the capacity of machines to harness computational speed. A disconcerting experiment proposed by Morel is "Quantum Gray," a pattern generated using a true random number generator (based on quantum physics) directed against typical concepts of order and composition. The goal of this proposal is to uncover a design logic that eclipses the binary of geometry and informality in order to produce a pattern of "perfect inequality." This pattern ends design's multicentury relationship with rationality along with the possibility for human reason to plan the world through the act of projecting. Computation as a form of artificial intelligence limits architecture to mere patterning, systems of buildings and spaces strictly controlled by algebraic parameters missing a readable logic from the vantage of human perception. Morel proposes an architecture driven by computing logic that is "invisible," not because it disappears but because of its omnipresence across any built or virtual environment. In this context, the architect does not draw, does not even conceive any form, but simply manages patterns of data.

Here poverty of experience lies in the unviability of a design synthesis beyond the mere machinic order of computation. But philosopher Matteo Pasquinelli refutes the myth of computation as an autonomous form of intelligence dissociated from society and humans.[64] As he argues, computation is not an alien form of cognition, but rather an instrument of knowledge magnification that perceives features and patterns of correlation in vast spaces of information beyond human reach. Knowledge magnification is neither compelled by an immanent impetus from within computational knowledge itself nor value-free, but is in fact an extractive apparatus that serves the interest of capital. Still, Morel's understanding of architecture as mere pattern formation divulges the capacity of the discipline of architecture to be reified within the machinic logic of computation. For Morel, it is impossible for the human mind to deconstruct and comprehend computational procedures. For this reason, most operations escape us. "Behind each petabyte of data," argues Morel, "are hidden other petabytes, behind each algorithm, approximation, and rounding operation are hidden thousands, millions of other algorithms, approximations and rounding operations."[65] If Benjamin identified poverty of experience in a society saturated by information, today the same poverty of experience is discernible in the extreme redundancy of algorithms and data that organize our existence.

Confronted with new forms of poverty, and following the work of predecessors who abandoned the conceit of "humanity," like those discussed above, Morel invokes the submission of design to the merciless logic of computation. His recommendation is to be taken seriously, without forgetting that computation is not an autonomous logic, but one radical instance in the millennia-long history of the organization and division of labor. Though Morel maintains that an architecture of computational "superintelligence" is yet to be produced, it arguably already exists—and a glimpse of its material and economic logic is visible in the architecture of data centers. These structures are the ultimate "built" form of the computation age because they host connection and storage systems that cannot be individually possessed. Data

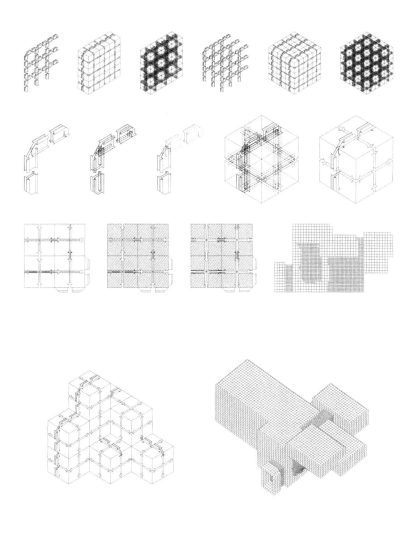

6.12 EZCT Architecture & Design Research, Universal House, 2009, isometric view.
© Philippe Morel.

centers originated as computer rooms, spaces dedicated to hosting the complex assemblage of racks, mainframes, and cables of early computing machines. These rooms became widespread with the advent of time-sharing operating systems, which allowed multiple computers to simultaneously share a major computer resource, or "server." The emergence of data centers, as they are known today, is directly linked with the rise of cloud computing, a form of digital sharing in which personal computers outsource computing power to large-scale hubs built in remote locations. As argued by Tung-Hui Hu,[66] the evolution of computer sharing from the emergence of time-sharing to cloud computing is enmeshed in the shift away from waged labor toward what Maurizio Lazzarato has defined as "immaterial labor"—an economy of flexible labor that includes myriad services and jobs, often unpaid, where production and delivery of information play a fundamental role.[67] The immaterial labor economy became pervasive with the advent of the internet and especially the "internet of things" that links many quotidian objects—from phones to cars—with computing devices. Thus the rise of the cloud is not only about technological innovation, but is a corollary to the technology necessary to maintain forms of labor based on freelancing and multitasking that can be performed everywhere and at any time. Yet, if cloud computing presents itself with an aura of immateriality in which our increasingly wireless technologies thrive undisturbed by the frictions of physical life, data centers as part of a vast network of physical infrastructures reveal the megastructural nature of our immaterial way of living and working.

The ubiquity of the ethereal internet paradoxically requires forms of extreme technological concentration and security in the form of data storages safely concealed within architecture. Data centers are perhaps the most elusive kind of building in the history of architecture. Often mythologized as generic architecture "without content," their built logic goes far beyond traditional parameters of design, such as order and form. Data centers are consequently impenetrable to analysis, largely because they are designed to host not humans but machines: humans are allowed in these extremely restricted areas only as controllers and caretakers. The architecture of data centers, in certain respects, belongs to the tradition of industrial architecture. As with the

fig. 6.13

250

architecture of factories, there is nothing symbolic about data centers; all elements conform to what the building does. Yet factories were often conceived and built according to a unifying modular system clearly manifested in the even distribution of the typical plan. The regularity of structure within factories was additionally instrumental in increasing the managers' control of workers. A panopticon effect is not required in spaces, like data centers, heavily controlled by cameras and minimally inhabited by humans. Data centers are instead assemblages of elements and spaces that cannot be reduced to a unifying building logic. While every element is standardized, the sum of these elements does not guarantee a legible whole. As noted by Pietro Bonomi and Nicolò Ornaghi, data centers reverse the traditional logic of modularity: a prefabricated and patented element or unit of a data center is conceived independently of the overall framework in which it is located.[68] Bringing elements together is a set of design protocols that mediates two conditions: the actual site and dimension of the data center and the layout of the machinery, which is organized according to a predefined layout that guarantees high levels of efficiency and security. Of utmost importance is security, a parameter fundamental to the data center as a successful financial enterprise.

In terms of architectural form, the data center is an illegible conglomerate of standardized elements that do not make a coherent whole. The architecture of data centers is both modular and ad hoc: their abstraction resides in the capacity to defy any notion of architectural order. Data centers do not have legible space or proportion. Their plans reveal a high degree of repetition (endless rows of server racks), and yet the overall composition is irreducible to the logic of one module or unit. To a certain extent, data centers revive the architecture of early factories, such as those built by the Portuguese Empire and the Dutch East India Company to ensure the logistics of their colonial trade.[69] As discussed in chapter 4, these factories functioned as places not for manufacturing but for storage. As such, they were strategically sited, heavily guarded, and their architecture was more concerned with efficiency and security than appearance. The common conception of data centers as "Platonic" abstract boxes is simply the projection of the indifferent appearance of their envelopes, which has nothing to do with what happens within the building. Envelopes are hermetically

6.13 Data center. Photo by Delfino Sisto Legnani, 2019. © Delfino Sisto Legnani.

defined not for aesthetic reasons, but simply to ensure a clear separation between inside and outside. Behind the blank façades of data centers lie inscrutable compositions of machines and a variety of technical equipment that cannot be discerned by a single individual. The intricacy of these interiors exceeds the division of knowledge because no individual, not even those directly involved in the design, building, and maintenance of data centers, can grasp the entirety of these infrastructures. Within these buildings, the elements that provide shelter are the least expensive equipment; consequently the term "architecture" references not the building but the organization of machinery within it. As Bonomi and Ornaghi argue, the architecture of data centers is purely technical, scattered, procedural, and is impossible to abstract into a concept or form.[70] A stable typological layout is therefore negated because the structure of data centers is constantly adapted to new requirements. Here we learn the true nature of architecture in the age of computation: generic standardized and replicable parts that come together in nontypological formations. The concept of type arose in the eighteenth century as an abstraction that allowed architects to reduce classes of buildings to general principles of spatial organization. Data centers resist the simplifying force of type and manifest a building logic that is beyond the conceptual reduction of abstraction. Instead, data centers induce abstraction, alienating the computer's user from computational machines. Of course, each computer is a machine, but within the internet of things, most of the computer's power is generated from servers which data centers conceal.

If Archizoom's No-Stop City and Morel's Universal House envisioned a building logic generic enough to incorporate everything that exists, data centers elude such overall order and manifest a condition that is deeply uneven and asymmetrical, a condition in which general principles succumb to the logic of financial maximization that results in an architecture of constant obsolescence and upgrade. The lack of legibility in the architecture of data centers parallels the main ideological principle of both neoliberalism and computation: the impossibility of reducing the world to a legible political order and the invocation of an unplannable but effective "cosmic order," the latter a concept advanced by early neoliberal thinkers against the paternalist and coercive order of the state. The so-called internet of things represents the technological embodiment of such a "cosmic order," and yet its implementation was far from "cosmic." As exposed in the architecture of data centers, the implementation of these infrastructures was impossible without an overt centralized and monopolistic economic and thus political power. An alliance between state and corporate interest is unveiled: the development of computation was heavily sponsored by the state, and it thrives today within the monopoly of big tech corporations. The political synergy of state and corporations allowed computation to reach an immense scale that embraces nearly everything that exists. Ultimately, it is the physical footprint of this expansive network, the new nomos of the Earth, that ensures the power of financial capitalism.

The role of architecture within this condition is paradoxical, as computing itself is a powerful form of architecture, and yet its project is diluted into a hypertrophic proliferation of specific expertises. Within this fragmentation, traditional forms of knowledge like geometry or mathematics do not allow the architect to decipher the state of things. Here abstraction is so encompassing and immensely powerful that it transcends the division of labor and paradoxically undermines the prerogatives of intellectual labor itself.

The Proletarization of the Architect

The "formless" architecture of the data center is an extreme case that demonstrates how the architectural project today is fragmented into subcontracted competencies and professional roles. This fragmentation is driven not by the benefit, or use value, of cooperation among different experts, but by the exchange value driven by profit. Hence every aspect of architecture, from design to construction, is fertile ground for surplus extraction. This tendency reduces architects to mere providers of artistic veneer behind which lies a complex conglomerate of financial and technical mechanisms that they can no longer control. The abstractions that mediate the production of architecture are so complex and ubiquitous that they exceed the planning and drawing that guided architectural and engineering work for centuries and were the original site of abstraction in architecture. Ironically the division of labor that separated head from hand and proletarized the builder is now proletarizing the architect as well. The end result of the proletarization of architectural work is the increased precarity of this professional figure.[71]

Among the architects mentioned in this chapter, Hannes Meyer deliberately addressed the proletarization of the architect: not as a problem but as an opportunity. His design and pedagogy were not just a *representation* of poverty of experience (as in his *Co-op Interieur*), but an attempt to translate this condition into a method of work, with the aim of shifting the role of the architect from master to worker. Meyer's idea of architecture found its mature elaboration in 1928 when he was appointed director of the Bauhaus. In contrast to Walter Gropius, the school's previous director, who attempted to unite the fine arts with industrial design as a way to redeem the latter with the former, Meyer argued that design, especially architectural design, had to be devoid of any artistic content. Rather he conceived architecture as a mere technical activity, which the architect was expected to perform in collaboration with a multitude of other technicians including builders. This radical anti-artistic position emerged from his critique of the ideological origins of the Bauhaus (and much of modern architecture) in the arts and crafts movement and its ambition to "artisticize" architecture and product design in an effort to "save" the role of the artist and architect from its inevitable professional downgrading.

Precisely this rejection of the "artistic" in architecture and design gave Meyer the reputation of a merciless functionalist. He was perceived as an advocate of a dry and soulless problem-solving approach to architecture. The fact that a Bauhaus student of Meyer (and Hilberseimer) enrolled in the SS and became the architect of the Auschwitz concentration camp makes the Swiss architect's alleged hard-core functionalist pedagogy even more controversial.[72] Yet, as has been noted, Meyer's idea of architecture, as it emerged from his design, writings, and especially his directorship of the Bauhaus, was far from apathetically functionalist.[73] Meyer wanted his students to learn and practice architecture with technical competency while being aware of the political and economic context within which architecture is produced. This meant that the architectural project was not limited to the visible form of a building or its materiality, but encompassed all the social and technical aspects of building production, including financing, engineering, construction, and use. Meyer encouraged students to approach the "technical" aspects of architecture not technocratically. He avoided the functionalist trap in Louis Sullivan's saying that form follows function, which suggests an affirmative, uncritical lens that doesn't question the given function.[74] Alternatively, by means of seminars and lectures on diverse topics, including political economy, history of construction, and philosophy, Meyer's students were trained to think about architecture not just pragmatically but also critically. For example, rather than relying on students' creative instinct, Meyer tasked them with extensive analysis of the requirements of a project prior to beginning their design proposals. Moreover, he insisted that historical knowledge was necessary to understand how the form of cities and architecture is not a matter of style but depends on the political and economic organization of society.[75] For Meyer, the proletarization of architectural work meant that students and architects accepted their position as workers among other workers. Consequently, he dismissed the romantic notion of architects as "masters" or "artists" who impart their creative genius in the form of orders to their subalterns. This is why he organized the studios at the Bauhaus in the form of vertical brigades where older and more expert students would assist younger students and where teachers contributed as consultants rather than masters. Moreover, by introducing real commissions into the studios, Meyer expected students to be paid, emphasizing that education was antecedent to profession and thus considered work, not just a disinterested intellectual pursuit.

Meyer's position on architecture aligns with how Benjamin understood the role of the writer in the modern age.[76] In his famous essay "The Author as Producer" Benjamin confronted two popular trends of his time: activism and objectivity.[77] The first trend consisted of writers who, according to Benjamin, were eager to express political support for the working class, but without questioning their class status as bourgeois intellectuals. In the New Objectivity movement, writers aestheticized the effects of industrial development without taking into consideration the exploitative nature of such phenomena. Against the false choice between activism and acritical objectivity, Benjamin advanced the idea of writers as producers who take a political position not on the level of content, but on how their work is organized within the social relations of production. For Benjamin it was the form of intellectual work itself as a professional apparatus rather than its ideological content that had to be addressed critically and eventually changed. Translated into architectural terms, this would mean that rather than expressing political content, architects should focus on the way their profession is organized: the institutions that support it, and especially how the professional apparatus and its disciplinary mentality inevitably reproduce the asymmetrical class relationships that—as we have seen—were the basis for the emergence of architecture as a discipline that served the ruling class and extracted power from workers. It was for this reason that Meyer wanted to erase the boundary between intellectual and manual workers by encouraging students to learn about building skills, in addition to their training as designers. By introducing students to salaried work he leveled their class status, enabling working-class students to afford their education while upper-class students recognized their education not as a privilege but as training for work. The proletarization of the architectural worker was not achieved by forcing young architects to endure unpaid training and work—as occurs today—but by making them properly salaried workers. We can therefore understand why Meyer was averse to the artistic side of architecture. He understood that the artistry of architecture reinforced its idealization as a romantic endeavor devoid of any professional technical or economic concern.

And yet Meyer was not at all insensitive to or intolerant of the aesthetic character of architecture (as is evident in the subtle and elegant look of his rather austere drawings and buildings). Any consideration of the appearance of architecture, however, could not obscure the larger reality of architectural production. He thus adopted a highly unsentimental way of presenting his projects with diagrams, graphs, and calculations of the building's structural or environmental performance, as is visible in the famous illustration of his project for the Petersschule. This attitude is also apparent in his competition entry for the Palace of the League of Nations (1926–1927) and his realized design for the School of the General German Trades Union Federation in Bernau, near Berlin (1928–1930). In these projects, program requirements were handled in a legible and consequential manner in order to ease not only circulation and inhabitation but also the management of both design and the construction process. For Meyer, legibility of building form, from the vantage of designers and builders but also users, was the most important datum of architecture. This desire informed his emphasis on Gestalt theory as a way to properly configure space according to specific conditions of perception and use. His commitment to legibility resulted in a diagrammatic architecture that intended to help designers eliminate excess, or what might be considered surplus. Rather than the expression of individual craft or creativity, Meyer's diagrammatic architecture expresses an enhanced typification of building in support of a legible model of construction and inhabitation. For example, in the Trades Union School, Meyer broke down the complex program into parts related to specific moments in the daily routines of residents. The faculty apartments, the community building, the student cells, and the school building were arranged as distinct units so as to make best use of their site condition, and yet were united in a clearly laid-out programmatic sequence. The choice of material responded to both comfort, durability, and cost; Meyer limited concrete to the load-bearing structure and floor. Partitions were then constructed in brick within the concrete skeleton that was left exposed, making the Dom-ino-like system visible (and not hiding behind the plastic effects of architecture as in many buildings by Le Corbusier).

Meyer's "crude" architecture is similar to Bertolt Brecht's "crude thinking." Meyer and Brecht were determined to make every aspect of reality a concrete causation comprehensible to all. This demand for general intelligibility was announced by the presumably simple-minded donkey whose small wooden representation adorned the beam of Brecht's living room with the inscription "Even I must understand it." In a way, Meyer's direct language—as both production process and formal resolution—suggests the possibility of an architecture in which even Brecht's donkey can comprehend form as a manifestation of the use value of social relationships, or cooperation of workers. Although mostly conceived and realized in capitalist countries, it is possible to interpret Meyer's architecture as an attempt to imagine a building form defined by its *use* where everything is reduced in order to support a good life full of light and fresh air. It makes sense, therefore, that Meyer tried (though with little success) to pursue this idea of architecture in socialist countries such as Soviet Russia and Lázaro Cárdenas's Mexico. An approach to architecture similar to Meyer's could even be attempted today by relying on technology to enhance a broader understanding of how buildings work rather than accelerating the division of labor and allowing a small group of experts and developers to control the profession. For Meyer, the objective of building was not technological progress per se, but the possibility of fair cooperation in which everyone could intellectually and manually participate on an equal basis. In Meyer's crude architecture we finally see the communal interests that Benjamin saw as the reward for radically embracing the poverty of experience. Once the abstraction of architecture is unplugged from the logic of capitalist accumulation it can become the most appropriate form for socialist life.

Acknowledgments

I would like to thank Cynthia Davidson and Thomas Weaver for their support in making this book possible. I thank them also for editing and publishing my essays through the years in *Log* and *AA Files*. Thank you, Matthew Abbate, for carefully editing the final version of the manuscript. The content of this book took form during three seminars I taught at the Architectural Association in London, Yale School of Architecture, and at the École Polytechnique Fédérale de Lausanne, School of Architecture, Civil and Environmental Engineering. My deepest gratitude goes to the students who took part in these seminars and who through their questions and comments helped me to sharpen the thesis of the book. In the last decade I had the fortune to supervise a group of PhD researchers at TU Delft and the AA in London: their work (and friendship) have been a big influence on many of the ideas that inform this book. Teaching is not simply a one-way transmission of knowledge but also—and especially—the sharing of a common intellectual and existential space. Thank you, Bernardina Borra, Brendon Carlin, Jingru Cheng, Amir Djalali, Fernando Donis, Georgios Eftaxiopoulos, Platon Issaias, George Jepson, Shiyu Jin, Hamed Khosravi, Christopher C. M. Lee, Lola Lozano, Enrica Mannelli, Olivia Neves Marra, Francesco Marullo, Gili Merin, Samaneh Moafi, Elena Palacios Carral, Lukas Pauer, Ioanna Piniara, Mathilde Redouté, Davide Sacconi, Aylin Tarlan. Big thanks to Martino Tattara, my partner at Dogma, whose collaboration and friendship have been an important point of reference for my work. Discussions through the years with Emily Abruzzo, Aristide Antonas, Neeraj Bhatia, Tatiana Bilbao, Marco Biraghi, Andrea Branzi, Andrea Cerutti, Michael Robinson Cohen, Peter Eisenman, Roberto Gargiani, Nikolaus Hirsch, Elisa Iturbe, Marson Korbi, Adrian Lahoud, Gabriele Mastrigli, Philippe Morel, Manuel Orazi, Jack Rusk, Tuomas Toivonen, Mario Tronti, Nene Tsuboi, David Turturo, and Christophe Van Gerrewey have been seminal for the development of this book and my work in general.

I'm profoundly indebted to Michael Robinson Cohen who helped me in editing the book and whose insightful remarks have been a major contribution. My deepest gratitude goes to my family—Luigi Aureli, Lucia Biscontri, and Annalisa Aureli—and to Maria Shéhérazade Giudici with whom I've the privilege to teach, work, and study and whose influence on my work is immense. Without her relentless support, helpful comments, and generous criticism this book would not have been possible. I dedicate this book to Maria and our daughter Sibilla Cecilia.

Notes

Introduction

1   Peter Halley, "Abstraction and Culture," in *Selected Essays, 1981–2001* (New York: Edgewise, 2013), 163–171.
2   Ibid., 163.
3   César Chesneau Dumarsais, "Abstraction," in Denis Diderot and Jean Le Rond D'Alembert, eds., *Encyclopédie*, vol. 1 (Paris: André le Breton, Michel-Antoine David, Laurent Durand, and Antoine-Claude Briasson, 1751), 45–47.
4   Ibid., 45.
5   F. Duchesneau, "Sémiotique et abstraction: de Locke à Condillac," *Philosophique* 3, no. 2 (October 1976): 147–166.
6   John Locke, *An Essay Concerning Human Understanding* (1689; London: Clarendon Press, 1979), 155–163.
7   Gary Fields, *Enclosure: Palestinian Landscapes in a Historical Mirror* (Oakland: University of California Press, 2017), 61–63.
8   Karl Marx, *Grundrisse: Foundations of the Critique of Political Economy*, translated by Martin Nicolaus (London: Penguin, 1993), 164.
9   Manfredo Tafuri, "Toward a Critique of Architectural Ideology," translated by Stephen Sartarelli, in K. Michael Hays, ed., *Architecture Theory since 1968* (Cambridge, MA: MIT Press, 1998), 16.
10   Meyer Shapiro, "Nature of Abstract Art," *Marxist Quarterly* 1, no. 1 (January/March 1937): 77–98.
11   Ibid., 84.
12   Piet Mondrian, *New Design. Neoplasticism. Nieuwe Beelding* (Berlin: Lars Müller, 2019), 51.
13   Ibid., 12.
14   Ibid.
15   Piet Mondrian, "Le home, la rue, la cité," *Vouloir*, no. 25 (1927): 276–281.
16   Yve-Alain Bois, "The De Stijl Idea," in *Painting as Model* (Cambridge, MA: MIT Press, 1990), 111.
17   Felicia Rappe, "The Viewer in Motion: 'Elementarization and Standardization' in De Stijl," in Helmut Friedel and Mathias Muhling, eds., *Mondrian De Stijl* (Berlin: Hatje Cantz, 2011), 72, 73.
18   Henri Lefebvre, *The Production of Space*, translated by Donald Nicholson-Smith (Oxford: Blackwell, 1991), 285–291.
19   Japhy Wilson, "The Devastating Conquest of the Lived by the Conceived: The Concept of Abstract Space in the Work of Henri Lefebvre," *Space and Culture* 16, no. 3 (August 2013): 364–380.
20   Lefebvre, *The Production of Space*, 229–291.
21   Ibid., 234–236.
22   Ibid., 262–268.
23   Ibid., 289.
24   Ibid., 364.

25 Łukasz Stanek, "Space as a Concrete Abstraction: Hegel, Marx, and Modern Urbanism in Henri Lefebvre," in Kanishka Goonewardena, Stefan Kipfer, Richard Milgrom, and Christian Schmid, eds., *Space, Difference, Everyday Life: Reading Henri Lefebvre* (Abingdon, UK: Routledge, 2007), 62–79.

26 Marx discussed the issue of abstraction most notably in his introduction to the *Grundrisse*. See Marx, *Grundrisse*, 81–114.

27 Ibid., 104.

28 Ibid.

29 Alfred Sohn-Rethel, *Intellectual and Manual Labor: A Critique of Epistemology*, translated by Martin Sohn-Rethel (London: Macmillan, 1978), 35.

30 Ibid., 2.

31 Tirthankar Roy, *India in the World Economy* (Cambridge: Cambridge University Press, 2012).

32 Hans Hollein, "Alles ist Architektur," *Bau* 1/2 (1968): 1–32.

33 Vera Keller and Ted McCormick, "Towards a History of Projects," *Early Science and Medicine* 21, no. 5 (November 2016): 423–444.

34 Ibid., 445.

35 Joan Thirsk, *Economic Policy and Projects: The Development of a Consumer Society in Early Modern England* (Oxford: Clarendon Press, 1978), 1.

36 Daniel Defoe, *An Essay upon Projects*, edited by Henry Morley (London: Cassel & Company, 1887), 14.

37 Karl Marx, *Grundrisse: Foundations of the Critique of Political Economy*, translated by Martin Nicolaus (London: Penguin, 1993), 83.

38 Defoe, *An Essay upon Projects*, introduction, quoted also in Tomás Maldonado, "Defoe and the 'Projecting Age,'" *Design Issues* 18, no. 1 (Winter 2002): 78–85.

39 Defoe, *An Essay upon Projects*.

Chapter 1

1 Karl Marx, *Capital*, vol. 1, translated by Ben Fowkes (London: Penguin, 1992), 284.

2 Juan José Ibáñez, Jesús Emilio González Urquijo, and Xavier Terradas, "Natufian Huts and Hamlets: Experimenting for a Sedentary Life," in Juan Luis Montero Fenollós, ed., *Redonner vie aux Mésopotamiens. Mélanges offerts à Jean-Claude Margueron à l'occasion de son 80e anniversaire* (Ferrol: Proyecto Arqueológico Medio Éufrates Sirio and Sociedade Luso-Galega de Estudos Mesopotámicos, 2014), 81.

3 Gill Harklay and Avi Gopher, "A New Look at Shelter 131/51 in the Natufian Site of Eynan (Ain-Mallaha), Israel," *PLoS ONE* 10, no. 7 (2015).

4 Lewis Mumford, *Technics and Human Development: The Myth of the Machine*, vol. 1 (San Diego: Harcourt Brace Jovanovich, 1966), 58–62.

5 Ibid., 60.

6 Marlies Heinz, "Public Buildings, Palaces and Temples," in Harriet Crawford, ed., *The Sumerian World* (Abingdon, UK: Routledge, 2013), 179–200.

7 Kent Flannery and Joyce Marcus, *The Creation of Inequality: How Our Prehistoric Ancestors Set the Stage for Monarchy, Slavery, and Empire* (Cambridge, MA: Harvard University Press, 2012), 260–297.

8 David Graeber and David Wengrow, *The Dawn of Everything: A New History of Humanity* (London: Penguin, 2021).

9 Flannery and Marcus, *The Creation of Inequality*, 275–281.

10 Ibid., 278.

11 Robert S. Homsher, "Mud Bricks and the Process of Construction in the Middle Bronze Age Southern Levant," *Bulletin of the American Schools of Oriental Research*, no. 368 (November 2012): 1–27.

12 Morris Kline, *Mathematical Thought from Ancient to Modern Times*, vol. 1 (New York: Oxford University Press, 1990), 11.

13 See Mario Liverani, *Uruk: The First City*, translated by Zainab Bahrani and Marc van de Mieroop (Sheffield: Equinox Publishing, 2006).

14 Mario Liverani, *The Ancient Near East: History, Society and Economy*, translated by Soraia Tabatabai (Abingdon, UK: Routledge, 2006), 73–79.

15 Ibid., 69.

16 Guillermo Algaze, "The End of Prehistory and the Uruk Period," in Crawford, *The Sumerian World*, 78.

17 Mumford, *Technics and Human Development*, 188–211.

18 Ibid., 191.

19 Ibid., 189.

20 Ibid., 192.

21 Graeber and Wengrow, *The Dawn of Everything*, 141–147, 313–321.

22 Peter Jánosi, *Die Pyramiden* (Munich: Verlag C. H. Beck, 2004), 43.

23 Ibid., 42–43.

24 Miroslav Verner, *The Pyramids: The Mystery, Culture, and Science of Egypt's Great Monuments* (New York: Grove Press, 1997), 62–101.

25 Herodotus, *The Histories*, translated by Aubrey de Sélincourt (London: Penguin Classics, 2003), 95.

26 Alfred Sohn-Rethel, *Intellectual and Manual Labour: A Critique of Epistemology*, translated by Martin Sohn-Rethel (London: Macmillan, 1978), 90–91.

27 Ibid., 88–94.

28 Ibid., 98.

29 Ibid., 94–100.

30 Mark S. Peacock, "The Origins of Money in Ancient Greece: The Political Economy of Coinage and Exchange," *Cambridge Journal of Economics* 30, no. 6 (July 2006): 637–650.

31 Sohn-Rethel, *Intellectual and Manual Labour*, 58–79.

32 Vitruvius, *Ten Books on Architecture*, edited by Ingrid D. Rowland and Thomas Noble Howe (Cambridge: Cambridge University Press, 1999), 56.

33 Maria Chiara Barone, *La colonna greca: origini costruttive* (Lausanne: EPFL Architecture, 2016), 191.

34 Spiro Kostof, "The Practice of Architecture in the Ancient World: Egypt and Greece," in Kostof, ed., *The Architect: Chapters in the History of the Profession* (New York: Oxford University Press, 1977), 3–27.

35 J. J. Coulton, *Ancient Greek Architects at Work: Problems of Structure and Design* (Ithaca, NY: Cornell University Press, 1977), 23.

36 Lisa Landrum, "Before Architecture: Archai, Architects and Architectonics in Plato and Aristotle," *Montreal Architectural Review* 2 (2015): 6–11.

37 Plato, *The Statesman*, translated by Christoper J. Rowe (Warminster: Aris and Phillips, 1995), 35.

38 Coulton, *Ancient Greek Architects at Work*, 15.

39 Ibid., 20.

40 Richard Seaford, *Money and the Early Greek Mind: Homer, Philosophy, Tragedy* (Cambridge: Cambridge University Press, 2014).

41 Ibid., 102–124.

42 Vitruvius, *Ten Books on Architecture*, 86.

43 Ibid., 21.

44 Carlo Tosco, "Gli architetti e le maestranze," in Enrico Castelnuovo and Giuseppe Sergi, eds., *Arti e storia nel medioevo*, vol. 2, *Del costruire: tecniche, artisti, artigiani, committenti* (Turin: Giulio Einaudi, 2003), 56.

45 Wolfgang Braunfels, *Monasteries of Western Europe: The Architecture of the Orders* (London: Thames and Hudson, 1972), 47–66.

46 Walter Horn and Ernest Born, *Plan of St. Gall: Study of the Architecture and Economy of, and Life in, a Paradigmatic Carolingian Monastery* (Los Angeles: University of California Press, 1980).

47 Ibid., 25.

48 Michel Foucault, *Discipline and Punish: The Birth of the Prison* (New York: Vintage Books, 1977); see also Gilles Deleuze, *Foucault*, translated by Sean Hand (London: Continuum, 2006).

49 James Bond, "Cistercian Industry in Medieval England and Wales," in Arnaud Baudin, Paul Benoit, Joséphine Rouillard, and Benoît Rouzeau, eds., *L'industrie cistercienne* (Paris: Somogy éditions d'art, 2015), 249–250.

50 Carlo Tosco, *Andare per abbazie cistercensi* (Bologna: Il Mulino, 2017), 22.

51 Nigel Hiscock, "The Two Cistercian Plans of Villard de Honnecourt," in Terryl Kinder, ed., *Perspectives for an Architecture of Solitude: Essays on Cistercians, Art and Architecture in Honour of Peter Fergusson* (Turnhout: Brepols, 2004), 157–172.

52 Jean-Paul Deroin and Gilles Fronteau, "La pierre à bâtir dans les premières abbayes cisterciennes de la filiation de Clairvaux au XII siècle," in Baudin et al., *L'industrie cistercienne*, 179–204.

53 Donata Degrassi, "Lavoro e lavoratori nel sistema di valori della società medievale," in Franco Franceschi, ed., *Il medioevo: dalla dipendenza personale al lavoro contratatto* (Rome: Castelvecchi, 2017), 16.

54 Dieter Kimpel, "La razionalizzazione dell'architettura religiosa gotica in Francia. Fattori endogeni ed esogeni," in Jean-Claude Maire Vigueur and Agostino Paravicini Bagliani, eds., *Ars et ratio* (Palermo: Sellerio Editore, 1990), 127–146.

55 Maureen C. Miller, *The Bishop's Palace: Architecture and Authority in Medieval Italy* (Ithaca, NY: Cornell University Press, 2018), 80.

56 Kimpel, "La razionalizzazione dell'architettura religiosa gotica in Francia," 133.

57 Dawn Marie Hayes, "Earthly Uses of Heavenly Spaces: Non-Liturgical Activities in Sacred Place," in *Body and Sacred Place in Medieval Europe, 1100–1389* (London: Routledge, 2003), 53–70.

58 Kimpel, "La razionalizzazione dell'architettura religiosa gotica in Francia," 130–132.

59 Dieter Kimpel, "L'attività costruttiva nel medioevo: strutture e trasformazioni," in *Cantieri medievali* (Milan: Jaca Book, 2005), 11–50.

60 Claude Reichler, "John Ruskin and the Europe of Cathedrals," in Emma Sdegno, Martina Frank, Pierre-Henry Frangne, and Myriam Pilutti Namer, eds., *John Ruskin's Europe: A Collection of Cross-Cultural Essays* (Venice: Edizioni Cafoscari, 2020), 213–222.

61 Richard A. Jones, "Gleaning from 1253 Building Accounts of Westminster Abbey," *AVISTA forum* 11, no. 2 (1999): 19.

62 John M. Jeep, ed., *Medieval Germany: An Encyclopedia* (New York: Garland, 2001), 294.

63 Kimpel, "La razionalizzazione dell'architettura religiosa gotica in Francia," 14–15; Jean Gimpel, *The Medieval Machine: The Industrial Revolution of the Middle Ages* (London: Pimlico, 1992), 114–119.

64 Cited in Tim Benton, "The Building Trades and Design Methods," in Diana Norman, ed., *Siena, Florence, Padua: Art, Society and Religion 1280–1400*, vol. 1, *Interpretative Essays* (New Haven: Yale University Press, 1995), 127.

65 Ibid., 6.

66 Robert Bork, *The Geometry of Creation: Architectural Drawing and the Dynamics of Gothic Design* (Burlington, VT: Ashgate, 2011), 29–53.

67 A debate on whether medieval orthogonal projections did follow specific scales has not been settled yet, but the latest analyses suggest that they did, and that any significant "mistake" in the extant documents might be due to issues of parchment conservation.

68 James Ackerman, "Ars sine Scientia Nihil Est: Gothic Theory of Architecture at the Cathedral of Milan," *Art Bulletin* 31, no. 2 (June 1949): 84–111.

69 Leon Battista Alberti, *On the Art of Building in Ten Books*, translated by Joseph Rykwert, Neil Leach, and Robert Tavernor (Cambridge, MA: MIT Press, 1988), 3.

70 Maria Paola Zaniboni, *Scioperi e rivolte nel medioevo: le città italiane ed europee nei secoli XIII–XV* (Milan: Jouvence Historica, 2015), 178.

71 E. R. Truitt, *Medieval Robots: Mechanism, Magic, Nature, and Art* (Philadelphia: University of Pennsylvania Press), 42.

72 Gimpel, *The Medieval Machine*, 147–170.

73 Benton, "The Building Trades and Design Methods," 129–130.

74 Marvin Trachtenberg, *Building-in-Time: From Giotto to Alberti and Modern Oblivion* (New Haven: Yale University Press, 2010), 297. On Brunelleschi as model for Alberti's theory of architecture see also Mario Carpo's seminal *The Alphabet and the Algorithm* (Cambridge, MA: MIT Press, 2011).

75 Trachtenberg, *Building-in-Time*, 301–307.

76 Ibid., 103–143.

77 Ibid., 375.

78 Ibid., 357–358.

79 Pier Vittorio Aureli, "Do You Remember Counterrevolution? The Politics of Filippo Brunelleschi's Syntactic Architecture," *AA Files* 71 (2015): 147–165.

80 John M. Najemy, *A History of Florence 1200–1575* (London: Wiley-Blackwell, 2008), 157–160.

81 Ernesto Screpanti, *L'angelo della liberazione del tumulto dei Ciompi: Firenze, Giugno-Agosto 1378* (Florence: Protagon editori toscani, 2008).

82 Arnaldo Bruschi, "Prima del Brunelleschi: verso un'architettura sintattica e prospettica," in Bruschi, *L'antico, la tradizione, il moderno: da Arnolfo a Peruzzi, saggi sull'architettura del Rinascimento* (Milan: Electa, 2004), 19–84.

83 Eugenio Battisti, *Filippo Brunelleschi* (Milan: Electa Architetture, 2002), 123.

84 Trachtenberg, *Building-in-Time*, 301–307.

85 Frank D. Prager and Gustina Scaglia, *Brunelleschi: Studies of His Technologies and Inventions* (Cambridge, MA: MIT Press, 1970), 85–109.

86 Antonio di Tuccio Manetti, *The Life of Brunelleschi*, translated by Catherine Enggass (Philadelphia: University of Pennsylvania Press, 1970), 55.

87 Leopold D. Ettlinger, "The Emergence of the Italian Architect during the Fifteenth Century," in Kostof, *The Architect*, 108.

88 "There is a further matter about walls that is not to be neglected. They must not be put up too quickly, or with hasty hands, or in one uninterrupted operation, nor should sloth be allowed to delay the work once in progress. Rather the work should proceed with *method and purpose*; speed should be combined with deliberation and proper care." Alberti, *On the Art of Building in Ten Books*, 75–76 (my emphasis).

89 Leon Battista Alberti, *L'arte del costruire*, trans. Valeria Giontella (Turin: Bollati Boringhieri, 2010), 106.

90 Werner Sombart, *The Quintessence of Capitalism: A Study of the History and Psychology of the Modern Business Man*, translated by Mortimer Epstein (New York: E. P. Dutton, 1915), 105–109.

Chapter 2

1   As defined in *Enciclopedia Treccani*, https://www.treccani.it/vocabolario /disegno/.

2   Michael Baxandall, "English Disegno," in *Words for Pictures: Seven Papers on Renaissance Art and Criticism* (New Haven: Yale University Press, 2003), 83.

3   Ibid., 86.

4   Ibid., 94.

5   Giorgio Vasari, *The Lives of the Artists*, translated by Julia Conaway Bondanella and Peter Bondanella (Oxford: Oxford University Press, 2008), 3.

6   Sergio Rossi, *Dalle botteghe alle accademie: realtà sociale e teorie artistiche a Firenze dal XIV al XVI secolo* (Milan: Feltrinelli, 1980), 146–181.

7   On the work of master gunmakers, see Rainer Leng, "Social Character, Pictorial Style, and the Grammar of Technical Illustration in Craftsmen's Manuscripts in the Late Middle Age," in Wolfgang Lefèvre, ed., *Picturing Machines 1400–1700* (Cambridge, MA: MIT Press, 2004), 85–111.

8   For a description of Johannes Formschneider's book, see Rainer Leng, *Ars belli. Deutsche taktische und kriegstechnische Bilderhandschriften und Traktate im 15. und 16. Jahrhundert*, 2 vols. (Wiesbaden: Reichert, 2002).

9   Rossi, *Dalle botteghe alle accademie*, 66.

10   Leon Battista Alberti, *On Painting*, translated by Martin Kemp (London: Penguin, 1991).

11   Such as Cennino Cennini's *Libro dell'arte*: see Cennino d'Andrea Cennini, *The Craftsman's Handbook*, translated by Daniel V. Thompson Jr. (London: Dover, 1954).

12   Morris Kline, *Mathematical Thought from Ancient to Modern Times*, vol. 1 (New York: Oxford University Press, 1990), 145–148.

13   Leon Battista Alberti, *On the Art of Building in Ten Books*, translated by Joseph Rykwert, Neil Leach, and Robert Tavernor (Cambridge, MA: MIT Press, 1988), 7.

14   Ibid.

15   Branko Mitrovi|, "Leon Battista Alberti, Mental Rotation, and the Origins of a Three-Dimensional Computer Modelling," *Journal of the Society of Architectural Historians* 74, no. 3 (2015), 316.

16   Alberti, *On the Art of Building in Ten Books*, 34.

17   Stephen Murray, *Plotting Gothic* (Chicago: University of Chicago Press, 2014).

18   François Bucher, "Medieval Architecture Design Methods, 800–1560," *Gesta* 11, no. 2 (1972), 44.

19   Filippo Camerota, "Renaissance Descriptive Geometry: The Codification of Drawing Methods," in Lefèvre, *Picturing Machines 1400–1700*, 175–208.

20   Liane Lefaivre and Alexander Tzonis, *The Emergence of Modern Architecture: A Documentary History from 1000 to 1800* (London: Routledge, 2004), 91–95.

21   Wolfgang Lotz, "The Rendering of the Interior in Architectural Drawings of the Renaissance," in *Studies of Italian Renaissance Architecture* (Cambridge, MA: MIT Press, 1977), 1–65.

22   Ibid., 40.

23   Wolfgang Lefèvre, "The Emergence of Combined Orthographic Projections," in Lefèvre, *Picturing Machines 1400–1700*, 223–224.

24   Ibid., 224.

25   Alfred Sohn-Rethel, *Intellectual and Manual Labour: A Critique of Epistemology*, translated by Martin Sohn-Rethel (London: Macmillan, 1978), 112.

26   Ibid., 113.

27   Ibid., 114–115.

28 Bernard Cache, *Toujours l'informe … géométrie d'Albrecht Dürer* (Lausanne: EPFL Press, 2016), 24.

29 Rolando Bussi, ed., *Misurare la terra—centuriazione e coloni nel mondo romano: città, agricoltura, commercio—materiali da Roma e dal suburbio* (Modena: Franco Cosimo Panini, 1985).

30 John A. Pinto, "Origins and Developments of the Ichnographic Plan," *Journal of the Society of Architectural Historians* 35, no. 1 (March 1976), 36.

31 Ibid., 36–37.

32 Ibid., 38.

33 Hans Belting, *Florence and Baghdad: Renaissance Art and Arab Science*, translated by Deborah Lucas Schneider (Cambridge, MA: Harvard University Press, 2008).

34 Massimo Scolari, *Oblique Drawing: A History of Anti-Perspective* (Cambridge, MA: MIT Press, 2012).

35 For an accurate account of the origins of "soldierly perspective," see Emile D'Orgeix, "Fortification and Military Perspective in Seventeenth-Century France," in Mario Carpo and Frédérique Lemerle, eds., *Perspective, Projections and Design: Technologies of Architectural Representation* (London: Routledge, 2008), 127–140.

36 Scolari, *Oblique Drawing*, 219. See also Pamela O. Long, "Picturing the Machine: Francesco di Giorgio and Leonardo da Vinci in the 1490s," in Lefèvre, *Picturing Machines 1400–1700*, 117–141.

37 J. R. Hale, *Renaissance War Studies* (London: Hambledon Press, 1983), 22.

38 Nicholas Adams, "L'architettura militare di Francesco di Giorgio," in Francesco Paolo Fiore and Manfredo Tafuri, eds., *Francesco di Giorgio architetto* (Milan: Electa, 1994), 114.

39 Ibid.

40 Francesco Benelli, "Diversification of Knowledge: Military Architecture as a Political Tool: The Case of Francesco di Giorgio," *Res* 57/58 (Spring/Autumn 2020), 148.

41 Massimo Mussini, "La trattatistica di Francesco di Giorgio: un problema critico aperto," in Fiore and Tafuri, *Francesco di Giorgio architetto*, 378.

42 Simon Pepper, "Sword and Spade: Military Construction in Renaissance Italy," *Construction History* 16 (2000), 13–32.

43 On the collective nature of military design, see Mary Henninger-Voss, "Measures of Success: Military Engineering and the Architectonic Understanding of Design," in Lefèvre, *Picturing Machines 1400–1700*, 143–174.

44 Ibid., 151.

45 Anthony Gerbino and Stephen Johnston, *Compass and Rule: Architecture as Mathematical Practice in England 1500–1750* (New Haven: Yale University Press, 2009), 31.

46 Eugene S. Ferguson, *Engineering and the Mind's Eye* (Cambridge, MA: MIT Press, 1994), 21.

47 Alexander Marr, "Pregnant Wit: Ingegno in Renaissance England," *British Art Studies*, no. 1 (2021), https://dx.doi.org/10.17658/issn.2058-5462/issue-01/amarr.

48 Henninger-Voss, "Measures of Success," 152.

49 Ibid.

50 Ibid., 164.

51 Roberto Rossi, "La Nuova Scientia: Rewriting the History of Operational Research," unpublished manuscript, 2017, 7.

52 Ibid., 9.

53 Henninger-Voss, "Measures of Success," 149.

54 For an overview of Vauban's achievements in military design and warfare, see Jean-Denis G. G. Lepage, *Vauban and the French Military under Louis XVI:*

269

An Illustrated History of Fortifications and Strategies (Jefferson, NC: McFarland, 2010). See also Paddy Griffith, *The Vauban Fortifications of France* (Oxford: Osprey Publishing, 2006).

55 Lepage, *Vauban and the French Military under Louis XVI*, 153–162.

56 Griffith, *The Vauban Fortifications of France*, 24–25.

57 Vauban wrote extensively about myriad subjects, but all his writings are empirical studies of concrete and pragmatic topics such as navigation and forestry. A complete list of his writings was made by Jacques de Gervain and André de Lafitte-Clavé in 1768 and is published in Lepage, *Vauban and the French Military under Louis XVI*, 280–281.

58 Sébastien Le Prestre de Vauban, *Les oisivetés de Monsieur de Vauban: ou Ramas de plusieurs mémoires de sa façon sur différents sujets* (Paris: Champ Vallon Editions, 2007).

59 Alberto Pérez-Gómez, *Architecture and the Crisis of Modern Science* (Cambridge, MA: MIT Press, 1983), 19.

60 Ibid., 19–22.

61 Ibid., 26–27.

62 Bryony Roberts, "Beyond the *Querelle*," *Log*, no. 31 (Spring/Summer 2014), 13–17.

63 Myra Nan Rosenfeld, "The Royal Building Administration in France from Charles V to Louis XIV," in Spiro Kostof, ed., *The Architect: Chapters in the History of the Profession* (New York: Oxford University Press, 1977), 173.

64 Pérez-Gómez, *Architecture and the Crisis of Modern Science*, 195–196.

65 For an overview of Colbert's policies it is still useful to consult Arthur John Sargent, *The Economic Policy of Colbert* (London: Longmans, Green, 1899).

66 Antoine Picon, *French Architects and Engineers in the Age of Enlightenment* (Cambridge: Cambridge University Press, 1992), 223.

67 Ibid., 197.

68 Cesare Birignani, "The Police and the City 1660–1750," PhD diss., Columbia University, 2013, 4.

69 On the art of policing see the seminal study by the philosopher Andrea Cavalletti, unfortunately not yet translated into English: Andrea Cavalletti, *La città biopolitica: mitologie della sicurezza* (Milan: Mondadori, 2005).

70 Birignani, "The Police and the City 1660–1750," 7.

71 Pérez-Gómez, *Architecture and the Crisis of Modern Science*, 238–266.

72 Picon, *French Architects and Engineers in the Age of Enlightenment*, 346–349.

73 Ibid., 165–166.

74 Paolo Morachiello and Georges Teyssot, *Nascita delle città di stato: ingegneri e architetti sotto il consolato e l'impero* (Rome: Officina, 1982), 23–40.

75 Jean-Nicolas-Louis Durand, *Précis of the Lectures on Architecture*, translated by David Britt (Los Angeles: Getty Research, 2000), 79–80.

76 Werner Szambien, *Jean-Nicolas-Louis Durand (1760–1834). De l'imitation à la norme* (Paris: Picard, 1984).

77 Jean-Baptiste Rondelet, *Traité théorique et pratique de l'art de bâtir*, vol. 1 (Sydney: Wentworth Press, 2018), 35.

78 Alberti, *On Painting*, 73.

79 Alberti, *On the Art of Building in Ten Books*, 35.

80 Jacques Lucan, *Composition, Non-Composition: Architecture and Theory in the Nineteenth and Twentieth Century* (Lausanne: EPFL Press, 2012), 23.

81 Christopher C. M. Lee, "The Construction of a Common Knowledge in Durand's Method," in Pier Vittorio Aureli, ed., *The City as a Project* (Berlin: Ruby Press, 2013), 170–212.

Chapter 3

1 I do not intend to search for the "origin" of the grid, and thus I don't want to repeat here the universalizing and "diffusionist" interpretation of the urban grid made by previous historical accounts such as the seminal 1946 study of the grid by geographer Dan Stanislawski. My intention is to trace a possible genealogy of the particular urban grid that originated as a system of land subdivision and later became instrumental in enforcing the regime of property. This regime, which emerged with modern Western colonialism, is arguably the basis of modern and contemporary capitalism. See Dan Stanislawski, "The Origin of the Grid-Pattern Town," *Geographical Review* 36, no. 1 (January 1946): 105–120; for a critical account of Stanislawski's history of the grid see Reuben S. Rose-Redwood, "Genealogies of the Grid: Revisiting Stanislawski's Search for the Origin of the Grid-Pattern Town," *Geographical Review* 98, no. 1 (January 2008): 42–58. For a general cultural history of the grid see Hannah B. Higgins, *The Grid Book* (Cambridge, MA: MIT Press, 2009).

2 Peter J. Wilson, *The Domestication of the Human Species* (New Haven: Yale University Press, 1989), 50.

3 Ibid., 30.

4 Rosalind L. Hunter-Anderson, "A Theoretical Approach to the Study of House Form," in Lewis Roberts Binford, ed., *For Theory in Archaeology: Essays on Faunal Remains, Aquatic Resources, Spatial Analysis, and Systemic Modeling* (New York: Academic Press, 1977), 287–315.

5 Kent V. Flannery, "The Origins of the Village Revisited: From Nuclear to Extended Households," *American Antiquity* 67, no. 3 (July 2002): 421.

6 Ibid., 424.

7 Erhan Bıçakçı, "Çayönü House Models and a Reconstruction Attempt for the Cell-Plan Buildings," in *Readings in Prehistory: Studies Presented to Halet Çambel* (Istanbul: Graphis, 1995), 101–125.

8 Hunter-Anderson, "A Theoretical Approach to the Study of House Form," 297.

9 See Mario Liverani, *Uruk: The First City*, translated by Zainab Bahrani and Marc van de Mieroop (Sheffield: Equinox Publishing, 2006).

10 V. Gordon Childe, "The Urban Revolution," *Town Planning Review* 21, no. 1 (April 1950): 3–17.

11 Liverani, *Uruk: The First City*, 34.

12 See Mario Liverani, *The Ancient Near East: History, Society and Economy*, translated by Soraia Tabatabai (Abingdon, UK: Routledge, 2006), 61–81.

13 Herodotus, *The Histories*, translated by Aubrey de Sélincourt (London: Penguin Classics, 2003), 95.

14 Alfred Sohn-Rethel, *Intellectual and Manual Labour: A Critique of Epistemology*, translated by Martin Sohn-Rethel (London: Macmillan, 1978), 90–91.

15 Nadine Moeller, *The Archaeology of Urbanism in Ancient Egypt: From the Predynastic Period to the End of the Middle Kingdom* (New York: Cambridge University Press, 2016), 249–300.

16 Barry J. Kemp, *Ancient Egypt: Anatomy of a Civilization*, 2nd ed. (London: Routledge, 2006), 163–244.

17 On the organization of labor in ancient Egypt, see Micòl Di Teodoro, *Labour Organisation in Middle Kingdom Egypt* (London: Golden House Publications, 2018).

18 Of course colonial tendencies are evident earlier in Mesopotamia, but the Egyptians of the Middle Kingdom developed this form of urbanism in an

astonishingly systematic way due their constant need of resources and their bureaucratic mentality. See Kemp, *Ancient Egypt*, 211–231.

19 Although colonies were established as independent city-states, there was always a strong political and economic alliance between the newly founded colony and the city from which it came. For powerful *poleis*, founding colonies was a way to resolve social discontent and political conflicts by allowing some of the population to leave the mother city and relocate elsewhere. It was also a way for mother cities to expand their political and economic influence by establishing friendly outposts useful for military campaigns and trade. See Paolo Morachiello, *La città greca* (Bari: Laterza, 2003), 52–69.

20 See J. P. Vernant, *Myth and Thought among the Greeks*, translated by Janet Lloyd and Jeff Fort (New York: Zone Books, 2006), 91–93.

21 On the planning of Greek colonies, see Aidan Kirkpatrick, "The Image of the City in Antiquity: Tracing the Origins of Urban Planning, Hippodamian Theory, and the Orthogonal Grid in Classical Greece," master's thesis, University of Victoria, 2015.

22 Kirkpatrick defines Olynthus as an "experiment in social cohesion" ("The Image of the City in Antiquity," 52). On the construction of the domestic environment at Olynthus see Nicholas Cahill, *Household and Social Organization at Olynthus* (New Haven: Yale University Press, 2002).

23 Aristotle, *Politics: A New Translation*, translated by C. D. C. Reeve (Indianapolis: Hackett, 2017), 36–40, 174.

24 For an incisive reading of how Hippodamus subtly subverted the isonomic order of the grid, see Luigi Mazza, "Plan and Constitution—Aristotle's Hippodamus: Towards an 'Ostensive' Definition of Spatial Planning," *Town Planning Review* 80, no. 2 (2009): 113–141.

25 See Neville Morley, "Cities in Context: Urban Systems in Roman Italy," in Helen Parkins, ed., *Roman Urbanism: Beyond the Consumer City* (London: Routledge, 2005), 42–58.

26 On the process of centuriation, see Rolando Bussi, ed., *Misurare la terra—centuriazione e coloni nel mondo romano: città, agricoltura, commercio—materiali da Roma e dal suburbio* (Modena: Franco Cosimo Panini, 1985).

27 Ibid., 20–27.

28 Ibid., 81.

29 Ibid., 82.

30 On the practice of surveyors in ancient Rome, see O. A. W. Dilke, "The Roman Surveyors," *Greece and Rome* 9, no. 2 (October 1962): 170–180.

31 See David Gilman Romano, "The Orientation of Towns and Centuriation," in Jane DeRose Evans, ed., *A Companion to the Archeology of the Roman Republic* (Hoboken, NJ: Wiley-Blackwell, 2013), 251–267.

32 On the concept of *res* in Roman Law, see Yan Thomas, "La valeur des choses: le droit romain hors la religion," *Annales: Histoire, Sciences Sociales* 57, no. 6 (December 2002): 1431–1462.

33 Ibid., 1440.

34 Ibid.

35 Cicero, *Tusculan Disputations*, translated by John Edward King (Portsmouth, NH: Heinemann, 1927), 70.

36 Adrian Randolph, "The Bastides of Southwest France," *Art Bulletin* 77, no. 2 (June 1995): 290–307.

37 Ibid., 292.

38 Ibid., 304.

39 John W. Reps, *Town Planning in Frontier America* (Princeton: Princeton University Press, 1969), 15.

40 Ibid., 19.

41 See David Friedman, *Florentine New Towns: Urban Design in the Late Middle Ages* (Cambridge, MA: MIT Press, 1989).

42 Marsely L. Kehoe, "Dutch Batavia: Exposing the Hierarchy of the Dutch Colonial City," *Journal of Historians of Netherlandish Art* 7, no. 1 (Winter 2015).

43 Ibid., 12. See also Charles van den Heuvel, *De Huysbou: A Reconstruction of an Unfinished Treatise of Architecture, Town Planning and Civil Engineering by Simon Stevin* (Helsinki: Edita, 2006).

44 Nicholas Blomley, "Law, Property, and the Geography of Violence: The Frontier, the Survey, and the Grid," *Annals of the Association of American Geographers* 93, no. 1 (March 2003): 121.

45 See Gary Fields, *Enclosure: Palestinian Landscapes in a Historical Mirror* (Oakland: University of California Press, 2017), 143. See also John L. Comaroff and Jean Comaroff, "Law and Disorder in the Postcolony: An Introduction," in Comaroff and Comaroff, eds., *Law and Disorder in the Postcolony* (Chicago: University of Chicago Press, 2006), 30.

46 Brenna Bhandar, *Colonial Lives of Property: Law, Land, and Racial Regimes of Ownership* (Durham: Duke University Press, 2018), 3.

47 Alessandro Bava, "The Grid and the American City," in Pier Vittorio Aureli and Maria Shéhérazade Giudici, eds., *Rituals and Walls: The Architecture of Sacred Space* (London: Architectural Association, 2016), 34–39.

48 Fields, *Enclosure*, 45.

49 Ibid., 93–170.

50 Ibid., 115–118.

51 David Armitage, "John Locke, Carolina, and the 'Two Treatises of Government,'" *Political Theory* 32, no. 5 (October 2004): 602–627.

52 Fields, *Enclosure*, 129.

53 Ibid., 97–144.

54 W. E. Tate, "The Cost of Parliamentary Enclosure in England (with Special Reference to the County of Oxford)," *Economic History Review*, n.s. 5, no. 2 (1952): 258–265.

55 Karl Marx, "Part Eight: Primitive Accumulation," in *Capital*, vol. 1, translated by Ben Fowkes (London: Penguin, 1992), 873–940.

56 John Pickles, *A History of Spaces: Cartographic Reason, Mapping, and the Geo-Coded World* (London: Routledge, 2004), 92–106.

57 Ann Bermingham, *Landscape and Ideology: The English Rustic Tradition, 1740–1860* (Berkeley: University of California Press, 1986).

58 Fields, *Enclosure*, 143.

59 William D. Pattison, "Beginnings of the American Rectangular Land Survey System, 1784–1800," thesis, University of Chicago, 1957.

60 Ibid., 45–50.

61 Ibid., 50.

62 Ibid., 67–80.

63 For a discussion of Cerdà's concept of urbanization, see Andrea Cavalletti, *La città biopolitica: mitologie della sicurezza* (Milan: Mondadori, 2005). See also Pier Vittorio Aureli, *The Possibility of an Absolute Architecture* (Cambridge, MA: MIT Press, 2011); Maria Shéhérazade Giudici, "Inconsiderate Hardness: The Avenue and the Grid, Paris-Barcelona 1853–1970," in her "The Street as a Project: The Space of the City and the Construction of the Modern Subject," PhD diss., Technical University of Delft, 2014, 237–241; Ross Exo Adams, "The Burden

of the Present: On the Concept of Urbanisation," *Society and Space*, February 11, 2014, http://societyandspace.org/2014/02/11/the-burden-of-the-present-on-the -concept-of-urbanisation-ross-exo-adams/.

64 Ildefons Cerdà, *Cerdà: The Fives Bases of the General Theory of Urbanization*, edited by Arturo Soria y Puig (Berkeley: Gingko Press, 1999), 79.

65 Francesc Magrinyà and Fernando Marzá, eds., *Cerdà: 150 Years of Modernity* (Barcelona: Actar, 2017), 23.

66 Cerdà, *Cerdà*, 50.

67 Ibid., 79–80.

68 Ibid., 5.

69 Miguel Corominas i Ayala, *Los orígenes del ensanche de Barcelona: suelo, técnica e iniciativa* (Barcelona: Universitat Politècnica de Catalunya, 2002), 169–170.

70 Ibid., 120.

71 See Heinz Ronner and Sharad Jharevi, *Louis I. Kahn: Complete Work, 1935–1974* (Basel: Birkhäuser, 1987), 26–27.

72 See Kathryn E. Wilson, *Ethnic Renewal in Philadelphia's Chinatown: Space, Place, and Struggle* (Philadelphia: Temple University Press, 2015).

73 Ronner and Jharevi, *Louis I. Kahn: Complete Work*, 26.

74 See Michel Foucault, *Discipline and Punish: The Birth of the Prison*, translated by Alan Sheridan (New York: Vintage Books, 1995). See also Gilles Deleuze, *Foucault*, translated by Sean Hand (Minneapolis: University of Minnesota Press, 1988).

75 Carl Schmitt, *The Nomos of the Earth in the International Law of Jus Publicum Europaeum*, translated by G. L. Ulmen (Candor, NY: Telos Press, 2006), 81.

Chapter 4

1 On Schinkel's trip to England, see Karl Friedrich Schinkel, *The English Journey: Journal of a Visit to France and Britain in 1826*, edited by David Bindman and Gottfried Riemann (New Haven: Yale University Press, 1993).

2 Ibid., 175.

3 Ibid., 177.

4 Alberto Grohmann, *La città medievale* (Bari: Laterza), 136–140.

5 Sebastiano Serlio, *On Architecture*, vol. 2: *Books VI and VII of "Tutte l'opere d'architettura et prospettiva,"* edited by Vaughan Hart and Peter Hicks (New Haven: Yale University Press, 2001), 92–105.

6 Myra Nan Rosenfeld, "The Royal Building Administration in France from Charles V to Louis XIV," in Spiro Kostof, ed., *The Architect: Chapters in the History of the Profession* (New York: Oxford University Press, 1977), 172.

7 Maria Shéhérazade Giudici, "Government and the Emergence of architecture d'accompagnement, 1584–1765," in Pier Vittorio Aureli, ed., *The City as a Project* (Berlin: Ruby Press, 2013), 155–156.

8 On the architecture of these two squares, see Hilary Ballon, *The Paris of Henri IV* (Cambridge, MA: MIT Press, 1991).

9 Giudici, "Government and the Emergence of architecture d'accompagnement," 161.

10 John Summerson, *Georgian London* (London: Pleiades Books, 1945), 50.

11 Stefan Muthesius, *The English Terraced House* (New Haven: Yale University Press, 1982), 19–22.

12 Ibid., 20.

13 Karl Marx, "Section 1. The Two Factors of a Commodity: Use-Value and Value," in *Capital*, vol. 1, translated by Ben Fowkes (London: Penguin, 1992), 126.

14 Ibid.

15 Muthesius, *The English Terraced House*, 28.

16 E. W. Cooney, "The Organization of Building in England in the 19th Century," *Architectural Research and Teaching* 1, no. 2 (November 1970), 47.

17 Muthesius, *The English Terraced House*, 27.

18 John Wilton-Ely, "The Rise of the Professional Architect in England," in Kostof, *The Architect*, 180

19 Andrew Ure, *The Philosophy of Manufactures* (London: Charles Knight, 1835), 13–14.

20 Karl Marx, "Part Eight: Primitive Accumulation," in *Capital*, vol. 1, 873–940.

21 Ibid.

22 S. D. Chapman, "The Transition to the Factory System in the Midlands Cotton-Spinning Industries," *Economic History Review* 18, no. 3 (1965), 526–543.

23 Karl Marx, "The Factory" in *Capital*, vol. 1, 548.

24 Carolyn Cooper, "The Portsmouth System of Manufacture," *Technology and Culture* 25, no. 2 (April 1984), 192–193.

25 Ibid., 194.

26 Ibid.

27 Karl Marx, "The Eighteenth Brumaire of Louis Bonaparte," in *The Karl Marx Library*, vol. 1, ed. Saul K. Padover (New York: McGraw-Hill, 1972), 245.

28 For an overview of the role of "factories" in Dutch colonialism see Fernand Braudel, *Civilization and Capitalism, 15th–18th Century*, vol. 3, *The Perspective of the World*, translated by Siân Reynolds (London: Collins, 1984), 207–234.

29 Georgios Eftaxiopoulos, "Stasis: A Critique of Flexibility in Architecture," PhD diss., Architectural Association, London, 2020.

30 Rem Koolhaas, "Typical Plan," in *S, M, L, XL* (New York: Monacelli, 1995), 335–350.

31 "Socially necessary labour-time is the labour-time required to produce any use-value under the conditions of production normal for a given society and with the average degree of skill and intensity of labour prevalent in that society." Karl Marx, *Capital*, vol. 1, 129.

32 Lindy Biggs, *The Rational Factory: Architecture, Technology and Working in America's Age of Mass Production* (Baltimore: Johns Hopkins University Press, 1996), 6.

33 Ibid., 15.

34 David F. Noble, *America by Design: Science, Technology and the Rise of Corporate Capitalism* (New York: Oxford University Press, 1979), 5.

35 Ibid., 6.

36 F. W. Wilder, *The Modern Packing House* (Chicago: Nickerson and Collins, 1905).

37 Frederick Winslow Taylor, *The Principles of Scientific Management* (New York: Harper and Brothers, 1911).

38 Quoted in Biggs, *The Rational Factory*, 50.

39 Reyner Banham, "Ransome at Bayonne," *Journal of the Society of Architectural Historians* 42, no. 4 (1983), 387.

40 Michael Osman, "The Managerial Aesthetics of Concrete," *Perspecta* 45 (2012), 67–76.

41 Ibid., 69.

42 Ibid.

43 Ibid., 74.

44 Claire Zimmerman, "Albert Kahn in the Second Industrial Revolution," *AA Files* 75 (2017), 30.

45 As cited in Charles K. Hyde, "Assembly-Line Architecture: Albert Kahn and the Evolution of the U. S. Auto Factory 1905–1940," *Journal of the Society for Industrial Archeology* 22, no. 2 (1996), 7.

46 Joshua, B. Freeman, *Behemoth: A History of the Factory and the Making of the Modern World* (New York: W. W. Norton, 2018), 121.

47 Quoted in Grant Hildebrand, *The Architecture of Albert Kahn* (Cambridge, MA: MIT Press, 1974), 101.

48 As cited in Hyde, "Assembly-Line Architecture," 14.

49 Marx defines labor power as "the aggregate of those mental and physical capabilities existing in the physical form, the living personality, of a human being." See Karl Marx, *Capital*, vol. 1, 270.

50 Francesco Marullo, "Typical Plan: The Architecture of Labor and the Space of Production," PhD diss., Technische Universiteit Delft, 2014, 28.

51 Louis Kahn, "Don't Let War Plants Scare You," *Nation's Business* 32 (1944): 27–28.

52 Adam Lauder and Lee Rodney, "Albert Kahn's Five-Year Plant and the Birth of 'Uncertain Space,'" in *Future Anterior* 12, no. 2 (Winter 2015), 38–61.

53 Ibid., 41.

54 Mario Tronti, *Workers and Capital*, translated by David Broder (London: Verso, 2019), 294.

55 Francesco Marullo, "Architecture and Revolution: The Typical Plan as Index of Generic," in Aureli, *The City as a Project*, 216–260.

56 Ibid., 239.

57 Tronti, *Workers and Capital*, 297.

58 https://sah-archipedia.org/buildings/MD-01-005-0114.

59 Detlef Mertins, *Mies* (London: Phaidon, 2014), 283.

60 Ibid., 283–284.

61 Ibid., 283.

62 Ibid., 492.

Chapter 5

1 For a general discussion of the term "form" see Adrian Forty, *Words and Buildings: A Vocabulary of Modern Architecture* (New York: Thames and Hudson, 2000), 149–172.

2 Rodolphe Gasché, *The Idea of Form: Rethinking Kant's Aesthetics* (Stanford, CA: Stanford University Press, 2003), 6.

3 Carl Schmitt, "The Age of Neutralizations and Depoliticizations," *Télos*, no. 96 (1993), 138.

4 For a discussion of Fiedler's influence on the tradition of "pure visibility," formalism, and modern architecture, see Renato de Fusco, *L'idea di Architettura. Storia della critica da Viollet-le-Duc a Persico* (Milan: Franco Angeli, 2003), 65–95.

5 The roots of architectural theory in psychology are discussed in Mark Jarzombek, *The Psychologizing of Modernity: Art, Architecture and History* (Cambridge: Cambridge University Press, 2000).

6 Mitchell W. Schwarzer, "The Emergence of Architectural Space: August Schmarsow's Theory of *Raumgestaltung*," *Assemblage*, no. 15 (August 2015), 48–61.

7 Ibid., 50.

8 The former St. Petersburg was renamed Petrograd in 1914, further renamed Leningrad in 1924, and returned to its original name, St. Petersburg, in 1991.

9 This and other links between German and Russian traditions of formalism have been investigated in Luka Skansi, "What Is Artistic Form: Munich-Moscow 1900–1925," in Christoph Flamm, Henry Keazor, and Roland Marti, *Russian Émigré Culture* (Newcastle upon Tyne: Cambridge Scholars Publishing, 2013), 69–88.

10 Victor Erlich, *Russian Formalism: History, Doctrine* (New Haven: Yale University Press, 1981).

11 Viktor Shklovsky, "Art as Device," in *Theory of Prose*, trans. Benjamin Sher (Chicago: Dalkey Archive Press, 1990), 1–14.

12 Ibid., 6–11.

13 Boris Ejchenbaum, "La teoria del 'metodo formale,'" in Tzvetan Todorov, ed., *I formalisti russi: teoria della letteratura e metodo critico* (Turin: Einaudi, 2003), 33.

14 For the linguistic origins of Malevich's approach to painting see Aleksandra Shatskikh, *Black Square: Malevich and the Origins of Suprematism*, translated by Marian Schwartz (New Haven: Yale University Press, 2012), 1–33.

15 Kazimir Malevich, "Suprematism," in Robert L. Herbert, ed., *Modern Artists on Art* (New York: Dover, 1999), 116.

16 Boris Groys, *The Total Art of Stalinism: Avant-Garde Aesthetic, Dictatorship and Beyond*, translated by Charles Rougle (London: Verso, 2011), 33.

17 Anna Bokov, *Avant-Garde as Method: Vkhutemas and the Pedagogy of Space* (Zurich: Park Books, 2020), 76.

18 Skansi, "What Is Artistic Form," 73–77.

19 Ibid., 74.

20 Bokov, *Avant-Garde as Method*, 160–282. See also Luka Skansi, "Insegnare architettura: Nikolaj Ladovskij 'spazio,' corso base al Vchutemas, Mosca, 1920," *Casabella* 847 (2015), 4–19.

21 Selim O. Khan-Magomedov, *Pioneers of Soviet Architecture* (London: Thames and Hudson: 1987), 21–24.

22 Bokov, *Avant-Garde as Method*, 320–322.

23 Labor understood in terms of psychic effort: ibid., 256.

24 Ibid., 256–262.

25 Maria Gough, *The Artist as Producer: Russian Constructivism in Revolution* (Berkeley: University of California Press, 2005), 2.

26 Ibid., 21–60.

27 Ibid., 22.

28 Ibid., 39.

29 Aleksei Gan, *Constructivism*, translated by Christina Lodder (Barcelona: Tenov Books, 2014), 22.

30 Khan-Magomedov, *Pioneers of Soviet Architecture*, 153.

31 Moisei Ginzburg, *Rhythm in Architecture* (London: Artifice Press, 2017).

32 Ibid., 14.

33 Ibid.

34 Guido Canella and Maurizio Meriggi, eds., *SA Sovremennaja Arckhitektura, 1926–1930* (Rome: Dedalo, 2007), 22.

35 Moisei Ginzburg, *Dwelling* (London: Fontaka Publications, 2017), 8–42.

36 Alessandro De Magistris and Irina Korob'ina, eds., *Ivan Leonidov 1902–1959* (Milan: Electa, 2009), 160.

37 For an insightful analysis of Leonidov's proposal for a Club of a New Social Type, see Richard Anderson, "A Screen that Receives Images by Radio," *AA Files* 67 (2013), 3–15.

38 Ibid., 4–5.

39 Ibid., 4.

40 Ibid.

41 Reproduced in Kazimir Malevich, *Die gegenstandslose Welt* (Dessau: Bauhausbucher, 1927), fig. 68.

42 Yve-Alain Bois, "From −∞ to 0 to +∞: Axonometry, or Lissitzky's Mathematical Paradigm," in Caroline de Bie, Arlette Brouwers, Jan Debbaut, Dees Linders,

and Marielle Soons, eds., *El Lissitzky, Architect, Painter, Photographer, Typographer* (Eindhoven: Municipal Van Abbemuseum, 1991), 27–33.

43 Danilo Udovicki-Selb, *Soviet Architectural Avant-Gardes: Architecture and Stalin's Revolution from Above, 1928–1938* (London: Bloomsbury, 2020), 35–43.

44 Groys, *The Total Art of Stalinism*. See also Ricardo Ruivo Pereira, "The Historiographical Invention of the Soviet Avant Garde: Cultural Politics and the Return of the Lost Project," in Sebastiaan Loosen, Rajesh Heynickx, and Hilde Heynen, eds., *The Figure of Knowledge: Conditioning Architectural Theory, 1960s–1990s* (Leuven: Leuven University Press, 2020), 227–242.

45 Marco De Michelis, "L'organizzazione della città industriale nel Primo Piano Quinquennale," in Manfredo Tafuri, ed., *Socialismo, città, architettura URSS 1917–1937* (Roma: Officina Edizioni, 1976), 151–169.

46 Sheila Fitzpatrick, *Everyday Stalinism: Ordinary Life in Extraordinary Times: Soviet Russia in the 1930s* (New York: Oxford University Press, 2000).

47 Rita di Leo, "L'operaismo tra comunismo italiano e esperimento sovietico," in Mario Tronti, ed., *Politica e destino* (Rome: Luca Sossella editore, 2006), 75–84.

48 The results of this research were published in Tafuri, *Socialismo, città, architettura*.

49 Manfredo Tafuri, "Il socialismo realizzato e la crisi delle avanguardie," in Tafuri, *Socialismo, città, architettura*, 43–87.

50 De Michelis, "L'organizzazione della città industriale," 157.

Chapter 6

1 Walter Benjamin, "Experience and Poverty," in *Selected Writings*, vol. 2, part 2, edited by Michael W. Jennings et al., translated by Rodney Livingstone (Cambridge, MA: Belknap Press of Harvard University Press, 1999), 731.

2 Ibid., 731–732.

3 Ibid., 732.

4 Ibid.

5 Detlef Mertins and Michael W. Jennings, eds., *G: An Avant-Garde Journal of Art, Architecture, Design, and Film, 1923–1926* (London: Tate Publishing, 2010).

6 Detlef Mertins, "Architecture, Worldview, and World Image in *G*," in Mertins and Jennings, *G*, 74.

7 The most thorough analysis of Le Corbusier's Dom-ino is Eleanor Gregh's "The Dom-ino Idea," *Oppositions* 15/16 (Winter/Spring 1979), 61–81. See also Tim Benton, "Dom-Ino and the Phantom Pilotis," *AA Files* 69 (2014), 23–47.

8 Le Corbusier, *Oeuvre complète*, vol. 1, *1910–29* (Zurich: Editions d'Architecture, 1964), 24–25.

9 Benton, "Dom-Ino and the Phantom Pilotis," 42–43.

10 Adolf Max Vogt, *Le Corbusier, the Noble Savage: Toward an Archaeology of Modernism*, translated by Radka Donnell (Cambridge, MA: MIT Press, 1998).

11 Pier Vittorio Aureli, "The Dom-ino Problem: Questioning the Architecture of Domestic Space," *Log*, no. 30 (Winter 2014), 153–168.

12 Benton, "Dom-Ino and the Phantom Pilotis," 36.

13 Le Corbusier, *Oeuvre complète*, vol. 1, 24–25.

14 Gregh, "The Dom-ino Idea," 77.

15 Benton, "Dom-Ino and the Phantom Pilotis," 43.

16 Henri-Marcel Magne "L'architecture et les matériaux nouveaux," *Art et Décoration* (1919).

17 Vogt, *Le Corbusier, the Noble Savage*, 24.

18 This tendency will surface in Le Corbusier's work, especially in his planning work, such as his Plan Obus for Algiers. For Manfredo Tafuri, the Plan Obus scaffold-like structure open to any possible residential infill manifests Le Corbusier's attempt to create a model where a maximum flexibility of occupation and dwelling corresponds to a rigid and abstract structural system. In this sense the Plan Obus can be consider a radical development of the Domino system. See Manfredo Tafuri, *Architecture and Utopia: Design and Capitalist Development*, translated by Barbara Luigia La Penta (Cambridge, MA: MIT Press, 1976), 128.

19 Ludwig Hilberseimer, *Grosstadtbauten e altri scritti di arte e architettura*, trans. Michele Caja (Naples: Clean Edizioni, 2010), 51.

20 Eduard Bernstein, *The Preconditions of Socialism* (Cambridge: Cambridge University Press, 1993).

21 On the rise of this subject, see Sergio Bologna, "I lavoratori della conoscenza fuori e dentro l'impresa," in *Ceti medi senza futuro? Scritti, appunti sul lavoro e altro* (Rome: Derive e Approdi, 2007), 108–136.

22 Ibid., 111–117.

23 Ludwig Hilberseimer, "Bewegungskunst," *Sozialistiche Monatshefte*, no. 27 (1921), 467–468; see also Edward Dimendberg, "Towards an Elemental Cinema: Film Aesthetics and Practice in *G*," in Mertins and Jennings, *G*, 53–69.

24 Ludwig Hilberseimer, *Metropolisarchitecture and Selected Essays*, translated by Richard Anderson and Julie Dawson (New York: GSAPP Books, 2012), 113.

25 George Simmel, "The Metropolis and Mental Life," in *The Sociology of Georg Simmel*, translated and edited by Kurt H. Wolff (Glencoe, IL: Free Press, 1950), 409–424.

26 Benjamin, "Experience and Poverty."

27 K. Michael Hays, *Modernism and the Posthumanist Subject*: *The Architecture of Hannes Meyer and Ludwig Hilberseimer* (Cambridge, MA: MIT Press, 1992).

28 Walter Benjamin, *The Arcades Projects*, edited by Rolf Tiedeman, translated by Howard Eiland and Kevin McLaughlin (Cambridge, MA: Harvard University Press, 1998), 8.

29 Walter Benjamin, "The Destructive Character," in *Selected Writings*, vol. 2, part 2, 541.

30 Adolf Behne, "Intérieur Co-op," *UHU*, 1926, 5.

31 Hannes Meyer, "The New World," in Claude Schnaidt, ed., *Hannes Meyer: Buildings, Projects and Writings* (London: Alec Tiranti, 1965), 91–94.

32 Ibid., 91–93.

33 Thomas Klaus, Erika Golo, et al., *The Co-op Principle: Hannes Meyer and the Concept of Collective Design* (Leipzig: Spector Books, 2015), 68.

34 Benjamin, op. cit.

35 Maria Mies, *Patriarchy and Accumulation on a World Scale: Women in the International Division of Labour* (London: Zed Books, 2014).

36 Nicholas Bullock, "First the Kitchen: Then the Façade," *Journal of Design History* 1, no. 3/4 (1988), 177.

37 Maria Shéhérazade Giudici, "Counter-planning from the Kitchen: For a Feminist Critique of Type," *Journal of Architecture* 23 (2018), 1203–1209.

38 Dolores Hayden, "Catherine Beecher and the Politics of Housework," in Susana Torre, ed., *Women in American Architecture* (New York: Whitney Library of Design, 1977), 22–49.

39 Sophie Hochhäusl, "From Vienna to Frankfurt Inside Core-House Type 7: A History of Scarcity through the Modern Kitchen," *Architectural Histories* 1, no. 24 (2013), 11.

40 Antonia Surmann, "The Evolution of Kitchen Design: A Yearning for a Modern Stone Age Cave," in Nicolaj van der Meulen and Jörg Wiesel, eds., *Culinary Turn: Aesthetic Practices of Cookery* (Bielefeld: Transcript Verlag, 2017), 52.

41 As quoted in Anne Lee Morgan, *Contemporary Architects* (Chicago: St. James Press, 1987), 853.

42 Roberto Gargiani, *Dall'onda pop alla superficie neutra. Archizoom Associati 1966–1974* (Milan: Electa, 2007), 11–12.

43 Ibid., 12.

44 Mario Tronti, "La società e la fabbrica," *Quaderni Rossi*, no. 2 (1962), 1–31.

45 Mario Tronti, *Workers and Capital*, translated by David Broder (London: Verso, 2019), 328.

46 Archizoom Associati, "Città catena di montaggio del sociale. Ideologia e teoria della metropoli," *Casabella*, no. 350–351 (July-August 1970), 43–52. For the English version of this article see Andrea Branzi, ed., *No-Stop City: Archizoom Associati* (Orléans: HYX, 2006), 156–174.

47 Ibid., 88.

48 Manfredo Tafuri, "Per una critica dell'ideologia architettonica," *Contropiano*, no. 1 (January-April 1969), 15–40.

49 Ibid., 22. For the English translation, see Manfredo Tafuri, "Towards a Critique of Architectural Ideology," translated by Stephen Sartarelli, in K. Michael Hays, *Architectural Theory since 1968* (Cambridge, MA: MIT Press, 1998), 23.

50 Archizoom Associati, "City Assembly Line of the Social," in Branzi, *No-Stop City*, 160.

51 On the work of LARO see Catherine F. McMahon, "Predictive Machines: Data, Computer Maps, and Simulations," in Arindam Dutta, ed., *A Second Modernism: MIT, Architecture, and the "Techno-Social" Moment* (Cambridge, MA: MIT Press, 2013), 436–473.

52 Ibid., 440. See also Jennifer S. Light, *From Warfare to Welfare: Defense Intellectuals and Urban Problems in the Cold War* (Baltimore: Johns Hopkins University Press, 2003).

53 Arindam Dutta, "Linguistics, Not Grammatology: Architecture's *A Prioris* and Architecture's Priorities," in Dutta, *A Second Modernism*, 3.

54 Stuart A. Umpleby, "A History of the Cybernetics Movement in the United States," *Journal of the Washington Academy of Science* 91, no. 2 (Summer 2005), 54–56.

55 Massimo de Carolis, "Non salvateci più. Sulla vocazione rituale dei mercati finanziari," in Dario Gentili, Mario Ponzi, and Elettra Stimilli, eds., *Il culto del capitale* (Macerata: Quodlibet Studio, 2014), 125–141.

56 Matteo Pasquinelli, "How to Make a Class: Hayek's Neoliberalism and the Origins of Connectionism," *Qui Parle* 1, no. 30 (June 2021), 159–184.

57 Norman Sanders, "A Possible First Use of CAM/CAD," in Arthur Tatnall, ed., *Reflections on the History of Computing: Preserving Memories and Sharing Stories* (Berlin: Springer, 2012), 43–56.

58 Ibid., 48.

59 A typical example of this kind of digital avant-garde is represented by Greg Lynn, *Animate Form* (New York: Princeton Architectural Press, 1999).

60 Philippe Morel, "The Origins of Discretism: Thinking Unthinkable Architecture," in Gilles Retsin, ed., *Discrete: Reappraising the Digital in Architecture*, special issue of *Architectural Design* 89, no. 2 (2019), 15–21.

61 Ibid., 16.

62 Ibid., 16–17.

63 Alan M. Turing, "On Computable Numbers, with an Application to the Entscheidungsproblem," *Proceedings of the London Mathematical Society*, n.s. 42, no. 1 (1937), 230–265.

64 Matteo Pasquinelli and Vladan Joler, "The Nooscope Manifested: Artificial Intelligence as Instrument of Knowledge Extractivism," *AI and Society* (November 20020), https://doi.org/10.1007/s00146-020-01097-6.

65 Morel, "The Origins of Discretism," 19.

66 Tung-Hui Hu, *A Prehistory of the Cloud* (Cambridge, MA: MIT Press, 2015), 39.

67 Maurizio Lazzarato, "Immaterial Labor," in Paolo Virno and Michael Hardt, eds., *Radical Thought in Italy: A Potential Politics* (Minneapolis: Minnesota University Press, 1996), 133–150.

68 Pietro Bonomi and Nicolò Ornaghi, "Less than Zero: Data Infrastructure, or Architecture as Service," *AA Files 77* (2020), 127–140.

69 James D. Tracy, *The Political Economy of Merchant Empires* (Cambridge: Cambridge University Press, 1997).

70 Bonomi and Ornaghi, "Less than Zero," 137.

71 The culture of architecture—especially in the last decades—has done all it could to exorcise the downgrading of the architect. The most obvious example of this tendency is the affirmation of the "archistar," a sort of hyperarchitect whose authorship hides the multitude of workers—from designer to builders—who are necessary to produce architecture. Yet the only economic rationale for this kind of architect is the financial valorization of buildings (and the places where they are built) by associating them to a "brand name." On this issue see Pedro Fiori Arantes, *The Rent of Form: Architecture and Labor in the Digital Age* (Minneapolis: University of Minnesota Press, 2019), 5–78.

72 Adina Seeger, "Fritz Ertl: Bauhaus Student and Architect at the Auschwitz-Birkenau Concentration Camp," in Philipp Oswalt, ed., *Hannes Meyer's New Bauhaus Pedagogy: From Dessau to Mexico* (Berlin: Spector Books, 2021), 453–458.

73 About this issue see especially Hubert Hofmann, "Memoirs of a Student of Architecture," in Oswalt, *Hannes Meyer's New Bauhaus Pedagogy*, 131–139.

74 Louis Sullivan, "The Tall Office Building Artistically Reconsidered," in *Kindergarten Chats and Other Writings*, ed. Isabella Athey (New York: George Wittenborn, 1986).

75 Ibid., 135.

76 On the comparison between Meyer's proletarization of the Western architect and Benjamin's theory of the author as producer see Amir Djalali, "The Architect as Producer: The Proletarization of the Western Architect," *Footprint: Delft Architecture Theory Journal*, no. 17 (2015), 12–20.

77 Walter Benjamin, "The Author as Producer," in *Selected Writings*, vol. 2, part 2, edited by Michael W. Jennings et al., translated by Rodney Livingstone (Cambridge, MA: Belknap Press of Harvard University Press, 1999), 768–782.

Index

Writing Architecture Series

Writing Architecture Series

A project of the Anyone Corporation
Cynthia Davidson, editor

Writing Architecture Series design:
Ben Fehrman-Lee

This book was set in Lexicon by Jen Jackowitz.
Printed and bound in the United States of America.

Library of Congress Cataloging-in-Publication Data is available.

ISBN: 978-0-262-54523-5

10 9 8 7 6 5 4 3 2